First published in Great Britain in 2006 by
Anchor Books
Remus House
Coltsfoot Drive
Peterborough
PE2 9JX
Telephone: 01733 898102
www.forwardpress.co.uk

Animal Antics

2006

Edited by Michelle Afford & Laura Martin

An Anthology of Poetry Celebrating the
Unique Bond Between People & Animals

Foreword

Animals can be our dearest friends and confidants; they can also destroy our homes, chew our shoes and dig up our lawns! Cute but terrible, they have the power to evoke all kind of emotions in us, from the joy, and more often than not shock, held in the miracle of birth, to the aching hole that is left when a cherished pet dies. Animal Antics 2006 spans the spectrum of these feelings to provide a magical anthology that will delight with tales and memories of our loyal companions.

This year's Animal Antics competition solicited your greatest response yet, with nearly a thousand poems being sent in to us. What a joy it was to read of the relationships and experiences you have had with the animal kingdom, and the photographs had us laughing and cooing for weeks!

As always, the standard of work was incredibly high making our task of choosing a winner, though pleasurable, extremely difficult. The top poem this year, 'Confessions Of A Kitten' by Rex Andrews, is one that we all agree conveys perfectly the cheeky pastimes of its subject. This, as well as nine other poems that particularly stood out to us, earned the worthy right to feature on our website.

All of us here at Anchor Books are sure that the poems and photographs presented in this beautiful anthology will provide as much pleasure to you as readers as they have for us whilst working with them.

Michelle Afford & Laura Martin
Editors

Contents of Poets

The Animal Poems

Confessions Of A Kitten

The world's my jungle, I'm the king
in full command of everything.
Your table legs are trees to me;
your goldfish pond's my open sea;
your backdoor's where I hone my claws;
your sideboard's where I wash my paws;
your shoe box is my hideaway
where, should a mouse or lizard stray,
I'm on it like a flash of light
to prove my case that 'might is right'.

I like to delve in curious places,
like leather boots with dangly laces;
sewing baskets, when they're full
of cotton threads and strands of wool;
a waste bin packed with crumpled paper,
bits of string and Sellotape; a
pair of socks; an unmade bed;
a window box; the garden shed ...
I don't care what these things are for,
they're simply something to explore.

To humans I'm a cuddly pet,
as sweet a kitten as you'd get
From John o' Groats to Timbuktu.
That's just the side I show to you:
- my *superego* in control,
I seem a pure and gentle soul:
I come in purring when I'm bid.
But underneath the mask, my *id*
is fierce and bloody if unchecked -
so kindly treat me with respect.

Rex Andrews

Congratulations Rex!
'Confessions Of A Kitten' has been chosen as the winning poem in this collection by our panel of editors. Your poem has won you our first prize of £1000!

Squirrel

His lithe and liquid body
pours and curls and sweeps
in a slither of propulsion -
in his flying, wingless leaps
from fence to tallest treetop
with one agile, nimble bound,
tail curling round the branches
as he winds his way to ground
where he forages his larders
to retrieve his winter stores
then streaks along fence edges
on fleet tightrope-walking claws.

Mercurial in motion
with his bushy tail behind,
he picks up bread for bird food
and sits down like humankind
to hand to mouth each morsel
in the way we humans eat
while I watch in fascination
for he looks so small and sweet;
then off he runs meandering
the way a river flows,
oblivious of enthralment
of spectators of his shows.

Joy Saunders

Commended

All commended poems
can be seen online at
www.forwardpress.co.uk

A Cat's Life

Reclining in a draped repose
With paw curled half across her nose,
Our cat seems constantly resigned
To sleep - and always disinclined
Towards exertion, though she'd be
Like lightning up the nearest tree
If from those partially closed eyes
She focused on new enterprise!

It seems to me she has life made
As most cats do - quite unafraid
To seek respect with graceful charm
Before she gently twists your arm
Towards whatever satisfies -
Then suddenly will scrutinise
Your every move - and patronise
With penetrating saucer eyes

But slowly I'm beginning to
Respect the feline point of view
Except, of course, I can't foresee
Myself curled on our lounge settee
For hours on end just marking time
Until I'm served with food and wine
To get away with things like that
I'll have to come back as a cat!

Jo Lewis

Commended

All commended poems
can be seen online at
www.forwardpress.co.uk

Senses Of Darkness

Drapes drawn to a close
The doors locked and secure
The black Persian's curled up
Eyes closed and demure

The old lady sighs
As she strokes his soft fur
The clock ticks in time
To his rhythmical purr

Rain pounds on the windows
Strong gales lash the door
The cat skits off her knee
His pads slip on the floor

The blind lady gets up
From where she was sitting
Chastises the cat who is
Clawing and spitting

Her senses become tuned
To the sounds of the house
The commotion she feels
Has been caused by a mouse

The cat brushes her ankles
Then nuzzles her hand
His rough tongue assures her
He does understand

Joyce Graham

Commended

All commended poems
can be seen online at
www.forwardpress.co.uk

Misty

(For Bryony and Ben)

Her shepherd's lantern leads us in the dark,
A white-tipped tail that sweeps a steady arc.
Her nose tracks scents in deepest autumn leaves,
Her eyes miss nothing when the night deceives.

And when November mornings dawn, she roves
The frosty fields and chases rooks in droves;
They flap their wings with supercilious stare,
Then tease her from their stronghold in the air.

In wintertime, with snowflakes on her nose,
She jumps the ice where her reflection shows.
In summer, surfs green waves of meadow grass,
And nips at bees and butterflies that pass.

She is the quietest creature, makes no noise.
She waits so patiently and sits with poise
To watch us fill her bowl. Then, once set down,
A pad of paws and gentlest crunching sound.

A connoisseur of puddles after rain,
She'll sip the water as we would champagne!
And with her thirst and hunger satisfied,
Flops down to dream, with brown eyes open wide.

Roger Kendall

Commended

Lyt, A faithful friend

Commended

All commended poems
can be seen online at
www.forwardpress.co.uk

A faithful friend,
With a heart of gold,
Reflects on time,
Growing old.
Eyes once keen,
With life and fun,
See only shadows,
Despite the sun.
A body once light
And full of vigour,
Now feels the cold,
Showing signs of rigour.
The passing days
That flow into years,
Old age descends,
Despite the fears.
Always there,
By my side,
Down through the years,
Her place of pride.
A faithful friend,
In role traditional,
Constant companion,
Love unconditional.
Twilight years,
Our time now measured,
A life fulfilled,
And memories treasured.

Stephen Humphries

Bailey

All the way across the town to see your little face
I fell in love immediately and took your owner's place
So small and sweet and innocent - a tiny little pup
Who knew what a little monstrous dog you would end up
Now he warned me you were bad and troublesome
But the smooth white coat and cheeky face were wholesome
The first time you wet the floor I shrugged, you're a pup
Then you barked, bit and chased and tore the place up
But something in that naughty face held onto my heart
Every naughty, evil, silly thing was just all your parts
For loyal, sweet and loving you could be when at rest
From tormenting the world with evil; what you loved best
I cried, I shouted, I pointed and I tore my hair out
But when a few weeks passed by, I couldn't give a clout
I laughed at your barking, and ignored all your growls
For a 'Bailey, shut up' sent you from naughty old howls
To licking and kissing and cuddling right up
To becoming my baby, my best friend, *my pup!*

Leanne Marshall

Commended

All commended poems
can be seen online at
www.forwardpress.co.uk

Narcissus At The Pool

Sleek phantom shapes streak silver in the pool;
Gilded gauze-meshed fins flicker lazily
In that half-lit world; green, leaf-patterned, cool,
Where tendrils weave a grotto fantasy.

He slinks out from the shadow of the shed,
Peers down, tail twitching, readying every claw.
The water mirrors and reflects his head.
Narcissus preens and then extends a paw.

About to strike, he halts, his eyes meet mine
And seek approval. He will kill for me.
Fish on my pillow - this the token sign,
Like mice on mats - mutual dependency.

He strikes a pose, just waiting for my nod
To compliment him for his sinuous grace.
Worship, as for some Nile, ancestral god,
He thinks he's due. Slit pupils read my face.

I stamp and shout. He stares, then darts away.
But not too far. He crouches and looks up high
To where the birds perch round the feeding tray,
Forgets the pool. There're other fish to fry.

D Nixon

Commended

All commended poems
can be seen online at
www.forwardpress.co.uk

Gossamer Child

Soft and sleek, so stealthily,
She slips into the night.
On velvet pads, with silent tread,
She'll vanish out of sight.

Blacker than black her satin coat,
Big golden eyes to see
All the night-time dwellers
In the shrubbery.

I stoop to give her supper,
But as I put down the plate,
Like quicksilver, like mercury,
She's out the garden gate.

Gossamer child, my lovely girl,
At moonrise out you go -
Child of the night, a fairy child,
You're free as air, I know.

She's always been a little wild,
Though *she* adopted *me,*
And how I love my gossamer child -
Dainty, lovely, free.

D Price

Commended

All commended poems
can be seen online at
www.forwardpress.co.uk

Ember My Pointer

I wonder as you rest
Nose twitching, paws outstretched
Deep in slumber,
What memories haunt your dreams?

Early in the morning mist
We walked through frosty fields,
Breathing steam
Across peaceful solitude.

You frolicked in the garden,
Shadow dancing in the sun
Tail unhinged -
Ecstatic in your game.

Languidly at midday
You lay and watched me work.
Adoring eyes
Followed my every move.

Later, we strode through woodland.
You leapt over logs and streams
Chasing the breeze
With graceful agility.

And now you lie exhausted.
Your glossy coat reflects the light.
All mischief spent -
I marvel at your being.

Brenda Artingstall

Commended

All commended poems
can be seen online at
www.forwardpress.co.uk

An Old English Gentleman

The sounds my cat makes are gentle,
His paws treading along the carpet,
Ears pricking at my movements,
He's an old boy and he knows.

His white-ginger face has whiskers,
Like a very old English gentleman.
Sometimes he looks like a walrus,
And I love his pale pink nose.

My cat's belly is an undercarriage
Of pure white curly strands.
His head is large and royal,
An aristocrat and it shows.

Oscar is a king-of-the-house cat,
With an expert eye for the best.
He has a regal way of washing
The tuna taste from his toes.

His eyes are green and misty,
Often hazel like my own.
Sometimes they meet and between us,
There's a love that flows and flows.

Christine Lacey

The Bump In The Blinds

We've got new blinds
Just like most people these days.
The only trouble is,
We didn't warn the cats, and they don't approve.

They used to have free rein,
An empty window ledge,
Where they could sprawl,
And ponder the outside world in complete peace.

With the coming of the blinds,
They gave us one of their looks.
You know, the one that says,
'What have you done now?'

Now they have to negotiate the blinds,
Their bulk treading carefully
Between the slats
And chain links.

Until they again
Sit in majesty,
Staring out on their domain.
The bump in the blinds.

Alan McKean

Westie Limericks

Our Westies love watching TV
Wildlife programmes are top of their tree
A rat or an owl
Will elicit a growl
But a cat prompts a leap off my knee.

Georgie, our Westie, is meek
If frightened, she lets out a shriek.
The wind up her tail
Will cause her to wail
And faced with a male dog, she'll freak.

Judy Mackie

I Love A Fuss

Without all the fussing
what would I do?
How would you know
that I really love you?

Out on a walk
the children we meet,
having all their fuss
is such a great treat.

My tail starts to wag,
'Hallo Suzy,' they say.
Oh, it's my heaven,
and they make my day.

Julie Brown

My Beautiful Smarti

She plays in the garden and bathes in the sun,
Each new day full of feline fun.
Chasing the mice and catching bees,
Watching the birds from beneath the trees.

She hides amongst the garden gnomes,
And chases ants from their homes.
Pats the fountain spray with one velvet paw,
The most beautiful cat you ever saw.

She ambushes grasshoppers with a furry bounce,
And catches spiders with a stealthy pounce.
Chases fallen leaves across the lawn,
Then lays down in the sun with a tiny yawn.

When nights draw in and there's a chill in the air,
Look by the fire and you'll find her there.
On her big soft pink pillow, fast asleep,
Except for loud purring, you don't hear a peep.

Julie Wealleans

PS ... I Love You

PS ... I love you,
you're devoted, loyal and true,
you release my inner anxieties,
my heart belongs to you.

You are my life,
my days and nights,
releasing me from the tension,
of life's daily strife.

My angel saviour, when I call
You never turn away,
bounding happily toward me,
with style and regal grace.

PS ... I love you!

You lay and wait, eagerly,
when I go away,
when I return home to you,
you yip and kiss my face.

So many things you've taught me,
so many things I've learned:
The emptiness inside me.
It was for you that I had yearned.

I'll never take for granted,
the lovelight in your eyes,
or the way your little tail wags
when you see me cry.

I'll honour you the best I can,
you're not just a friend of Man.
I'll tell the world and all will know,
my dog, my friend, I love you so.
Protected from the worst I'll be,
as long as my dog stands by me.

PS ... I love you!

Jodie Flanders

Welcome Sheba

Hello Sheba, my new dog, welcome to our home.
We hope you'll always want to stay with us, with no desire to roam.
I saw you first, a week ago, clear in my mind's eye,
I knew you'd be the one I'd choose, now I wonder why.
It wasn't just the size of you, or the colour of your hair,
something deep inside of me whispered, 'I'm in there'.
Which of my dogs is in your flesh, has come back to be with me?
Or maybe there's some of each? One day I'll surely see.
I only know a vision plain came to my inner mind,
I saw two dogs, 'hind kennel doors, I knew just what I'd find.
The first one out was big and bold, liked playing with her toy.
Then you came upon the scene, you showed such utter joy.
You just came straight up to me, thrust nose into my hand,
as if to say, 'Now let's go home - together we'll be grand',
and Sheba, like I said before, my mind had been made up,
by God or by some being, like a reincarnated pup.
We were meant to be together, of that I have no doubt,
so now we'll work in harmony, wherever in or out,
and with God's blessing, we'll have happy times galore,
which I believe will be approved, by those who've gone before.

Sheba found me 22/12/99. This was written 23/12/99
I have always made a point of accepting my dogs for what they are
and not comparing them with past friends, treating each as an individual
with its own strong points and its own weaknesses. Sheba is different;
in her I see something of every dog that has ever owned me.
She is the third rescue Alsatian I have had, named Sheba.

Brian Muchmore

29

My Best friend

You are always there listening and waiting,
For the sound of my key in the door,
You are always so gratified to see me,
As you rush to me and hold up your paw.

However badly I've behaved,
However badly the world has treated me,
However awful I look or feel,
However poorly you walk or are,
You hobble to greet me.

I am the centre of your little world,
With your wet nose and wagging tail,
Whoever comes or goes in my life,
Your faithfulness will never fail.

You sense when I'm unhappy,
And you nudge with your nose,
Then you lick me and paw me,
Until my mood comes to a close.

Lady, you and I are inseparable,
You're my baby, confidant and best friend,
Unlike all the human relationships,
Ours will never end.

Susan Jenner

Taz

Hi, my name is Taz and life is so much fun
Because I'm small and pretty, I'm loved by everyone
We play all sorts of lovely games, I've got a big balloon
And when I catch and pull the string it bounces round the room
Sometimes they say I'm naughty but that don't bother me
I turn on my appealing look and land upon their knee
I started out a rescue pup, but now, as you can tell
I'm loved so much by everyone, my life is really swell.

Audrey A Allocca

Clever Mouse

I am a little mouse
I eat the best things in the house
It's nice when the cat is asleep
But I always have a peep before I do my leap
Onto the cat's head
Which is like a soft bed
Then, if he wants to chase me
He has to chase himself instead!

O Tate

A faithful Companion

Our dog loved to go on family holidays
We would all drive to Glasgow to stay for a long weekend.
Up early to catch the ferry to Arran Isle of purple heather
And high mountain peaks.
Landing at Brodick's broad bay
Country scenes and walking groups
Away from the hum and crush and stress of city rush.

Arran optimism, we joked and walked along
The flat, smooth way by the edge of silver-grey sandy beach,
Often the sky hung heavy with threatening rain.
All hoped that we'd reach the red sandstone castle
Of Brodick nestling in dark trees,
Before wet swept down from the high Goat Fell mountain.
Remembering his later days,
It is good to gaze back in memory and think how he enjoyed his holidays.

Freda Grieve

My Spaniel 'Beldie'

This is about my spaniel, she is a lemon roan
And things have never been the same
Since she came along

I looked around for a long, long time
To see what I would get
But I knew she was the perfect one
The moment that we met

She was only 9 weeks old, a bundle full of fun
And nothing could prepare me
For the weeks that were to come

Training her and walking her
Getting her to stay in bed
And not forgetting all the times the puppy needed fed

But now she's nearly 2 and she fills my heart with joy
I wouldn't put my Beldie back, or her squeaky toy

She's grown up with the children
Who sometimes have been rough
But Beldie takes it in her stride
She really is so tough

I play with her, give her treats and take her for a walk
And sometimes when she looks I think
If only she could talk
Her eyes are full of mischief
As she runs around with glee
She may just be a dog
But she means the world to me

So when you read this poem and the verses I do send
It's not only about my dog but about my special friend

Pauline Norrie

Bark To Bach

I couldn't bear the lifelong yolk
Unrelieved by my daily walk, where
I can embrace tree boles, but not oak,
It's too rough upon my coat.
Nor black budded pewter ash
Growing by the old mill flash
With weeping willows hanging there
That's the heron's lair, not that I'm afraid.
But as my friend Angus says,
It's the beech and elm that have the
Squirrel drays, that give great fun
To chase and bark and see them run
For refuge in hollow trunks and high branches
And like the clacking grouse take their chances, amongst
Bracken and alder saplings by the stream
But it's of the silver birch that I dream
That stand of white bright trees with hallelujah limbs
That stretch to Heaven with their hymns.
The scent of rabbit and fox lie near,
Field mice and vole have nature's fear, their survival.
And I can feel the red kite's eyes.
He'd strayed from his moorland lies
And sits in the limes that lead to the hall.
He could snatch me in a flash, and so I keep to the path
Close to Mick. He always has a stick.
Hornbeam windfall from winter's gales.
We turn by the chestnut rails and head for home.
Now where did I leave that bone?
I buried it beneath the larch.
It's safe. Now time to listen to some Bach.

Hayes Turner

Not A Poodle

Mr Dog, I call him
But Charlie's his name
A Bichon Frise, not a poodle
Who enjoys playing a game

He's only a loaner
Who we care for each year
When his owner's away
In some exotic frontier

His fur may be curly
Soft and bright white
But he's butch and right macho
And up for a fight

With an air and a grace
And that loveable face
He will win your affection
And command your attention

But heed what I say
And don't dare get it wrong
'Cause his demeanour will change
With an expression that's strong

He may be all cute
And try hard to please
But he's *not* a poodle
He's a tough Bichon Frise.

David Ironmonger

Felix

At 6 weeks old he came to me
A bundle of ginger joy
He stole my heart and he came free
My lovely Felix boy

He was such a happy kitten
But naughty as most kittens are
With Felix though I was totally smitten
And he was my favourite cat by far

He grew into an intelligent cat
Who knew my every mood
He loved to sit upon my lap
Until it was time for food

At night on top of me he'd lay
Squashing me flat to the bed
In the early hours he'd sneak out to play
With the mice under my neighbour's shed

We had good times for many years
When suddenly his master died
My Felix helped me through my fears
And on him I relied

Not long ago he passed away
Where did the years all go?
I miss his purr more each day
While my love for him still grows

I treasure each moment over the years
And sometimes although I feel sad
When I think of him I shed no more tears
Because of the fun time the two of us had.

S Withey

Fat Cat

I'm a fat cat, a scat cat, lazing in the road
I'm a bed cat, overfed cat, a very heavy load
I'm a fluffy cat, a scruffy cat, I live around the bend
I'm one to trust, not a bit of rust, a very loyal friend
I'll always be a lap cat, purring out with glee
A cute cat, a mute cat until you shout out 'tea'
Not for me the alleyways, the scavenging for food
I much prefer the indoors, the people aren't so rude
Not for me the wild cats, getting into fights
Scattering when the humans start turning on their lights
I'm a fat cat, a scat cat, lazing in the road
I'm a bed cat, overfed cat, a very heavy load

Kelly Peanut (13)

Clara

Whiskers twitching round a shiny pink nose
She quietly glides upon her toes
In one bound she's on the chair
And soon she's circling my hair
Gently stretching and curling her spine
She cosily settles and her tail entwines
Around my neck - ah joy sublime
I am hers and she is mine.

Her purring deafens in my ear
Her warmth gives me comfort and cheer
Her claws extend and then retract
Into my shoulders and my back
Soon she settles down to sleep
A tranquil peace we both then keep
She is mine and I am hers
As gentle snores combine with purrs.

I called her Clara - can't think why
Many years have since passed by
Clara has long since left this life
And I became a busy wife
Three children grew up in my home
Now they have to their own homes gone
But nothing ever took the place
Of Clara - the cat so full of grace.

Joyce Beard

Pyewhacket

Pyewhacket is my dainty, pretty cat
I got her from a stray cats' home but that
Cannot disguise the fact that she
Was once a witch's cat, but we
Don't tell a soul
Cos no one would believe that rigmarole

I know she was a witch's cat because
At midnight she creeps in on silent paws
And climbs upon my bed
To check that I'm not really dead
Then settles down
To sleep beside me on my eiderdown

She hates like poison my old battered car
And knows, two days before, I'm going far
Away, and suddenly goes shy
And simply won't come nigh
Fearing that I'll pick her up
And take her with me
Where the ancient witches sup

Her green, hypnotic eyes stare in my face
To keep me very firmly in my place
And, now and then, she butts my lip
To seal our strange relationship
And when she purrs
She is not mine
She knows that I am hers.

Tony Jennett

Robin My Special Friend

(In loving memory of a special dog)

Robin was my special friend
Friendship I thought would never end
Until one day he hurt his paw
Breaking off one tiny claw
I thought I would take him to the vet
That was my biggest error yet
I hope that through this simple rhyme
This will not happen another time

With twice-weekly dressings to his paw
Pills and injections by the score
I thought, *this really cannot be real*
My poor dog's paw just will not heal
Pounds and pounds I had to spend
Never dreaming we were near the end
I did something I never should
I trusted my vet - thought he was good

Eventually Robin began to ail
The drugs had made his kidneys fail
There was no more the vet could do
He said, 'The final decision's up to you,'
I held my Robin close to me
The vet did his deed - then charged his fee
'Goodbye my boy,' I cried and cried,
'To help you, dear, I really tried.'

Jet's now arrived, my little pup
And through his antics, cheered me up
We are really having lots of fun
And swimming lessons have begun
Obedience is rather slow
Jet's got quite a way to go
The most important thing we have learnt yet
Is never, never trust your vet

Shirley Mills

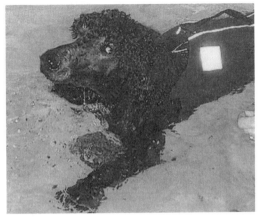

Mighty Huntress

Through night-dewed glade lit wanly by the misted moonlight, barely seen,
with fairy steps that scarce were wont to bend a bowing blade of grass
she passes, fleeting as a shadow falling on a trickling stream;
she pauses, glancing hence and thither, eyes as sharp as splintered glass,
the haughty huntress, fearless, fulgent in the soft and silv'ry sheen,
her eyes reflecting, yellow, awesome, fixing fear on all who'd see,
and knowing death might be mere moments from this frozen, fearsome scene.
But now she turns, her interest fading, shadows dancing, floating free,
then back she wends and homeward ambles scorning prey beneath her worth;
she knows that there is better booty, finer furrows she can plough,
and saunters through the open doorway, pasting careless pats of earth,
despising slaves who 'wait her presence, then commands with fierce 'miaow'.

John Wood

Chloe

Precious little Chloe - restless, trusting, alert, short,
Inveterate tester of new odours with a nasal snort.
Tiptoeing up, she'll poise with cagey canine's practised stance,
So's not to dislodge evidence from roadside grass and plants.
Her twitching nose she'll run along a spindly waving stem
Imbibing olfactory data quite unknown to men.
Thus in that catalogue of all the smells that ever were
Are numbered now another - one delectable scent more.

She terrorises wildlife, the neighbourhood she'll call
To watch a dead leaf waft across our garden in the fall.

Daintily tripping her erratic course along the street,
She challenges each garbage bag and tossed-out toy we meet,
Sometimes upon our customary après breakfast amble
Without the slightest forewarning or hint of a preamble,
Abruptly, she'll resist the leash, onward decline to go,
And firmly planting little bum steadfastly in the snow,
She'll look up at me, quizzically - those wide and guileless eyes,
So unambiguously blunt, with nary spoken word,
Say, here I sit unless I'm carried all the way homeward,
Until Hell freezes over, or the stone Madonna cries.

Anthony E Newman

Taking The Wee-Wee

What a performance
What a keruffle
Trying to get a wee sample
From our little Jack Russell.

Forget about pistols
It's specimen bottles at dawn
As we trail round behind
Waiting for her to perform.

She gives us a look
That says, 'That's disgusting.
I'm not going to go
Even tho' I'm busting'.

It makes people laugh
Gives them a reason to talk
As we repeat this performance
Each and every walk.

But there is one thing
Of which you can be sure
As soon as we get home
She'll stand by the door.

We'll turn our backs
Put the key in the lock
And down on the driveway
Vicky will squat.

Then she'll wag her tail
As if to re-enforce her stance.
'What, me pee in that bottle?
You haven't a chance'.

Christine Collins

Best Of friends

Squeak's a lovely Patterdale bitch,
She gets in a state, and all of a twitch,
When Charlotte goes to school each day,
She goes for a walk, and then does nothing but lay,
3.30 comes and the dog wakes up,
Charlotte comes home and says, 'Hello pup!'
The two of them are like the terrible twins,
And when they play football, Squeak always wins.

Charlotte is six and Squeak is four,
And the dog goes mad when there's a knock at the door.
It's lovely to see the two of them play,
And to give them love, it's true what they say,
A pet is for keeps and a companion too,
And you don't really realise until it is you.
Charlotte and Squeak are the best of mates,
And I'm finishing now 'cause it's getting quite late.

L D Kelman

Jet

Jet sits here below my feet,
Gnawing his bone, that he must eat,
Crunching, cracking, ears pricked high,
A breath or two, and then a sigh,
He watches out my every move,
His long black coat, so shiny and smooth,
He stops for a second to give a count,
Is that Fuzzy behind the couch?
He hears a noise and stops to stare,
Jumps up alert, leaving carpets of hair,
Well it's bedtime now, in the kitchen he bundles,
Into his basket with Fuzzy a-trundle.

Carolann Sutton

A Cat's Instinct

With coat so smooth and ears erect
I have no power nor circumspect.
No cause to reprehend or question why
I chase those birds who soar so high.
Maybe some know and understand
So long ago in a distant land
I was perfected in graceful form
Beside Euphrates river born.
If deserted far from home
A natural instinct lets me roam.
That inborn gift, devoid of care,
Of finding morsels when pantry's bare.
I pad the hoof on boats for rice
And in their holds catch many mice.

Arthur S Ford

A True Friend

Time for a walk -
Two bright pleading eyes.
I moan and I groan.
He's heard my sighs
Seen through my lies -
Yet will settle for less,
An apologetic caress.

Not much to ask
For the love he gives,
For all that he takes -
Bad temper, mean mood
Deserving his censure,
Does he only see good?

Impatient I shout
'We'll walk in the woods
And run in the fields
Watch coots on the pond.
Yes, yes old friend,' more gently now,
'We'll smell God's clean air,
Ah, it will do us both good.'

Eileen Symes

Robin Redbreast

Oh little robin redbreast
How finely you are dressed
Like the master of the hunt, you wear your Sunday best
That bright red waistcoat you wear upon your chest
No top hat on your head
But tails you wear instead
How you stand so proud
Surveying your domain from branches bowed
The best-dressed bird in county and town
Your bright fashion, you wear the crown
Never afraid of man
Scurrying for grubs, worms and morsels, when you can
I have to admire your cheek
From one so tiny and meek
And yet you make your living
For one who's always giving

Terry J Powell

The Watch Cat

black as night
from head to toe
this cat with yellow eyes

he sees things
beyond this realm
not seen by human eyes

a yowling cry
that calls alarm
and wakes you in the night

this cat companion
and pet familiar
that keeps a watchful sight

no ghost intruder
nor supernatural
can stealth beyond his watch

his whiskers twitch
his ears rotate
his tail begins to flick

he leaps with faith
he's lightning quick
he's claws and yowls and more

to sound the call
that something's there
then sit up in bed aware

look around
acknowledge existence
of the mysteries beyond

pet his head
deliver a kiss
then return to safe and sound

Debby Weinberger

Briar

Chips are down
Nice try, keep flying
Out in the night
Feed the cat
In through the doorway
Out of the city
In the garden so pretty
Neat as ninepence
Second to none
Briar the cat, our family home
Encouraged by all
Friendly cat, stroking a pleasure

Lean on me brother
I am a cat lover
Pictures taken just like other
Venture out to rat
No one notices his pad
Underneath the ledge on shelf
Briar enjoys sleeping on cookery books
Running up and down stairs
Phone please answer
Briar is at home
Friends appear in small numbers
Please put the cat in the kitchen
Out of the way
The children have come to play
Out goes Briar into the shed
Sorry, sorry I must come in
I want to see what's going on
Some food is left upon the shelf
Briar helps himself to cake - funny feline our cat!

S M Thompson

Untitled

I have a pink-toed tarantula
she has her own glass box
she's very pretty to look at
with her graceful ways and her hairy pink socks
you don't see her very often until it's time to be fed
and from time to time she'll spin a new web
she cunningly catches a cricket or two
as my cats look on, calculating what they'd like to do
and when she outgrows the body she's in
it's no problem, she just sheds her skin
a shiny new spider will slowly climb out
a fascinating sight to see for this there is no doubt
so I'm speaking as a spider lover, I think they're misunderstood
they are not vicious or scary and do nothing but good
so next time you see one out of the corner of your eye
just gently get a glass and put it outside

Sheryl Price

52

Nissi

The strangest day of my life,
Was when I looked upon my own reflection,
By a means of a 5 foot mirror,
At first I accepted my own delusion ...

Who was this standing in front of me,
Baring its teeth and growling my way?
Then of course it hit me,
It was I, my anger beginning to fade ...

I look back on that day,
As I do most as time passes by,
My family is all here with me,
As I let out a contented sigh.

Kimberly Harries

The Widget

The Widget is covered in short black hair,
It drops them everywhere - but does not care!
It walks around all nonchalant - as if it owns the place,
I am sure it thinks it is part of the human race!
So much so it insists on sitting in my chair,
And there is only one way to get it off there.
The way To the Widget's heart is its one desire,
We are both happy when it's curled up by the fire!
The Widget wouldn't entertain food from a tin,
I've tried - it gets wasted and just ends up in the bin!
It can have a mad half-hour playing with its ball,
Flicking it up in the air and patting it down the hall.
When it's in the garden it will try to climb the fence,
But The Widget wasn't graced with good balance or sense!
I can guarantee it will trip and fall - but carry on with grace,
As The Widget never ever likes to lose face!

I think The Widget could be deaf as when it's in the hall,
It never ever comes - no matter how long I call.
When dark clouds appear and it begins to shower,
Its back lowers and, with tail between legs, it cowers.
The Widget doesn't need me - but I need her,
To say 'hello' in the morning when I start to stir.
The Widget is very territorial and likes a good fight,
'Who are you to come in my garden? You don't have the right!'

The Widget has beautiful eyes - a shade of green that's pale,
The Widget got her name from the movement of her tail.
The Widget looks at me in a very special way,
And I know exactly what she is trying to say.
She is always asking for biscuits that make her nice and fat,
The Widget is my good friend and my little black cat!

Lara Wiseman

Houdini

Our rabbit, Houdini,
Was an escapologist.
Tunnels were his forte,
Chewing through cages.
Nobody told him
Rabbits are meek and mild.
It was best to avoid his rages.

Our Houdini was a wild child
A biter, a snarler, a leaper
He ate up next-door's carrots in one go.
Even a prize chrysanthemum
They'd reared from seed, for show.

Oh, he was a stealer, a terrier, a smuggler
After a night on the tiles
Digging up the leeks across the street
We found him tearing fur out of his chest
We put it down to summer's sultry heat.

He made a nest, went broody, stayed at home
We were perplexed.
One morning, there they were
Houdini's tribe, in white and spotty vests.

He was a her. She lost the will to roam
Stopped growling, settled down to
Asda's pellets. We missed the reprobate.
She had to be rechristened Rabbit Kate.

Sheena Blackhall

Guess My Friend!

Guess who?
My pet.

Guess where?
At my place.

Guess when?
3 years ago I got to
know this cat.

Guess why?
She's my best friend,
my silent life companion ...
just like me, though much
smaller and more hairy ...

And

Guess what?
Her name is actually *Guess*
though in Swedish,
of course.

Vineta Svelch

Zorro The Cat

I wanted to be a piano player
But I was born to be a cat. So,
I work my paws along sofas and chairs
In long, long runs, and short electric
Bursts. Sometimes I hit the goldfish bowl
A sideways swipe, a high C.

Under my paws, like music,
A world unfolds: of night patrols,
Rat interceptions at 12 o'clock high
On walls where debated lands intersect
In yowls, like air raid sirens.

My blues roll unwinding like a ribbon
Across my big book neighbourhood:
Its dustbin full stops, back alley sentences
And the path where I lost an eye.

Look
From my favourite tree, the maze
Of backstreets runs in lines and blocks
And stories.

You think you are on top. But rise at five,
Before the commuters and the cars,

I own this place.

Michael Brett

Proxy Pets?

We had to move, found a flat,
Patio to garden, ideal, yet ...
It broke our hearts that
The lease said we could have no pet.
In the farmhouse we'd collected
Cats, dogs, guinea pigs and rabbits,
So sadly new homes were selected
With friends who knew each one's habits.
No one said anything about 'outside',
With crusts, water and some grain
New pets came from far and wide,
Soon we'd acquired a crowd again.
A hen pheasant became quite tame,
Three ducks flew in for soggy bread,
I shooed those off before foxes came ...
Who played ball with 'Grands' before bed!
Squirrels kept a beady eye
For any titbits left around,
Magpies and gulls also try
Finding scraps others haven't found.
The prettiest (happily not in the house),
With twitching nose and largest ears,
Is a tiny little mouse,
When others leave, silently appears.
Though I miss my pets a lot
These wild ones try to fill the hole,
Gaining their trust on this spot
Has done so much to console.

Di Bayshawe

Cat-Astrophe

Dear Friend, please do not think that our place is a mess;
Although it's untidy a lot, I confess.
On the floor you may find a spool or some lace,
And unless you are blind, you may witness a chase.
Here's *Keeper* and *Casper*. Which one will attack?
Oh! *Keeper's* knocked *Casper* right onto his back.
Observe even further. Here comes one more cat.
It's young kitty, *Scooter*, who gets in the act.
He waits for his chance, with mischief he's bursting.
In a minute he'll pounce. For that he is lurking.
And now, down the hall sneaks the quiet cat, *Casey*.
He's followed by the crazy one whom we have named *E-Z*.
They play solo hockey with round, tiny objects ...
But wait! They're distracted. Now they've found a new project.
Whoops! Out of the blue now appears that sly *Casper*.
He pounces on *Keeper*. Oh what a disaster!
There's growling and hissing: *A cat-astrophy*.
They've awakened dog, *Rocky*. Oh, now what will be?
He runs after *Casper* to settle the fight.
He bumps into *Keeper* - *Casper's* dashed out of sight -
With a bark *Rocky* chases poor *Keeper* away,
For *E-Z* is *his* cat! And *he* wants to play.
But now just to add to the crazy commotion:
Enter, *Sparkly,* the kitten, a timebomb in motion.
There's nothing that scares him, not even the broom,
It's like a tornado when he enters a room.
He chases each cat, first one then another,
Then curls up with *Unc Scooter*, or *Keeper - grandmother.*

Helen Dowd

Polly Perkins

(Miniature Yorkshire Terrier)

Please meet Polly Perkins
What a sheer delight.
She was once a roving pirate -
But now she's quite all right.
She can still be quite a handful -
If things don't all go her way.
I'm pleased to say she's only a dut -
When perched upon my duvet.
Upon taking me for a romping walk -
A Rottweiler she puts in his place,
In her own snappy doggy lingo -
Avast! She challenges Ace.
Ace looks across and trembles
Not believing his cunning eyes.
Polly Perkins keeps on yapping
Keeping back her big surprise.
What she cunningly fails to tell him
Is about her good friend Blue,
Who's a bloody great big Alsatian
And was also once a pirate too.

Darryl Benson

Charlie's Rescue

On the first day of a new year, I thought it was my last.
My strength was almost gone, my hopes were sinking fast.

My head was hanging low from lack of food, so weak
Life's scars upon my skin, I could not stand or speak.

The wind, so bitter-cold, chilled me right down to the bone.
I remembered once a time when I knew the warmth of home.

As I sat beside the road, no one seemed to see or care.
At times someone would pass, but they would only stare.

To stop the pain and hunger, I waited there for death,
But then I saw an angel before I took my final breath.

She hovered there above me, against the cloudy sky,
And as her arms reached for me, I knew I would not die.

Her smile was warm and friendly, I felt no sense of danger.
Her eyes were full of love and compassion for a stranger.

Her hands were warm and gentle as she helped me to her car.
Her voice as reassuring as sweet memories from afar.

She took me to her home and there gave me a warm bed.
Tired and worn, I drifted off, as I lay down my weary head.

For days I lay there sleeping, howling winds outside the door.
Food always there beside me. I could ask for nothing more.

There were times when I would shiver from the sickness and the fright,
She would lie down close beside me and hold me oh so tight.

Her body gently warmed me along with blankets soft as down,
And I was grateful and so thankful for this angel I had found.

Slowly she did heal me, and took away my pain,
And replaced it with such affection, I began to love again.

In my eyes she saw the love and a promise not to leave.
Today there's still no need for words, she knows my every need.

I will always protect her from all harm and with her I'll abide.
I will always love her faithfully and stay close by her side.

Joyce Gorum McGee

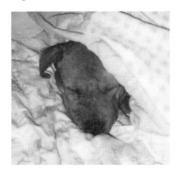

Smartie

Wherever he goes he brings a ray of light into the world
He is a small, sleepy old dog
Yet he acts like a human
So intelligent, friendly and charming
He loves every aspect of his life
And every day he deserves a special treat
So in the summer he lies in the sun
And in the winter he warms by a blazing fire
His chestnut eyes sparkle and shine when he is happy
And when he trots along his velvet ears bob up and down sweetly
His balding nose shows his age
But still after all these years he remains so loyal.

Sophie Peppercorn

My Friend

When no one was there by my side
When I had no one to confide
My secrets and my feelings to
I prayed for a friend and then got you

You came and made the thorns of my life
Turn into roses
You turned the Earth into Heaven for me
Loneliness you turned into happiness and glee

I wonder what would happen
If I hadn't got you
I would have remained a loner
For all the while I grew.

I thank the Lord and the heavens above
For my dear friend Jimmy
Who for me is my friend
My pet and my love!

Pravi Prakash

My Dog

My pug's called Ziggy,
When hungry does a jiggy.
He sleeps with me in bed,
He lies across my leg.
He always snores,
And gives his paws.
He had bulgy eyes,
When he sees custard pies.
He likes to fetch ball,
He comes when I call.
He has a curly tail,
Which wags without fail.
He has little black ears,
And has no fears.
Except for tweeting birds,
They get on his nerves.
He has a wrinkly face,
He loves chips and plaice.
I'll love him forever,
Whatever the weather.

Wendy Cooper

My Pet Dog

Theo enjoys sitting in the sun,
He must think it is fun.
He loves chasing a ball,
And comes when he is called.
He hates sticks,
But likes giving licks.
He is black and white,
And up for a fight.
He has big brown eyes,
And is very wise.
Theo doesn't like hailstones,
But loves his gravy bones.
Theo loves puddles,
He gets lots of cuddles.
He loves lots of walks,
And watching the hawks.
Theo loves sitting in a toy pram,
While eating his ham.
Theo is never far away,
As I taught him to lay,
So close to me,
That's how we will be.

Rachel Cooper (15)

Jazz

My boxer was sweet,
She lay at my feet.
She was white in colour,
There was no other.
She was like a sister,
I don't half miss her.
My dog loved the sea,
And she loved me.
Her name was Jazz,
She was like Taz.
She was mad over the ball,
She was so very cool.
She loved to chase sticks,
I got lots of licks.
She was only six.

Wayne Cooper (13)

Daisy

The first time that we saw you, you were jumping up and down,
So desperate for human company, even though those before us,
Had so cruelly let you down,
You were this ball of fadeless energy, aching to be found,
You hid beneath my long skirt, and seemed so reluctant to come out,
You were meant to me with us, that was in no doubt.

We brought you home, and started by changing your name,
Drew a line from your past, put closure on frustration, hunger and pain,
From now on you would be loved, never rejected again.
The mange and the worms we got rid of,
Your bad experiences we're still trying to erase,
Allergies, hyperactivity, destructive tendencies, we have faced.

So the little neglected bundle grew in confidence and weight gain
Stopped snapping and growling when scared,
Trusts the human hand once again,
Now you love nothing more than to cuddle up beside us,
Snoring and dreaming away, life is now very simple
You give us love and we give you the same.

Kae Elliott

Cocky

Our Ginger is a learned cat,
He knows about this, he knows about that.
For if he's standing at the kerb,
Traffic does not him disturb;
Making use of 'green cross' code,
He then proceeds across the road.
It did not take him long to learn,
He does the same on his return.
It seems to us, it could be fact,
His nine lives remain intact.
We think he wants to live forever,
Because he is so blooming clever!

Bill Austin

Healthy Appetite

My cat murdered a fly this morning
the first clue was a buzzing thunderstorm
as the black creature whizzed across the floor
like a puck on an air hockey table

Flightless, the fly couldn't -
and for all the noise seemed pathetic
a skewered insect-kebab on claw
until she got up and left it

My kitchen is now a cemetery
for flies and moths and spiders
I don't look forward to mice
and birds, the future prey of my tiger

Domesticated she may be
in the house but not outside
where she roams, an avid huntress
exercising her instincts on flies

My cat murdered a fly this morning -
amusement for a minute
it's pointless really I suppose
to wonder why she did it

Sophie Collard

Wintercat

Easing her silver shoulders
through a narrow doorway gap,
she comes, fresh from the cold outside,
to curl, purring, on my lap.

Each night she lies in stolen heat
on our cosy eiderdown.
Her purr, so soft, soothes us to sleep
as frost coats the dreaming town.

Her half-closed eyes are green
as the leaves that are to come,
but this morning she is Wintercat,
in a patch of winter sun.

Elise Gwyn-Williams

Megan

Since the first day I saw her
I've loved her so
I remember her being so small but sweet
With her smoky black coat shining in the sun
She was playful from the start and always jumped up to say hello

Soon she grew tall and proud
Though still adorable as ever
Megan the Labrador
She's beautiful to admire and look upon
I can't wait to see her with her bubbly personality

She's a naughty girl at times, but wouldn't hurt a fly
The house looks a mess with her chewing everything and anything in sight
I find it funny when she struggles to drag herself off the sofa
And when she's barking madly while chasing the birds in the sky
I love taking her for walks and stroking her when she's going to sleep

Megan is amazing and has many years ahead of her
I'm looking forward to spending them together!

Sarah George

Untitled

I saw you sprawled before me,
all black and white fur;
which the air had escaped from.
Pointed towards the back door
that led to the outside
you cherished and always sought for.

It seemed, at the last, that these walls were too small
to contain your sweet spirit;
and to gaze at birds and blue sky was more a necessity
than food or water.

Too late had I returned to comfort your finality,
to stroke your soft brow
and furrow my fingertips beneath your silken coat.
I could not will you to life again,
so I bundled you, as best I could,
and gave in to lament.

Tiny creature, which I had called my own from the beginning.
You have surpassed the meagre pleasures of this world
and gone on to unite with all things.
May your gentle life not go without reward.
It did not go unnoticed by those who so loved you.

Valerie Cruz

Tosh's Perplexity

Tosh, the handsome coal-black cat,
Picked listlessly at the kitchen mat.
For all his life, next door there'd been
His black 'n' white princess 'n' his tabby queen.
Abandoned now; so full of woe:
And he'd never even seen them go.
They'd been catnapped. It was plain,
He'd never see either of them again.
No food, no tray, no comfy sofa,
No willing ladies to groom him over.
Being welcome no longer at number fifteen
Was a bitter blow to his self-esteem.
He shook his head, and straightened his tail
He was handsome Tosh, the cat's miaow.
His feline grief he'd soon overcome,
With the flighty piece at twenty-one!

Joyce Dobson

A fishy Tale

A trio of fish, Flip, Flop and Flap
Took it in turns to take a nap.

Flip went first, Flop was next
Flap, the youngest soon got vexed.

'It's always me who has to wait
While they swan about like lovesick drakes!'

With that he blew a bubble so huge
He burst the heater's element tube.

Losing his cool ended the squabble
They died in an instant because of that bubble ... !

Betty Lightfoot

Clairvoyant

My cat's gaze is shifting
Moving side to side
She's watching fairy dancing
Her eyes open wide.

I feel them coming closer
Though I cannot see
Peeping through the flowers
They've come to look at me!

Mano Warren

What Did I Do?

What did I do?
Did I pee on the rug?
Did I chase next-door's cat
And eat that dead bug?

Was it me who knocked over
The mug full of soup?
Are you sure I'm the culprit
Of all this dispute?

Can you prove it in court
That I am the one,
Who made love to the teddy bear
Left there by your son?

I'd just like to say
Before blame gets dished out,
That I'm not the one
That you need to clout.

My last owners, they left me,
They blamed me for all.
I can't help but wonder
What all that was for.

I thought I was doing
The right thing by them.
I thought that they loved me
But that was back then.

Now that I've found out
A pretty good place,
Please don't get mad
If I want to chase.

It's just I'm so happy
To be here with you
I know you'll forgive me
'Cause you need me too.

Liz Di Marcello

Our Bertie

Relaxed he is,
A soft and
Furry feline,
Yet tough and strong,
Graceful and athletic.
When sleeping,
A curled question mark,
Purring softly,
Until ...
A sudden noise brings
Instant alertness,
Luminous eyes stare
Intently,
Head and body taut
Until ...
The threat is past.
Mystical,
Independent,
Can be affectionate,
Or aloof,
Playful,
A voice that sings of
Things unknown,
Except to him.
Deigns to share our lives,
Allows us to discover
Parts of his personality,
Yet likes his own space.
Is a law
Unto himself.

Kathleen M Scatchard

The Beast In The Dark

Two lights awoke me, shining through the night,
Glowing bright and red, sure gave me a fright.
Both moved left to right as if it were meant to be,
I got up, looked closer; those two eyes stared at me.
The hairs on my neck tingled, all stood up on end,
My heart sank to my feet with amazing descent.
The eyes had an appearance; bulk, shape and form,
Tingles and goosebumps stung me like a thorn.
As a dog bearing hackles, came an urge to growl,
Staring at this dark form, surely mean and foul.
Growling in reply, as if making talk with me,
The eyes seemed familiar but what could they be?
Reaching out a weary hand, filled with icy fear,
I reached into a fur coat, affront of me, so near.
The creature was now silent, hackles had dropped,
My hand lay motionless as my heart near stopped.
The form of a canine stood right affront myself,
Ice-cold sweat, backed off, used cautioned stealth.
A wet tongue across my cheek, sending mighty fear,
This was surely closer now, in front of me, so near.
Maybe I had watched, perhaps many horror film shows,
Yet this stood in front of me, a cold, moist, sniffing nose.
Then suddenly I recalled again and let out such a howl,
I was at my sister's home, her dog, this beast so foul.

C R Slater

Venus

It happens fairly often
A thought pops right into my mind
And my expression starts to soften
When I wish for magic of some kind
The kind that will return
A very special friend I had
Her friendship you had to earn
And she could sometimes drive you mad
Stubborn but fantastic
Just like the planet, a truly shining star
And she was absolutely, madly in love with our family car

I remember the time, out for a walk one day
When she suddenly ignored me and went to sneak away
I caught her by the collar and looked her in the eye
There was something in her mouth, this she tried to deny
I begged her to open the jaws so firmly closed
And with a little sigh, a forest mouse was suddenly exposed!

Another time we found her in obvious delights
Head in the dishwasher among some dirty knives
A long pink tongue clearly on a mission
This quickly became an accepted household tradition

The time with Venus eventually had to end
And there is no magic that can give me back my friend
It sounds like the oldest cliché, but I'll tell you this
For me, she is still here - in my memory she still exists

Asa Brorsson

Dog Gone!

The fat cat sat on the mat,
But you always sat close by me.
The weight of your head lying heavy on my feet.
Your deep brown eyes gazing adoringly at me,
Melting my heart.

The fat cat slept on the mat,
But you were glued to my side.
Your warm breath on my legs,
Reminding me that the one place on Earth you would choose to be,
Was close to me.

The fat cat purred on the mat,
But your happiness depended on my *being*
And, little did I know,
My happiness depended on yours.

The fat cat still sits on the mat,
But my feet ache
Under the weightlessness of your leaving.
My heart swells with the emptiness of your loss,
Threatening to tear me in two.
The fat cat sleeps on.

Deborah Anderson

Kitten Love

I play with anything
You throw my way,
To see you laugh
It makes my day!

You always smile
When I'm being funny;
Bouncing around
Like a frightened bunny!

When you stroke me
I purr like crazy.
Your soothing touch
Makes me feel lazy.

When I'm tired
I like to sleep;
On your lap,
Around your feet.

I know I'm cute
When I roll around.
I strut about;
My head held proud.

I'll chase your finger,
Chase your toes.
I aim to please,
And love you loads!

Kimberley Hill

My family

Jas bounds past me in the lounge
Our pitbull of nine years
He almost knocks me to the floor
Which brings me close to tears

He's being chased by our new cat
We've had him for eight months
Tabby miaows and Jas then barks
And so our neighbour jumps

Hot on the tails of both of them
Is Guinea who's from Rome
He's the hamster who makes up
Our backward, happy home.

Terry Lander

Scruffy, The Rabbit

Builders like to crane their necks,
They find it very funny,
That grumpy creature on the lead,
Is a small and fluffy bunny.

Scruffy is Houdini in fur,
He's always liked to roam,
So now I take him up the street,
Make him more content at home.

I've found him on the neighbour's lawn,
Having eaten her pretty flowers,
He'll look at me with innocent eyes,
Then dodge us both for hours.

Every day is the great escape,
The prisoner plans his day,
Perhaps he'll jump from my daughter's arms,
Then quietly bound away.

Or tail in the air he starts to dig,
He decimates the lawn,
He's planned it all so very well,
Begun his hole at dawn.

He looks so guilty every day,
He knows he is a sinner,
He lives his life as free as he can,
Then pops right back for dinner.

Julia Ford

Tiger

I held a tiger in my hands.
A cub abandoned. Briefly tame.
He wore the Devil's warning brands.
Amazed, I stroked his pelt of flame.
He snarled - the harbinger of grief.
I felt his pure white killer teeth.

I saw a tiger in a cage.
He slowly paced from side to side
and, smouldering with pent-up rage,
recalled his wilderness denied,
while safe spectators gawped and said,
'What time's this hunter being fed?'

The cities burst beyond the gates.
The loggers ply their rampant trade.
The highways hurtle ruler straight.
The jungles patched with light and shade
reveal their pools of poisoned ink.
The tiger's territories shrink.

Thus from Siberia's cold despair
across to monumental Wall
and from Sumatra's secret lair
to mango swamps of East Bengal,
as regress hastens his retreat,
the tiger glares against defeat.

When creatures rescued by the ark
through human greed do not exist
and God, confused, is forced to ask,
'Now which is Man and which is beast?'
I'll whisper to relieve His qualms,
'I held a tiger in my arms.'

Peter Gillott

Cleo's Poem

In the memory of our sunshine and candlelight,
With your short illness and brave fight.
Our dear Lord reached down from high above,
Selected my dog, the one I loved.
The time had come for me to say goodbye,
Now my heart is broken so I cry.
You understood every word I said,
Even knew when it was time for bed.
The funny way you pawed my leg
Even told you not to beg.
Now my days are so full of sorrow,
But for you, dear Cleo, there is no tomorrow.
As I write this poem just to share,
To all pet owners that really care.
    God bless.

E fensome

Salmon

eyes shine like a sunrise
got to get there got to get there
the journey near its end

fight the river rapids
got to get there got to get there
the spawning of new life
got to get there got to get there

and the chance to compete
got to get there got to get there
and make the circle complete
got to get there got to get there

David Chapman

Not All Angels

When I was undone by sorrow,
When despair had reign in me,

I asked the Lord
To lift my burden;
I asked my god
To comfort me.

Not all guardians dwell in Heaven.
Not all angels shield with wings.

For when no words
Could ease my heartache,
You purred His love
And mourned with me.

Lorraine Sautner

Jade

Oh what a cat this feline can be
Purring and miaowing and rubbing on me
There in the morning when early I rise
She'll curl and she'll roll and then earn her prize
Of a tickle of ear and a rub of the tum
Then off up the stairs to my bed she will run
She'll curl on the pillow for all of the day
Come hail, rain or shine, that's where she will stay
Then on my homecoming, our Jade, she will rise
With a yawn and a stretch and no sense of surprise
She'll deem to descend once more for a prize
And she'll eat of the fare, be it wet or it dry
Though if she dislikes she will simply pass by
If the weather is fair, to the garden she'll venture
But she's old and she's wise and it's no new adventure
For soon she'll return and without any care
She'll roll all around, cover carpets with hair
The wife, she will curse and holler and shout
But Jade takes no notice, she just rolls about
Then in the evening, of zest she is full
Curtains, carpets and cushions she'll pull
'Oh put out the cat,' my wife, she will say
For though she is quite good, she is funny that way
But it's time to repose and Jade seems to know
For she's under the table, laid ever so low
So then, through some coaxing and maybe deceit
She comes once again and curls at my feet
Then into my arms, what a day she has led
You've had a hard day Jade, it's time for your bed.

MAW

Peculiar Honour!

I'd had a bad day and wasn't feeling all there,
So was taking it easy in a big armchair.
Socks came in and sat on my lap
To be petted and fussed, and have a short nap.

Tension eased as I stroked his fur,
Socks felt likewise judging by his purr.
When he'd had enough, he upped and went outside
To prowl around and see what he could find.

Suddenly he came bounding in through the door,
Stopped dead at my feet and started pawing the floor.
What on Earth is he doing? Irritation aroused,
I looked down - he had a dead mouse!

He'd brought me a present and, though not my first choice,
I had to pet him and be seen to rejoice -
He'd brought it to me personally and laid it down on the mat,
Which is the highest honour you can get from a cat!

Kathy Rawstron

If Cats Had A Code

(Inspired by 'If' by Rudyard Kipling)

If you can sleep in bed when all about you
    Are losing heart and blaming it on you,
If you can trust yourself to laze throughout too,
    But know the power of a plaintive mew;
If, though they're late, you bring them by just waiting
    Fast to your side exclaiming: 'Here he lies!',
And being feted, have them also hating
    Themselves for thinking 'lost' 'cause: 'He's too wise!'

If you can scheme and make them think they're master
    When what they think are thoughts that serve your aim;
If you can snatch a triumph from disaster
    Or, failing, make them think that they're to blame;
If you just care to hear when praise is spoken,
    Know twisting round a leg's a trap for fools,
And know, if things get ripped, or even broken,
    They'll stoop and patch 'em up: play by your rules:

If by your guile you keep on always winning
    And for obedience don't give a toss,
And choose what food you want when you're beginning
    To fancy a nice snack: know you're the boss;
If you can force their heart and nerve and sinew
    To serve your turn whenever you have gone
And got into some scrape and to your rescue
    They race shouting out loud to you: 'Hold on ... !'

If you can stalk a dog and keep your fur too,
    Can squawk and sing - and missiles cannot touch,
If neither foes nor loving friends can stop you,
    If you can court and woo - but not too much;
If you can fill the unforgiving minute
    With sixty seconds' worth of sleep or fun,
Yours is the House and everything that's in it,
    And - which is more - you'll be a Cat, my son!

Diane Elizabeth Maltby

To Tabby

I love my cat, she's furry and fat and I love her half to death.
She's affectionate and sweet and loves a treat, but she has barracuda breath.
She jumps on my lap and takes a nap and wrestles with my slipper.
With eyes of green, she is so serene, but she smells like a rancid kipper.
She is fairly stout with a neat little snout that is dainty, wet and pink,
Such a pretty feline and her only crime is her halitosis stink.
For thirteen years I've stroked those ears and played with her flabby belly.
I've fed her turkey, changed her water when murky, but her mouth is very smelly.
It's not her fault she can't gargle with salt or even use a toothbrush.
But when I come home and she's been all alone, she greets me with a rush.
She's lovely you see and I think you'll agree, if I may be so bold,
She's frisky and sleek, lithe and chic for someone who's so old.
But live in fear and don't get near if she should start to yawn,
Your stomach will churn, your nostrils will burn and you'll wish you'd never been born!

Sarah Scott

My Three Cats

I have three pet cats, you see,
Two aged 16½ and one aged 10½, full of love, I agree,
They have been with me since kittenhood began,
And they give me lots of support, who needs a man?

The 10½ year old cat, called Lucky, was found very ill,
Cat flu, and full of worms, but he got over these with lots of pills,
His love has never let me down, that's true,
He cuddles into me, and I know what to do.

Give them all support and love,
I'd be lost without them, they are God's blessings from above,
Dalcroy and Tiger say, 'I love you' in their way,
And they yowl 'Hi' whenever I say 'Hi', this is their reply they say.

They helped me over my sad days,
When I lost my father, they gave me support in their own way,
They hardly ever left my side,
And told me off in their way, whenever I cried.

I know if anything happens to them, in the future years,
Their memory will flood me with tears,
And how I hate it when people don't want animals they get, you see,
And won't look after them, they just want to be free of responsibility.

I know one day the sad day will come,
When I've got to lose them, it won't be much fun,
They have all been so happy and show me that they care,
And they all give me lots of love, a love beyond compare.

Barbara Holme

Thoughts Of Walks

(In loving memory of Prince, 13.05.93 - 07.07.05)

I'm lying here just waiting,
Walkies anticipating,
Last time I took a peep,
She was still asleep.

Now, there's movement of the head,
She'll soon be out of bed,
And then there is no doubt,
She'll have to take me out.

I don't believe it! Gosh!
She's gone to have a wash,
And now! Well, I'll be blessed!
She's having to get dressed.

It really is a bore,
This waiting by the door,
She knows that I can't wait,
To get out of the gate.

And yes, I think it's wrong,
That humans take so long,
And so I have to say,
Intelligent? No way!

P Crawley

The Talking Cat

My life is relaxed in the house of treasures
My owners treat me very well
They give me food when I want it
They open the door when I want to come in
I like living in paradise.

I may get in their way
They may trip over me
I'm not going anywhere, I'm going to stay
The pitch of my miaow may be too loud
This cannot be helped; I am only a pussycat
I like living in this paradise.

I mustn't really grumble at what my owner's done
She's just thinking about who's going to fill my boots
When the tragic time comes and I'm gone
If my owner spots on her sofa a tear
I won't have to close my eyes because I won't be there
Because, mark my words, she will swear
It's nice living in paradise.

My legs aren't strong and my eyes are weak
At this stage of my life
There is a new cat on the scene
I'm finding it hard to adjust to his ways
I really wish that I was in a dream
I must tell you before I close my eyes
Come on and try it, it's nice in paradise.

Robert Bradley

Beloved Suki

When I brought you home by car,
You never made a sound,
Just looked up into my face,
Your blue eyes made my heart pound.

From that day you were so beloved,
Your Siamese mew was music to my ears.
You were so clever in all that you did,
Even though at times there were a few fears.

Then came a day we had to part,
For I was travelling to another land.
I tried so hard to find you a home,
Some sent you back for they couldn't stand,

Your ceaseless prowling and mewing for me.
So each time I welcomed you back with love.
Still, it was getting near the time I had to depart,
How on Earth could I leave you behind my dove?

Eventually you were taken by a friend,
Who just kissed and cuddled you as you fretted.
Then I used to receive news by mail,
Saying that at last you had finally settled.

And still those letters I keep dear because,
Each one bore your paw mark upon a page.
Suki, you had to go to Heaven, staying in my heart,
As a little stone that will never leave, even as I age.

Marj Busby

Black Cat

The big black cat
Sat with its claws out
Ready to catch the mouse or bird
The little old lady had it spayed
A long time ago
It sat and sat and watched and watched
The mouse run across so many times
Until it worked out how to catch it
It laid down flat upon its back
And was resting, watching, hoping
To catch its prey for its dinner that day
But the little old lady was wise
She saw in its eyes that she gave it a surprise
A shoe up the bum, boy, did it run
Until it learnt to play nicely

L Bevan

Tess

Messy Tessy
Our troublesome pup
She'd make the mess
Yet we'd clear it up

The little sister we never had
She's now fourteen years old
She'd always love seeing our grandparents
At their old house in Mold

If she's in a mood
She'll cause you alarm
If she begs you to tickle her
Then clutches your arm

Running around, when you say walk
Just by putting on your shoes, she can tell
My dad spelt it out to my mum years ago
She started running about. Tess could spell?

A real little growler
Who would never pause
At ignoring her dinner
When she's after yours

Look at the floor
Oh my, what a mess
Don't give me that look
You're not innocent Tess!

Dan McPheat

My feline Friend

She's affectionate and beautiful,
Proud and independent,
Walking with her tail held high,
So very cute and elegant.

Loves to sit upon my lap,
Sleeps next to my bed,
Wakes me up in the morning,
By tapping on my head.

Hooks poor frogs out from the pond,
Stalks birds for hours on end,
Chases cats who dare come near,
Her territory to defend.

We understand each other,
Body language comes into play,
My cat I could not part with,
I'm glad she came my way.

Doreen Kowalska

Our Beautiful Cat

Was that Sooty I heard in the night,
Scratching the door, giving us all a fright?
Her dignified mewing and quiet way,
Is always with us, even to this day.

Sometimes, at about 4am,
I hear her softly padding again,
Across the room she comes to my bed,
And puts her paws gently on my head.

That is the signal for me to get up,
Open the door, let her out without a fuss.
I often repeat the old ritual without thinking,
Stumbling out of bed, wearily blinking.

Then realise, heart sore,
As I get to the door ...
No. She's not there.
Not now.
Not anymore.

Kathleen Moran

My Mrs White Whiskers

She snuggles into my arms,
Her eyes gazing into mine.
Her seductive gaze, a secret weapon
That hypnotises, captivates,
And flames the heart,
Into acquiescence of her desires.

The one look that said,
'You are going to take me home'.
A stare to which I strangely succumbed,
Somewhat reluctantly!
(An experience leading to one cat becoming two!)

Now purring deeply,
She sleeps upon my breast.

Suddenly it seems time to take stock,
To take in every aspect, every loved expression.
Every idiosyncrasy that is hers and hers alone,
To be stored away in the vaults of the heart.
Suddenly scared, suddenly aware of
How short each life span is -
One for every 7 x 14.

She stretches, flexing her toes,
Her rich purr becoming a sedate snore.

My Mrs White Whiskers
Mishka, my cat.

Anita Richards

My Little Girl

My little girl's got curly hair
And a face so fair
Big brown eyes
Induce a thousand sighs.

Completely devoted
Happiness emoted
Bright as a buttercup
My faithful, gorgeous pup.

Jayne Eccleston

Ode To George's Moggy: Boots

I've always lived in comfort
with owners Maureen and George,
nothing's too good for this cat,
every day I'm allowed to gorge.

On tasty fish, chicken and rabbit,
milk I'm allowed to lap,
no water purr-lease - I'd rather die,
fresh cream from George on tap.

It keeps them happy and sweet
if I deign to bring home the odd mouse,
delighted, pathetically grateful,
for this I've the run of the house.

Just lately I haven't been too well,
but they said I'm more family than pet,
I couldn't eat! My mouth was sore!
So they took me along to the vet.

He gave me a good once over,
tablets would help with the cure,
just pay the bill, keep an eye open,
on Friday they'd see me once more.

So I went back again on Friday,
my mouth was still very sore,
out came some teeth, they polished the rest,
but money; they wanted some more!

George of course is bankrupt,
to work is a bitter pill,
he has to turn in weekends,
who else will pay the bill?

Now this Boots is made for walking,
and I smile now, even more brightly,
on a regular basis, out on the tiles,
on Bacardi Breezers, nightly.

Ann McDermott

A Tale Of Three Kitties ...

Three cats all up to mischief, on the tiles, out late,
A furry, fluffy army - Monet, Jackson, Tate.
To look at them you'd think they were just moggies out at night,
Until they jump the shadows and break out into the light.
In darkness they seem scary, three sets of eyes that stare,
But in the light you see three personalities are there.
They may seem united, to fight with sharpened claws,
But really they're just pussycats with gentle, squishy paws.
Monet is the lady, if human she would lunch,
If she could choose, she'd live in Kent, the poshest of the bunch.
She takes strokes when she wants them, she doesn't like to share,
She swaggers round the alleys with her nose up in the air.
Jackson is a tiger, but he's like a teddy bear,
His size makes people fear him, till he smothers them with fur.
See, he just likes to cuddle and snuggle on your lap,
He'll eat his tea then run to bed, his favourite place to nap.
Tate's a little minx, she is mischievous and fun,
She's Daddy's girl, as when he calls, she's always first to come.
She swirls around his legs, her miaow one of her charms,
So cute and sweet, you just can't help but hold her in your arms.
She may be small, but she cat eat! She snuffles like a hog ...
Intelligent, she is a whizz! Plays fetch just like a dog.
Every cat is different, aloof or sweet, sincere,
Protective, quiet, angry, the differences are clear.
Regardless of their quirks and faults, they're all our family,
We don't just choose our animals, they choose us too you see.
Though we love them and we're happy that they're here with us each day,
Remember they are wild and it's them who choose to stay!
Take it as a compliment, these felines love you too!
So try not to be cross when they've been out and rolled in poo!

Selena Ledgerton Cooper

Sleepy Cat

Curled up in a ball on the chair,
dreaming away the hours,
your little paws chase the air.
Whiskers twitch.
Your mouth utters little warnings
and your lips curl, showing your fangs.
Your ears scan around slowly,
as you listen for things in the dreamworld.
The end of your tail
moves from side to side.
Where are you, and what are you chasing?
Little, sleepy cat.
You will soon be awake in the real world,
purring, asking for some food
and a saucer of milk.
But for now, as you stretch
and go back into that place of adventures,
sleep well my precious friend.

Linda Knight

Best Of Pals

A mazingly adorable
B eautiful and bossy!
C ute and cuddly
D reamy and demanding
E ndearing and entertaining
F ussy and fearless
G reen eyes so gorgeous
H appy and home-loving
I nteresting and impossible
J umps high and looks at the sky
K nowing and knowledgeable
L oveable and loves to be groomed
M ysterious, a mouse-catcher
N osy and noisy
O bstinate - owns my chair and bed
P sychic, purring pet
Q uestioning, querying looks
R evels in rolling over
S oft and smooth, snoozy
T alkative, a tail-chaser
U npredictably unusual and understanding
V etted, versatile
W hite bib and white feet - wonderful
eX citing and extraordinary
Y es, why I wonder, 'y' do we share this close relationship?
Z exy and full of zest.

Stella Bush-Payne

Cat, Bat, Rat

Cat, Bat, and friend, Rat,
had gathered for their morning chat.
Cat told all where he'd been at,
stories Cat would tell off-pat.
But Bat and Rat who both knew Cat,
if frank would say his tales were tat.
The fact he pulled them from his hat,
did not escape friends Bat and Rat.

Bat and Rat had followed Cat,
and found Cat sleeping on a mat.
So Bat and Rat employed a gnat,
then Bat and Rat watched Gnat nip Cat.
Cat jumped up and left the mat,
but when he landed Gnat was flat!
So Bat and Rat and one flat Gnat
Left Cat asleep where he was sat.

Martin Colclough

Coodie

(Dedicated to the loving memory of Coodie)

A stealthy shadow lurking in the corners
Waiting for the time to pounce
Deep dark eyes and chocolate fur
Once the godfather on our street
Old and tired, he wanders still
Respected by the rest
Not stealthy anymore, he miaows
A noisy kind of pest
He eats what we eat although he shouldn't
He never leaves my side
We don't know if he is deaf or ignorant
We still can't tell if he is blind
Sometimes a clever lad he is
He knows how to get his way
He'll miaow in a corner
Or miaow on your lap
Even if he is inches away
He uses his age to get what he wants
Although I don't know what I'd do
If this ancient cat didn't pester anymore
As he's well past his sell by date
He's much older than he should be
But when he does I know for a fact
We'll never forget our Coodie.

Barbara Fox

It's Not The Same Without You

Your life with me is now over
You were a true and trusting friend
Now you're living with the angels
Any pain you were in will now mend
I hope that you are very happy
In your new home in the sky
I still miss you so very much
And when I think of you I cry
I miss all of your funny little ways
I was able to tell the time by you
I knew you'd be sitting there waiting
When I came home from work at two
You were as gentle as a kitten
With you I never had to scold
You used to lie across my feet
To keep them from getting cold
If I was sad you came to find me
And rested your head on my knee
I know you were trying to tell me
'It's OK Mum, you still have me'
But now I haven't got you
For you had to go on ahead
I can't bear to look at your chair
Or to see your empty bed
I'll never be able to replace you
Not that I ever want to try
But maybe if I get another dog
It will stop me wanting to cry

Margaret Ward

My Cat And I

My cat stands still in a dream of captured prey
Purring gently, not caring at all about global warming

I watch him look around, whiskers twitching
Licking his lips at some past meal, or maybe one to come

His fur bristling, as if its very softness was alive
He moves on, silently like the night

He owns his path as if by right, and saunters
Forward, swaying to an unheard symphony

I catch his gaze and he dismisses my presence
As a senior royal would a footman or a maid

He reaches the open door and pauses as if to say
'This step should be cleaner', sighs and enters in

I have often wondered of this handsome feline king
Am I his owner, keeper, friend, or maybe just his slave?

Sam Kelly

Megan And The Painters

I couldn't find my scratchboard,
My toys had disappeared,
Much chaos reigned around me
- My sanity, I feared.
Dust sheets, ladders, brushes, paint
Around me I could see,
Three strange men in overalls
All over, seemed to be.

For three long days they worked here,
(I disappeared from view)
The banter was amusing
With insults, not a few.
But when the work was finished
The hallway was transformed;
Will they start another room?
I'll keep you well informed.

Anne Gray

The Streaker

Oops-a-daisy
I know it drives him crazy
But I think it's a crack
When I shut me beak
And leave a streak
Dripping down his back.
He'll go up the shop
Without changing his top
Not noticing people's sniggers,
Until he is told
By someone bold
And suddenly it figures,
That I have leaked
And he is streaked
But I know he'll be forgiving,
For with the amount I do
If the sayings are true
He should be the luckiest man living.

Marlene Parmenter

That Stare!

Without a spoken word, Lucy stares at me -
And in her silent way is telling me she is ready for her treat.
How do I respond? How do I act?
I obey that stare without a second thought.
True to say there must be a power in a silent way -
A value without the need of any spoken word
At other times her stare will be to tell me she is now ready
To go out and about. Why can't it be - there is a cat door of her own?
Tell me please - why do I feel this need to obey her every command
Without a spoken word?
Lucy is her name.

R P Scannell

The Return

(In loving memory of my cats!)

In the dark I know you're there
so silent at the foot of the stair
waiting for a loving touch
for someone adored, oh! so much
I raise myself in darkened room
and stare around into the gloom
contented at your presence there
your absence has been hard to bear.
If I could *see* that lovely face
or look into those shining eyes
or touch your fur
or hold you near
to hear your purring in my ear
or lick my nose with rasping tongue
so happy to be here among
the ones you love but had to leave
the ones who *miss* you and still grieve
yet - in the dark I *know* you're there
so silent at the foot of stair ...

Margaret Hanning

Misty

I'm just a pretty little cat
Sleeping quietly on the mat
A little love is all I need
And fish for my evening feed
A gentle stroke of my luscious fur
Makes me roll and gently purr
I love my mistress and she loves me
Lifelong friends we're meant to be
Sometimes I surprise her with a mouse
Which I boldly bring into the house
I know this thrills her a great deal
For she lets out a little squeal
I often like to look at myself
In the mirror above the shelf
And I'm quite delighted with what I see
For there's no kitty more beautiful than me
I love to stretch out on the rug
And fall asleep, warm and snug
And I'm often woken by the smell of fish
As Mummy prepares it in my dish
I suppose I'm rather a pampered cat
But I feel I deserve that
As I really am so very sweet
And a more adorable cat you'll never meet

Lesley Karen Collins

Retrieved

Shandy, I don't want you
go away from my side.
No pleading in your eyes
so proud and self-assured.

I will not be taken hostage
into wet, hairy bondage,
have you rule from the couch
barring my way out.

I will not have my friend's intentions
thwarted by your snarls.
I just want my freedom
not a freaked-out jealous guard.

I lay whimpering on my bed
spiked with barbs of wire.
Upon reflection in the mirror
see no signs of life.

The sun shone upon the golden coat
of the Labrador in need.
He so full of promise,
I so full of greed.

Your head held high, most dignified
made others stop and stare.
Your jaunty walk as you passed by
I tagged along beside.

Shandy, you kept your pledge,
not one day did I regret.
That you were wrapped up in that skin
was just a huge mistake.

Brenda Atherton

Monty

Is she brown or is she red?
What goes on inside her head?
What would she say if she could talk?
Does she really want to go for this walk?

What makes her bark and what makes her pant?
Why does she always go for the expensive plant?
What makes her chew the bottom of the door?
What makes her sometimes mess the floor?

Why do noises make her cower?
Why does she shake her coat in a shower?
Why does she always look for food?
Why doesn't she know that belching is rude?

What makes her run to the little child?
Why doesn't she run off to the call of the wild?
Why does she look at you when having a dump?
Why did she chew my favourite pump?

What makes her give you so much devotion?
Why when she is sick do you feel such emotion?
Why are humans sometimes so very cruel?
Why does a dog love any bleedin' fool?

Because a dog needs a master to give it routine.
Not a bully who treats them so bloody mean.
What a dog gives can never be written.
Once you've loved, forever smitten.

Tommy

Lost And found

On road
in headlights
not dead
back broken
legs useless

raised its head
car missed it
stopping now
leave it/kill it
push it to one side

midnight, November
moonlit, misty
reversing, avoiding contact
not dead

silence now
a lonely road
raising head
eyes meeting
stooping, thinking.

Lifted carefully
cradling body
on seat, head lifted
eyes watching

carefully driven
lights on porch
bell rings
long fingers gentling
head raised, eyes bright
not dead yet.

T Webster

Humphrey

I brought her a present, why does she scold?

A mouse, a rabbit, *not* a bird, I was told.
Such a *fuss* was made of its golden feather,
she was lucky to get any in this terrible weather.

How can I please this woman?

The mouse is easy, just out of the hole.
The rabbit more fun, in fact quite a challenge.
But the bird takes care, patience and skill,
you wait for hours before clinching the kill.

How do you please this woman?

It's true, I received tremendous acclaim,
two weasels last month assured me of fame.
If you want fresh meat it's there to catch,
just go out, you've got your own hatch.
But *then*, she complains about mess on the floor,
if it's not to come in, then why my own door?

How can I please this woman?

Judith Hereford

A Dog's Life

As I laid there in the grass,
I watched as a dog ran past.
I thought how wonderful it would be,
To be so happy and carefree.
All they do is eat, drink and run,
And fall asleep in the boiling sun.
They don't have to worry about the problems we face,
Their lives are just filled with wonder and grace.
They can do what they want when they want to,
I'd love to be a dog, wouldn't you?

They always look so peaceful and sweet,
Running around on their small furry feet.
They can sleep all day and sleep all night,
It doesn't matter if it's dark or light.
They make you laugh, but are loyal too,
And will always be there for you.
They can fool around and have fun all day,
And can learn new tricks like 'sit' and 'stay'.
I'd love to be a dog or cat,
And have an easy life like that!

Clare Beavis (13)

A Dog's Tale!

My little dog was brought to me when he was just a pup
Looking in the box I saw two big brown eyes look up
His little tail was wagging as he jumped upon my knee
And each time that I moved, he would be right there next to me

We toyed around with names and in the end we called him Jed
We got an engraved name tag and a comfy little bed
He's seven and a bit now and he's still as cute as ever
I learn more about his qualities as we spend time together

I think he knows instinctively when things don't go as planned
He'll come and sit right by my side, he seems to understand
The best time of his day by far is walking through the park
He hears the clinking of his lead and then begins to bark
He cannot get out quick enough, this makes me chuckle too
As I sometimes wonder to myself just who is walking who!

Even in the dark of night you'll see his eyes shine brightly
His glossy coat reflects the moon, his proudness shows through slightly
He has his cheeky moments though, at Christmas more so too
He saw something to his delight, I didn't have a clue
Christmas party planned and so I went to the salon
I came back to the house and half the Christmas cake was gone
Laugh or cry, I couldn't decide, oh what a sorry state
I supposed in the end, it was just his way of helping me lose weight!

He brings us so much happiness, despite when things aren't right
He's always there to bring us joy, through morning, noon and night
The price we paid to buy him was a very little cost
But he's worth his weight in gold to me, without him I'd be lost

Michelle Jayne Watson

HRH The Cat

My cat's a little nightmare, he drives me round the bend
When I fuss and feed him, he pretends to be my friend
But when I shoo him off the chair or won't give him his way
He'll claw the carpets, trip me up, and really spoil my day

He lies in feline comfort, there upon my favourite seat
Basking by the window, soaking up the morning heat
And like a stupid human, I will find another chair
That's really not as comfy, but I have to leave him there

His crafty green eyes open as he sees I've given in
I'm sure I noticed as I passed a smugly, catty grin
And when my Lord wants feeding, I'd better not be slow
His attitude is simply this ... you follow where I go

And if I ever go away, I know he'll have revenge
The minute I get back, he drives me slowly round the bend
The problem isn't that he's missed me or the love I gave
The simple truth is that his lordship simply missed his slave

J Johnson

Smudge, The Ginger Cat

I, the stranger, dish in hand,
Tentatively offer the hand of friendship,
You look disdainfully,
Questioning my appearance,
And the sudden withdrawal of that familiar voice,
Plus gentle touch that soothes a feline.

As a temporary replacement, I have to win your trust,
Hoping the words holidays,
They'll soon be back,
Register in a cat's non-vocabulary.
By sustaining a food supply, we co-operate,
You oblige by devouring the contents of a tin.

You search the house in anticipation of an arrival,
Whilst awaiting the return of the host,
And the usual routine,
Until then, it's you and me,
And in some reassuring way,
You hold out the paw of friendship.

Ann G Wallace

Ozzy, Blue And Pansy Too

'I'm artful,' hissed Ozzy
as he stalked through the door.
'Say anything different
and feel my tough paw.'

'Caught mice last night,'
to the others, Blue said.
'At the sight of my fangs
two dropped down dead.'

'Don't call me Furbaby,'
Pansy spat.
'I like your mightiness
that wicked cat.

Is anything more thrilling than
slurping cream till you feel sick?
Between us we know everything
for sure, all dogs are thick.'

Lies and bragging increased
as the hour got late
no stars in the sky
storm lashing the gate.

Hell and mayhem
soon rampaged all around
those three scaredy-cats
made not a sound!

Nikky Ingram

Right Shoe

Now Puppy, where's my right shoe?
I'm sure I put it here!
Puppy, where *is* my right shoe?
I'm losing my mind I fear
Puppy, where's that right shoe?
It was here a moment ago
Where *is* my right shoe?
Oh Puppy, stop nibbling my toe
Now Puppy, where's my right shoe?
This game of hide-and-seek I hate
Oh Puppy, where *is* my right shoe?
Grief, now I'm running late
Ah Puppy, there's my right shoe
Where else would it be?
Puppy, there's my right shoe
So obvious, why didn't I see?
Puppy, there's my right shoe
I should've looked there at the start
Puppy, there's my right shoe
In Puppy's basket, now isn't she smart?

Lynne Garner

To Benji, Our Cat

(Died April 2004)

The house is quiet
The chair is bare
Our Benji's gone
He's just not there

We miss him so, he had to go
He couldn't eat much any more
He was in pain
Through every paw

No more telling us
In his way
What he wants
'Please empty my tray.'

I hope he's happy
Where he rests
He had to go
He's now at rest.

Ann Homewood

Our Sooty

Our Sooty from the rectory came when he was just a kitten
With holy spirits our Sooty was never smitten
He was a holy horror when he was very young
Walking down the garden path, from behind the flowers he sprung
He would grab you by your ankle and think it so much fun
We would shout at him, that sure made him run
He was a born hunter, was our Sooty cat
He would chase anything; birds, mice and even rats
When I went to work I had to leave him home alone
When I returned he would come to meet me before I reached home
How did he know it was me on my bike before I reached our gate?
He looked at me in as much to say, 'I'm hungry, hurry up, you're late.'
I really loved you Sooty, now you have gone to your resting place
I will always remember you Sooty, no other cat could you replace.

Harry Skinn

Lucky

Our first cat was black and white
We called him Lucky for it seemed right
We thought it was a she at first
Discovered later when we searched
Male or female it remained our Lucky
Bright little cat and very funny
He loved to stick his nose in bags
Shopping bags, handbags too
We thought some day he might rue
A lovely cat and so very clean
Never a scratch and never mean
He loved to play out in the snow
Throw a ball and see him go
Like a dog he would bring it back
Lay it at our feet, proud of his catch
One day Lucky just went missing
We searched the streets within our vision
High and low we searched around
No trace of him was ever found
Whatever happened, we never knew
Maybe a child thought he was a stray
Took him home for his protection
A lovely cat with great affection

J Prentice

Jimmy

I have a colour-fed canary
I keep him in a chromium cage
It's hanging in the kitchen
And he thinks the world's his stage

For when I'm frying bacon
Or boiling the kettle to make some tea
He just throws back his head
And sings a splendid melody

And when the sun shines through the window
He really sings his very best
He puffs out all the feathers
On his tiny crimson chest

And when the light begins to fade
That's when he ceases to sing
He draws a leg up to where it's warm
And tucks his head under his wing

E D Bowen

My friend Pippin

One day a little kitten came to live at our new house.
He had a coat of black and white, as smooth as any mouse.

But, oh dear me, his small white face was smudged from side to side;
You'd think that with a face like that he'd want to run and hide.

We wondered what to call him, Lil Pippin came to mind.
There was, of course, the name of Smudge: that might have been unkind.

I always said he was a cat that thought he was a dog!
Especially when he tailed me like he was lost in fog.

When I went in the garden, my friend was always there,
And when I sat down for a rest, he curled up by my chair.

What fun we had from day to day, sometimes he'd act quite mad;
But he had the loveliest nature of any pet I'd had.

And then one day my pet fell ill, I really did feel sad;
For Pippin was to leave me when he was just a lad.

His life was short some folks would say; just four years old was he,
But in that time he'd surely given a life of *love* to me.

Angela Constable

Triumph

Oh Claude, how you have suffered,
And yet never once complain;
Your philandering days are over
But that hasn't made you less vain.
You say knowingly, eyes sparkling green,
'Remember, I'm a cat, eight lives still remain!'

Majestic prince, each feature carefully carved,
Clad in thick fur of glossiest black,
Legs perfectly furnished with little white socks,
Oh how you once strutted with knack!
But now, but with head still held high,
You hop on three legs, tail hits the floor - smack!

You were shot in the leg; Man's cruelty.
Yet you never lost faith in humankind;
With loyalty and affection abounding,
Pretending that you don't mind,
You play with the others, scuffle in the grass,
And groom yourself with pride; your habits, as ever, refined.

Linda Benson

Weasels In Disguise

Pink snouts twitching
Tufty ears alert
Whiskers bristling with excitement
Tails curled around each other

No movement now at all
Furry bodies still
Eyes widen
Pupils dilate

Their victim is in sight
The old black cat pauses
His eyes narrow
Though his sight

Is more mole-like
Than black panther
His joints
Stiff and sore

The weasels slink down to the ground
They ululate together
Moving seamlessly towards him
Separating as they draw closer

The old black cat spots them both
He swears loudly, stands up
And clouts each weasel on
His ginger, tufty ears

Maggie Falconer Drew-Taylor

Afghan Hound

Prefers her own road - not yours.
Stops and stands looking
As poets do at nothing.
Howls when a violin strikes chords
Or bows arpeggios.

Sharp-eyed, a natural hunter
On a hair-trigger
Her stride suddenly ricochets
Like a speeding bullet where
Black dots of birds take cover.

Recalls each detail of a route previously taken,
Each sliver of grass once eaten
In passing.
Exactly repeats what she did
Last week, yesterday, last summer.

Each new walk in her wise head
Like small, well-fitted wooden pieces
Forming part
Of a finished picture,
Swiftly takes on the old walk's colour.

Easy in open, wind-blown spaces
On rocky heights
Or yellow sand dunes.
Herself sand-coloured.

Doesn't fetch thrown sticks
Or break into saltwater
As most other dogs do.
Probably once held to be sacred to Ra,
Her eyes have about them the scarab's texture.

Alan C Brown

Fathom

Fathom is a sheepdog,
Faithful, loyal and true.
Although she's not a working dog,
She could do what a working dog can do.
She is happy and she's healthy,
Although not in her prime.
Her coat is glossy, her eyes are brown,
Likes country walks all the time.

Fathom is so friendly,
She aims to protect and please.
Her reaction to the front doorbell
Makes her bark at whoever she sees.
Her back is black, her paws are white,
And her tail is bushy and long,
But she has an affectionate nature -
Remembers you after you have gone.

She's just a pet at home,
Not a working dog in the fields.
She loves a chew, not a bone,
But her penitence is real.
For when she's wanting to be made a fuss of
She's all submissive and coy,
One might say, a perfect pet
For any girl or boy!

Hilarie Grinnell

The Dog

Hey, why does Dad get angry,
All grumpy and depressed?
Why does he take me walking
When I want to sit and rest?

Hey, what are all those colours
Up there in the sky?
They come after the rain
And on sunny days, through the windowpane.

Who is that other dog
In the water on the floor
And in the shiny thing
Hanging on the wall?
He looks like me
But has no smell at all.

I sit and think of asking you,
But then we start to play.
Running through the fields,
On a lovely sunny day.

And I always follow you,
When going to the shops,
Because sometimes I get a treat,
Crisps and candy pops.

I'm always pleased to see you,
I'm glad that you're my friend,
You give me food and comfort,
On you I can depend.

C Rowley

Jet-Black Cat, A Special Friend

When you first came to our home, so small, rich black colour,
deep yellow-green eyes full of mischief.
Often you sat on my shoulder, purring to your heart's content.
Sweet, innocent face, white whiskers, pink nose,
something deep within your character told me you were a special
friend to have, an air of mystery around you, for a cat so young,
like you, had been here before.
When I was ill you came to my bed, snuggled close to me, gave me
your warmth, those eyes telling me I'd be alright. I would stroke you,
feeling the electric from your jet-black coat, on the road to recovery
from your unconditional love.
Jet, that was your name, jet-black cat, and you grew to be a fine feline,
long, strong, puma-like features, such a sweet nature, you would
not hurt a fly (rather odd for a cat).
Though you did bring birds home to show what cats normally do and
the odd mouse to show your appreciation to the master of the house.
Long, hot summer days were your favourite, you always found the right
place to sleep, in a ball with your pink tongue poking through your
teeth, with a sigh, not a care in the world, dreaming cat dreams,
the sun shimmering on your jet-black coat, oh how I envied you.
Ski came to our home, young just like you Jet, though you were boss,
you were kind to Ski and best friends, the odd squabble now and
again, mainly on whose lap to sleep.
Over the years I watched you mature, I'd call you Big Boy, and you
would greet me with your loving eyes, I'd give you a hug and kiss
like one of the family. Indeed you met my family, my daughter loving you, wanting to take
you home.
Years have gone by, now that you are old, I see that you are weak and
fragile like some cats go. It breaks my heart to see you sick and I wish
I could turn back the clock and make you alright, like you did to me.
Oh Jet, what a special friend you were - I shall miss you for evermore.
Your spirit lives on.

Terry Lane

Chelsea

Short, sleek coat of chocolate-brown,
With fluffy spots of baby down.
A shy little puppy from the start,
With deep, soulful eyes to melt your heart!
She snuggles in for cuddles as she sleeps on our settee,
Gambolling through her puppy dreams, head upon my knee.
When she awakes she's full of fun -
Bunny jumping around everyone!
She's full of mischief, there's no doubt -
Sometimes we have to sort her out!
Out in the garden she loves to play -
Watching the birds for half the day!
A water baby she's sure to be,
As she rolls in her water playfully.
At puppy school she's taught them all,
How to tip up the bowl and then swiftly roll!
Such a special part of our family,
Our Chelsea girl will always be.

Kim Thompson

The Ugliest Kitten

Steeped in snow in the cold of the year,
The cats' home struggled, food was dear.
Helpers were few and times were tough,
When a pregnant cat came from a man who was rough.

Four kittens born on Christmas morn,
Where a star had stood high until almost dawn.
Two were tabby, one was grey,
And one just no one could give away!
The ugliest kitten had a twisted tail,
Too many toes and a body frail,
But the Christmas spirit was there that day,
And the vet who called didn't take her away.
The runt of the litter was named Little Belle,
But what of her future? Who could tell?

Soon in the new year, adopters with pride,
Came to consider, consult and decide.
The first kitten homed was the long-haired grey;
Charlotte and Josh took her away.
With so little thought, their parents agreed,
And off they went with their usual speed.
Sadly a puppy was next on their list -
And now my tale has a terrible twist.
They found that the puppy was so much more fun -
And a half-grown kitten went on the run.

The two tabby brothers then left for a farm,
To kill the rats that do so much harm,
But the farmers really didn't much care,
And I'm sorry to say that they're no longer there.

Then to the home came a woman with hair,
That was wispy and grey, and I declare,
That she had a definite squint in one eye;
If I said she looked nice, I would tell a big lie.

By this time young Belle was nearly a cat,
But the wispy-haired woman didn't mind that.
She had learnt in her life, where the way had been steep,
That beauty is very much more than skin deep.
So I'm happy to tell you that Belle had a spay,
A cushion, good food, toys and lots of play.
And I often remember that evening in May,
When the ugliest kitten went home to stay.

Jane Huggins

To A Basset Hound Puppy

All the old fellow's haunts
Await your inspection and delight.
The twanging smells
That pleased his well-loved nose
Will tickle yours with equal pungency.
When you pad in his ponderous wake
The good old boy will be there
Trundling earnestly beside you.
His rekindled idiosyncrasies
Stirring a poignant lurch
Of recollected laughter.

Gaily explore the paths of his bequest,
Yet carve lanes of your own discovery.
For your individuality must be
As sturdily defined -
And they will love you,
Not only as his kind memorial,
But because no basset can ever be
Completely like another ...

Joan Howes

A Tribute To Spaniel Eyes

(For my dad)

Have you ever looked into a spaniel's eyes,
And wondered what they say?
Their eyes hold the wonders of their lives,
Their thoughts, wants and hopes.

When you walk into the room,
Their eyes are full of apprehension and longing.
Then, when you look at them, they change,
They become alert and full of expectation.

Have you ever noticed that ...
The spaniel's eyes can reflect your own moods.
When you are sad and worried, just look into their eyes,
They are also sad and worried too.

Sometimes you are cross with them,
Shout at them and send them to bed.
But, don't look at their eyes afterwards,
Because the hurt, sorrow and sadness in them will melt your heart.

A spaniel communicates through his eyes,
You can see adoration for his loved ones,
Excitement and surprise.
You can feel the love that emanates through them.

Anger, now there's an emotion,
One you see a lot nowadays.
But not in a spaniel's eyes,
Anger is one emotion that a spaniel's eyes never speak.

A spaniel's eyes convey so much,
They show a mind full of emotion.
From love to disappointment, dolefulness to happiness.
But the look in a spaniel's eyes
Is always true to their hearts.

Andrea Humphreys

Pet Subject

Fifteen summers Bella's seen,
Not a bad span for a cat!
Young enough still to be chasing her tail;
Too old to tackle a rat.

She sleeps away the daylight hours
On a chair or somebody's bed;
And only stirs her stiffening limbs
When she's ready to be fed.

But she's on the prowl most every night,
Depending on the weather;
Keeping watch on the silent street,
She and the moon together.

The yellow eyes are still as alert,
The claws as sharp as ever;
She may be less than agile now,
But she's every bit as clever!

John Coombes

Untitled

When I was little I had a dog,
That was invisible you see.
My mother called him make-believe,
But he was very real to me.
Sometimes we'd go out for a walk,
Or play down by the park.
I tried to teach him to fetch sticks,
To roll over and bark.
But one day, my dog, he ran away,
And I felt so unhappy.
Until my dad came home that night,
With a real live dog for me.

Jay Berkowitz

An Ode To A Duckling (By Ella The Bernese Mountain Dog)

Oh dear, little duckling
Why do you look so sad?
Have you just lost your mum and your dad?
Although I may look big, scary and black
Rest assured, I would never attack!
I'll be your mum
I know it won't be the same
We'll have to think what to call you
Ella is my name
I can't dig up worms
Nor swim too good
In fact I can't teach you
All that a mother would
So please, please little duckling
Let me be your mum
I'll do my best
To make you less glum.

Ann Gibson

Bird Brains

Would you just look at that!
Those birds are attacking the cat
And they persistently do so each day
The cat knows full well and
Keeps trying to tell them
Things aren't meant to happen this way

The situation's absurd
Cats are meant to chase birds
But this lot have not read the rules
They just make a beeline
For my cowering feline
Who's in danger of losing his cool

He knows that those things
Are just cat snacks with wings
And he's fervently anxious to eat them
But the birds do not on the whole
See themselves in this role
And continually contrive to defeat him

He makes chattering threats
And flicks his tail as he gets
All ready to spring into action
But with egos inflated
They taunt him and bait him
Then attack him when he tries to catch one

Rita Palm

Tyson

We got my dog, Tyson,
At only 8 weeks old,
Troublesome and mischievous,
And also very bold,
His first time in the park,
He was a bit unsure,
I taught him how to sit,
And to give me his paw,
Always destroying his toys,
Running around and barking,
He makes so much noise,
But when I'm feeling sad or down,
He's always there for me,
I love him so much,
He's the best dog there could be.

Jodie Norville (18)

Cleo

I have a cat named Cleo
She's very black and sleek
The things that she gets up to
You think, *what a cheek!*

She'll hide in ambush
Till someone goes by
She's hiding in the bushes
Her paw strikes out, she misses, nice try!

I caught her just the other day
She will help herself to tea
When no one is looking her paw goes in the tin
Thinking, *mmm, all for me!*

She really is her own boss
Laying down the law
With her pals, Bonnie and Gizmo, she'll keep them in their place
With one strike of her paw - ouch!

J Thompson

Vince

Some say that cats are capable of precognition,
practise telepathy and psychovision.
It's all a question of their grouped vibrissae,
hybrids of complex aerials and Sky dishes.

You think he's dumb? That purr is sycophancy,
he chooses laps according to his fancy,
he's no compassion for the disadvantaged tailless:
Look down! I'm here! Want in! Don't think me senseless!

Strolling along the keyboard of computers,
lashing his tail in semaphoric boosters,
claiming the sybaritic life like any paragon,
hobnobbing with Chris Smart and Dr Johnson ...

His ancestry is traced back to the Sphinx,
and though he'll have no children - he's been fixed,
he still marks out his territorial quarters,
wiping his whiskers on book covers, table corners.

His fur, like life, is mixed-up black and white,
witches' familiar, creature of the night.

Pat Earnshaw

for Bill

My old dog sleeps, and while he sleeps, he dreams;
I see his legs twitch, hear his little cries.
I hope he runs in sweet Elysian streams,

In fields of clover, under bright blue skies.
His cataract-dulled eyes see little now,
He cannot hear my heavy-hearted sighs:

'I will not let you suffer, Bill,' I vow.
But still I want him with me for as long
As life and time and mercy will allow,

And his old heart still sings a cheery song,
And he to me, and I to him belong.

Jane Bigg

Man's Best Friend

We took a walk round Battersea
One bright and fine June day,
We saw a lot of dogs
And then we came away.

Then we made a second trip
To give a dog a home,
They showed us you, in quarantine,
You laid there all alone.

They didn't know how old you were
For you'd been taken in, a stray,
Though you were sick, with kennel cough
Still found the strength to play.

I guess we fell in love with you,
You took to us as well.
The vet said we could bring you home,
So this we did, pell-mell.

Six years on, still with us,
My husband's pride and joy.
You're with him every step he takes,
You lovely, lively boy.

And so it seems we're stuck with you
Right to the very end.
Now we really, truly know
Why dog is Man's best friend.

Joyce Walker

Casey

We were born in a woodshed sixteen months ago
There were nine of us, and we knew no other way
So we romped and capered and played; suckled and slept
Loving our togetherness, the wriggling, snuggling mass
Of little bodies that knew nothing about fear.

But all that changed when I came back one day
I had been foraging for leftovers at the old lady's door.
There was a chilling silence in the shed as I crept in -
My brothers were gone; the bed we shared was empty.
I couldn't believe it, in a frenzy I looked for my sister
And she was there; thank God she was still there.
I never saw them again and feared the worst.
I grieved because we didn't say goodbye.

Life went on for another month or so,
My sister thrived; she was the pretty one
Who raced to meet the challenge of life head on.
She melted hearts with her roly-poly ways.
I was tall and skinny and just plain scared.
Like a gawky teenager, I had no social skills.

One autumn day, three women called to the yard.
They had heard about the pups that needed homes;
My sister, bless her, rushed straight out to greet them.
I hid in the shed and prayed; *please look at me.*

Then one of the women came in to where I sat
Trembling, trying to look pretty and trying to be kosher.
Hunkering down before me, she offered her hand
And spoke the words that are written in my heart:
'I think you're gorgeous, will you come home with me?'
She gathered me up, dangly legs and all
And carried me out of the shed and to her car.

Eimer Lynch

Wednesday Morning

When the dustman's dreaded dustcart
Drums the urban road,
And its groaning grey-geared heart
Grinds its ghastly load,
Our cats in cupboards cower,
Ears aback in terror's hour,
Horror-wide their eyes,
Wide in dread surmise.

Godfrey Ackers

Observations By The feline's Slave

(Photograph by Vicki Thompson)

Furry and frisky and friendly feline,
For fourteen years you have been mine,
Or am I yours? It's hard to say,
You eat and sleep away each day,
With indifference to toeing the line.

You sleep on the end of the bed,
But it really does have to be said,
You choose the best place,
Leaving me little space
To find somewhere to lay down *my* head.

The years are just showing, a tad,
You've not quite the speed that you had.
You laze in the sun,
With a spasmodic run -
Just to prove you are still the 'top' lad.

But to other young cats say beware,
Tread into our grounds with due care.
This is his domain
And you will not remain
Very long, when he spots you are there.

Some days he will tolerate 'friends'
With indifference, his gaze merely lends
A haughtier air.
He just doesn't care,
But his 'kingdom' he fiercely defends.

This beautifully marked tabby cat
Still agile and lean, never fat,
He's ours to the end,
This cuddlesome friend,
We love him, and really, that's that!

Penny Wright-Thompson

Woofy Dog Song

(To the tune of Monty Python's 'Lumberjack Song')

I'm a woofy dog and I'm OK
I woof all night and I woof all day.
He's a woofy dog and he's OK
He woofs all night and he woofs all day.

I pee on trees; I eat my lunch
I go to the lavatory.
On Wednesdays we go shopping
And have buttered scones for tea.

I pee on trees; I run and jump
I like to eat wild flowers.
Then chase all the scaredy-cats
And hang around in bars.

I pee on trees; I wear pink bows
With a tiny bell on my collar.
I wish I'd been a pussycat
Just like my dear papa!

I'm a woofy dog and I'm OK
I woof all night and I woof all day.
He's a woofy dog and he's OK
He woofs all night and he woofs all day.

David McDonald

The Tiger

Deep in the undergrowth I see movement,
a rustle in the bush.
I'm having difficulty spotting him,
the cover far too lush.
I feel I'm being spied upon,
he's looking for his lunch.
I feel he's getting closer,
I hear a small twig crunch.
But alas it's not the jungle,
it's the garden behind my flat.
That's not a giant tiger,
just my little ginger cat.

A Wilkinson

If A Dog Could Speak

You do not know me, though I seem familiar
A companion and friend and guardian when needed
A wolf in sheep's clothing, and a saviour at that
I would give up my own life for yours in a trice.
The secrets in my life are secrets in yours
For I gave you magic and faith enough to care
Belief in the other world, as real as my senses
A masterful hunter and a beacon for danger.
Together, by teamwork, we saw in the dark
And out of the darkness you then saw the light
Through terror and torment we survived the dark night.

Stephen Page

Lady

'Lady' is our cat, we call her that
Because she is an aristocrat
That's what she really wants us to think
Green, haughty eyes and paws pearly pink

Sometimes she views us with pure disdain
If her affection we try hard to gain
Mere mortals to her must all take their place
Till she is quite ready to consider their case

We'll coax her and wheedle
And rattle her dish
Then she'll soften towards us
At the magic word, 'fish'.

Doreen Gardner

The Cat Flap House Hotel

I moved into a cottage within a quiet cul-de-sac,
Neighbours to the left and right and facing front and back.

Sometimes waking in the dark, I'd feel alone and bleak,
That feeling left me suddenly! In fact, less than a week!

For some ambiguous reason, only felines can foretell,
My tiny home has now become - the Cat Flap House Hotel!

Across the nation everywhere, when darkness lingers down,
Doors are opened late at night and kitties hit the town!

It's a common misconception cats like being out all night,
I've studied this most carefully; the cats say I am right!

Snoopy Kitten lives on the corner and gets thrown out till light,
She flies right in and cuddles round the heating tank all night.

A ginger tom called Toby sneaks in quietly from next door,
Eats his fill, then commandeers the cushions on the floor.

Tortoiseshell Lady Kira thunders through the window to say,
'I need a lot of stroking - all night will be okay!'

A tabby thug named Tigger makes other felines flee,
There's a nightly truce as he sprawls about upon my best settee.

Smokie - a laid-back stray languishes on the front door mat,
Shoots in when the door is opened, snuggles up to another cat.

Pepsi and Koko clamber round when exhausted I fall into bed,
They share it with Portia the Persian who wraps herself round my head.

For those who think cats hunt at night or wonder where they roam,
Check the Cat Flap House Hotel - they've booked into my home!

Leigh Crighton

Best Of friends - Best Of Health

(To my beloved rescued horses, love Susannah)

'Come on babies! Come on in,'
Their heads looked up, I gave a grin.
Suddenly it's chaos as they went racing by,
Bucking and rearing playfully as they fly.
My eyes started weeping with warmth and glee,
When I saw them all coming just to greet me.

Moody and low I felt when I came,
But their joyous gallop puts me to shame.
So when they all came in at last,
I closed the gate as they passed.

Suddenly a snicker came from the gate,
It was old woolly Flo - she's always late!
She came on in to get her tea -
Then she leant round to cuddle me.

It's strange how each one could have died,
But my girls and I fight to keep them alive.
So any money that should come our way,
Will help to let our friends, the horses, stay.

S Walker

So Surely Missing The Sight Of Shellydog!

(Dedicated to my darling son Peter - 8th May 2004)

Such a pretty dog; young and old delighted by the sight of her
She brought a smile to everyone's cheek; wildly, deliciously sleek -
Off-white fluffy coat, cute curled tail, watchful ball catcher,
First-cross breeding between a sheepdog and a Tibetan terrier.

Later: Shellydog would stumble and stare at a wall or the air,
Hover around your feet; try to climb the stairs with defiant defeat,
Slightly dim-sighted and hearing completely and utterly deplete -
She walked the grounds around and around - not knowing just why!

They'd been watching the clock since early morning -
Stalking the room, making conversation, waiting, waiting,
Lingering in petting, stroking, looking, staring - cuddling.

Shellydog was given a last meal of special titbits: crispy bacon,
Cheddar cheese savouring, from a big blue bowl was quenching,
The vet and nurse were gentle and caring, laid her on her rug
Before sleeping, sleeping ... 2pm, no more waiting, waiting!

. . . Around the house now, wailing, wailing, tears unending
Close her eyes she's empty staring, yet still warm and soft -
Oh how sad a loss, an eighteen-year span of joyous blending.

The bluebell woods surrounding are fading, sadly fading -
So will always be remembering and coupling with departing
Of a faithful companion passing into her own doggy haven
So quietly, so peacefully, so surely ready to walk on - walk on.

Joan Sullivan

Honey And I

I saw the sun in the heavens,
I felt the wind in my hair,
I heard the sounds of hoofbeats
resounding through the air.

The spirit of flight was in her
as we sped across the Earth.
Hurdling all the fences,
and kicking up the turf.

A feeling of ultimate freedom
puts me on a temporary high.
A need to keep going and going,
this feeling just will not die.

We blend as one together,
fluent in all that we do.
Oblivious to the line still waiting
to prove they can do it too.

The moment of dawning has broken,
at last I know what they mean.
A horse and rider in harmony;
at last my fulfilled dream.

Yvonne Wreath

Dizzy

Born of parents I did not know
In a place I cannot show
For time has passed and I'm middle-aged
I'm slowing down where speed once raged
I skipped and jumped and chased the breeze
Now I trot and find I wheeze
I still like to walk the woods of home
To smell the scents and be free to roam
My boss and I - we don't go far
Cos I get excited when in a car
But every day I chase my ball
Not far mind, as I'm not too tall
My legs aren't long and have no pace
Just long enough for me to chase
Things that move - but not too fast
So I may catch up and not breathe my last ...
I'm mainly black, with a chest that's white
I've very good teeth that rarely bite
I once nipped the vet who was rather slow
In feeling my bits after an hour or so ...
My nose is cold and wet like a bog
I guess it should be - for I'm a pet dog!

Alan R Coughlin

Head Butted

All shiny black with fluffy tail,
at right angles to my greedy mate,
his hungry jaws jammed
in his plate.

A position you will seldom see,
'cause it happened accidentally,
I swear, it wasn't fixed -
the bowls were placed haphazardly.

The determined Persian that I am
calmly doing all I can to eat ...
it is not easy ... it's a farce,
my head's jammed under the tabby's arse!

Gabriela Alexander

Our Pet, Zeus

Zeus who was born to us on Mother's Day
To his mother, who was twelve, whose name was Jay Jay
Zeus, a little pup who came here at four months old
So dominant was he, although so small, yet a little bold

Chasing me around the room, thinking it was a game
Knowing he couldn't dominate me all the same
He was just a little bundle of joy, whilst giving a little yap
Knowing even then we loved, and cared, for this little pup

Now our dog Zeus is five years of age
So placid is he, never gets in a temper, or even a rage
His paw aloof, with his head on one side, looking with his
big brown eyes obediently
Shaking his hand continuously, till down he lies

One day he was taken to the vet, and upon the bus
Well, he cried, and cried, and made a big fuss
Some people patted him kindly, upon his back
I suppose by then he was thinking, *this is my luck*

Soon to be home again, after seeing the vet earlier
Giving him a biscuit. 'Well, that is much better
Than going on a bus, although it was just a ride
So why all that fuss, Zeus?' As his ears propped to one side

He is such a character, even so, even giving his toys away
To the dog next door, thinking they could together play
The dog never returned them, perhaps thinking they were a present
'That is what you get, Zeus, for being so pleasant'

When I come home he gets inquisitive and then he sniffs
Knowing fair well for him, there may be a few gifts
Animals are so funny, perhaps each one of a kind
When they are taught properly, a friend we may find

So when we own animals, just be kind but firm to the end
Then we will know their antics, and will surely be a friend

Jean P McGovern

Big Bad Ben

I called him 'Big Bad Ben' because he was mean
the meanest dog that I had ever seen
he weighed ten stone and I'm telling you
there wasn't a thing in the house he didn't chew
he chewed the carpets and he chewed my fleece
he even chewed my slippers and my false hairpiece
he would bound around the house night and day
and demolish anything that got in his way
nervous visitors would get as far as the drive
and say, 'How are you? Is that dog still alive?'
The poor postman nearly had a heart attack
when Big Bad Ben jumped and landed on his back
all the neighbours would scream with fright
whenever Big Bad Ben came into sight
but I loved that old dog and he loved me
he had a loving side that no one else could see
as he lay by my feet at the end of the day
I would stroke his head and his eyes seemed to say
'I'm not really so bad, just high-spirited you know'
and we'd both fall asleep in the firelight glow
I usually woke to the sound of him snoring
or so I thought until I found him gnawing
through something else that had caught his eye
then all too soon we said goodbye
Ben passed away and I felt so lost
as I counted all his teethmarks and weighed up the cost

Doreen Pankhurst

Our Battersea Babe

Her dull brown eyes were wary behind the metal grille,
Judging, could she trust us, she watched us, tense and still.
Her cellmate, an Alsatian pup, was a boisterous little chap,
But 'Nutkin' kept her distance, with a fearful, warning yap.

We knelt upon the concrete floor, made silly, soothing sounds,
And inch by inch she came to us, slunk low across the ground.
Her nose was warm, her coat was dull, her ears were folded flat,
Then we saw the smallest tail-wag and, doggone it, that was that.

The kennel maid was frank with us, 'She doesn't fetch or play.
She's a very nervous lady, you'll need patience every day.'
Our journey home was 'hairy', the moulting didn't cease,
By the time we reached our doorstep, the Volvo had a fleece!

We let her get her bearings and she dashed about the place,
But always she came back to us, that look upon her face.
Am I really going to stay here, will this be my new home,
Or will you go and dump me too, abandon me to roam?

We changed her name from Nutkin (she didn't seem to mind!)
Meg's temperament was wonderful, so loyal, sweet and kind.
Her nervousness continued, loud noises made her shiver,
Fireworks, storms and revving cars, they all got Meg aquiver.

But bit by bit we got there, put her demons all to rest,
Encouraged her to play again, chasing frisbees with the best!
She doesn't have a nasty bone inside her, that's a fact,
She may have been ill-treated but her character's intact.

And three years on she is our joy, we love her oh so much.
Her acorn-coloured fur's so soft, it's beautiful to touch.
She's truly one of us now, part of this family,
We're so grateful for the day we got our babe from Battersea!

Christine Sutton

Polly The Parrot

My boss he once had a parrot,
A most peculiar bird,
When we were around,
She said very few words.

She might say thank you,
When she was fed,
But if she didn't, she'd fly,
For your finger instead.

She didn't like ladies,
That she made clear,
But on a man's shoulder she'd ride,
And maybe nibble his ear.

One day he asked would I clean out her cage,
For once I was brave and said no,
I'm sure he was joking for he just laughed,
And said, 'Alright, you can go.'

When she felt alone,
She would chatter all day,
But if she felt a presence,
Then quiet she'd stay.

One day she was free,
The dog nearly caught her,
We found she could swear,
I wonder who taught her?

Iris Covell

I'll Meet You At The Rainbow Bridge

So, we must part, and I must weep
To send you to eternal sleep,
No more to stroke your downy fur
Or hear the comfort of your purr.

I could not keep you in my care,
But in my heart you're always there,
You made us laugh, you were a clown,
With tricks from daybreak to sundown.

Your mischief and the games we'd play,
With love and laughter filled the day,
In just five years, nine lives were spent,
To us, your happy soul was lent.

I'll meet you at the Rainbow Bridge,
Where there's no suffering or pain,
With all the pets I've loved and missed,
In sweet reunion once again.

Brenda Maple

Lulu

(My grandma's black Labrador)

She is as black as the night
As playful as a lion cub
As sneaky as a sly fox
As greedy as a pig
As timid as a tiny mouse
As naughty as a toddler having a tantrum
As cuddly as a teddy
As soft as a silky rug
As silly as a clown
As fast as a cheetah
As friendly as a best friend
As clever as a dolphin
As strong as a donkey
As loving as a heart
As cute as a bunny.

Polly Borden (9)

All About Matty

Every time you come to me
My heart fills up with love
You always seem to know exactly
When I need a hug!

I know you will be waiting
When I return back home
With you around for company
I never feel alone.

You give me so much pleasure
And always make me smile
You're a big part of our family
Just like another child.

Your loyalty astounds me
You never wander far
I only have to call your name
And *bingo!* There you are!

Yes, Matty, you are special
I'm so blessed to have you
And I know if you could speak you'd tell me:
'Mum, I love you too!'

Carol Biddle

Meg And Jess

Two little balls of fluff down on the farm
We all fell in love with you, who could harm?
We went for one and came home with two
Are we mad? Some say too true!
These two little balls of fluff with names unknown
In a short space of time, look how they've grown
They look up with those sad eyes which seem to say
Unconditional love and loyalty are coming your way
They are so full of life, so full of fun
And faithfully follow you, they were bred for the gun
The origins of these two deep-rooted in Spain
The land of conquistadors, so easy to train
Spaniels that's true, no more and no less
These two loyal friends called Meg and Jess

Peter Ellis

Gary Cooper And The Emerald-Eyed Lady

The sexiest tom I ever did see
Is a cat called Gary Cooper and he's living with me.
The very wildest of lovers in his headstrong youth,
Now he sleeps beneath my covers 'cause he's long in the tooth.

A peaceable, home-loving kind of guy ...
A Prufrock sort of cat ... rather shy ...
Living life on the razzle dazzle
Had been wearing him to a frazzle.

He was glad to quit fighting and wooing at last ...
To rest where it's shady, recalling his past ...
With an emerald-eyed lady reclining at hand
To worship, adore him and tell him he's grand.

There were many they loved and some whom they trashed,
There were nights they were flying and days when they crashed.
Now they laze here together remembering the past,
Their moments of sorrow and joy unsurpassed ...

Reliving the scandals of palmier days
When rocking and rolling was their favourite craze:
Mick's parting from Jerry, Nicole's from Tom Cruise,
The fall of John Kerry, the death of Ted Hughes ...
Iraq and Al-Qaida had them wailing the blues.

From a lifetime devoted to spiritual quest ...
Taking trips to the east ... exploring the west ...
They learned which enlightenment suited them best.
The scope of their knowledge, their wisdom is vast ...
So they'll doze here together 'til they breathe their last.

Elisabeth Anne Guss

Tales Of An Old Cat

(In memory of Amber RIP July 05)

I've only got one kidney
My fur's a little thin
I've lost 2 claws
My teeth are brown
I've wrinkles in my skin

I broke my hip when I was small
It really was quite bad
I limp along
The best I can
But rarely am I sad

My latest problem is my heart
It's made me feel quite ill
I cough and cough
And catch my breath
Oh no! Another pill

All in all I'm not too well
My life is one endurance
The veterinary bills
Keep mounting up
Thank God for pet insurance!

I cause my dad a lot of grief
This is plain to see
But when I go
There'll be no doubt
He thought the world of me

Pete Cribbdon

Showtime

I'm sick of sitting in a box for hours and hours on end
I think sometimes I'll howl and howl ... I'm going round the bend
With chalking, brushing, combing and watch out for the scissors
Snipping bits off here and there, you'd think my coat was feathers.

Then, here we go, the lead is on, pulled tight round my throat
Does she ever stop to think I might be sick or choke?
Back legs pulled out, front legs like sticks, tail held up on high
All this fuss and bother, it makes me want to cry.

On the table for inspection, what is it that they think?
Looking at my teeth ... what next? And yes ... my gums are pink.
What colour do they think they are, black or blue or grey?
They could be red if I bite hard and then I'd run away.

Off we go around the ring ... just walk there and back.
I have to try my very best if I want that sausage snack
I know it's in her pocket, I can sniff it in the air
If she doesn't give it me I'll pretend that I don't care.

Back in line, like statues, the judge takes one more look
I wonder what she really things and writes down in her book?
I can't stand still much longer, I've got cramp in my tail
Hooray ... I'm first ... yes I'm the best, I knew I couldn't fail.

Tonight I'll curl up in my bed and dream of greater things
Like chasing rabbits down a hole ... much better than *showrings*.

Ruby Bennett

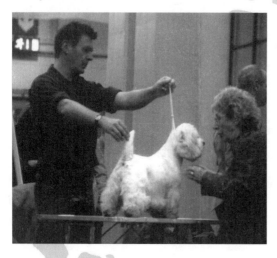

My Pet Kitten (Mojo)

My pet Mojo
Has lovely soft fur,
He lies in his basket
But he doesn't half purr.

My cat Mojo
Has lovely bright eyes,
And his arrival was
A birthday surprise!

My cat Mojo
Has pads on his paws,
If you tease him
He will use his claws.

Meaghan Hunt (8)

Our Yorkie

Some say that animals are dim,
But we don't get much fuss, it's him.
A Yorkshire terrier is he,
A lion in his mind he'll be.
Down to the garden gate he'll go,
Tail erect and eyes aglow.
Some passing female will succumb,
To stroke his ears and tickle his tum.
Of his cutie-pieness he's reassured,
And with this game he's never bored.
Indoors he comes to rest awhile,
And on his face we're sure, a smile.
He's not a young dog anymore,
So this attention his ego does restore.
Never say that animals are dim,
For we don't get much fuss, it's him.

I M Jones

My Pet

She twitches her nose all day long
She's got a toy ball that goes *bong, bang, bong*
She sits in sawdust and cleans her fur
Her name is Ruby and I love her
She eats lettuce and carrots with her big teeth
And in her hutch she goes to sleep.

Chloe Doran (8)

Marvellous Mabel

Marvellous Mabel, the ballroom cat
Sits and watches the dancers -
She knows each step
Off by heart
She has no need to rehearse.

The music fills her ears
And she fondly thinks
Of past romances -
Her loves of long ago
With twinkling toes
And soft purrs.

Their endearments echo
In time with the beat
Of the music -
Soulful eyes look at you
And her fur is aglow.

Marvellous Mabel, the ballroom cat
Sits and watches the dancers -
She loves the rhythm
She loves the beat
She loves to see the dancing feet.

All this adds up to just one thing
She is the queen of swing.

Marvellous Mabel, the ballroom cat
Sits and watches the dancers -

Beverley Beck

Walking The Dog

Small brown dog with little legs,
Tugging the lead with energetic zest,
You would think he had never been walked before,
Never been out of the door.

We walk up the hill,
Little legs scurrying on the ground,
Panting for breath with every tug,
Ears alert, listening to every sound.

A man is coming down the hill,
A big Labrador on a strong lead,
He smiles at us with goodwill,
The dog walking obediently at his side.

My dog stiffens at this view,
And bursts into a bark so loud,
Trying to scare this intruder away,
A terrier's nature to be true.

But this gentle intruder does not care,
He walks forward without a fear,
Noses meet with wagging tails,
A friendly moment the two dogs share.

We depart and go our separate ways,
Small brown dog starts tugging again,
Fierce little dog with a heart so soft,
Faithful to the end of his days.

Louise Bett

Mao, The Cat

You know what it's like when you come home and there's no one to swear at,
Then rambling along, stopping to rub against your leg comes the cat.
He thinks he is the king of the whole house, even the bed.
You think you're his master, but it's you being led.
You want to let off steam, rant and rave about your day
But out comes his fluffy ball and that look that would say
Here I am, now play. I tell him I'll swap him for a budgerigar, be less work
But he knows I don't mean it and with that ball goes berserk.
He's really fussy about what he eats,
Beans on toast will do for me, but for him, oh no, the best cuts of meat.
He leaves hair on the carpet, balls of the stuff.
Never cleans up after himself, I'm always saying enough is enough.
I know tomorrow when I come home again he'll be just the same.
But that's what I have him for, his friendship and trust, although he's a pain.

Brenda Ferguson

Requiem for A Puss

Companion of my home and hearth,
A dozen years upon my path,
But your lithe form no more I see,
Just one small mound beneath a tree.

Cats are mystics of the creature world,
Whether sphinx-like or by fireside curled,
There are enigmas in their emerald eyes,
I think of them as somehow strangely wise.

Unlike dogs, cats will never fawn,
Nor give a welcome on the lawn,
With wagging tail and bounding stride,
And rolling of the eyes beside.

Cats have more dignity than that,
His dress, if human, a top hat,
But yet these prideful pets can love,
When fussing like a furry glove,

Upon the lap or round the ankles,
And nothing in her ever rankles,
My finding always has been that,
Every puss is an aristocrat.

Did Christ our Lord caress a cat?
Be perfectly assured of that,
His holy hands ran through the fur,
His ears delighted at the purr,

I think that even when He rose,
After disposing of His foes,
That He who had such love for us,
Would have paused to pet a puss.

Derek Sones

Best Of Friends - Best Of Health

Oh darling dogs you've had your days,
Of showing off in your special ways.
Those days of walking proud in the ring,
What love and joy you all did bring.
Rosettes a-flutter, bags of food,
Certificates of 'First', it was all so good.
Retired now and dogs of the house,
Could not be bothered to catch a mouse.
Fox terriers they are, all white and black,
Will patiently wait till we all come back.
Those pleading eyes and slobbering kisses,
Will stir our hearts to obey their wishes.
'Just a little biscuit now, please Mum or Dad,
And we'll give you love - best you've ever had.'
We do not mind the muddy paws,
For in this house there are no laws.
Our dearest friends we know you so well,
Your stance, your eyes will us tell.
What is on your minds is for us to know,
Oh dogs of ours, we love you so.

Marie Knott

Puppy Life

We have you now Brynn, our little puppy dog,
When we take you out we all have to jog.
Full of life and fun, always jumping up,
A very mischievous little pup.

You are a Staffie and we love you lots,
But please stop chewing our favourite socks.

Your nose to the floor as you hoover the streets,
Eating everything in sight, even sticky sweets,
Tissues, cans of pop and bottle caps galore,
All much too interesting for you to ignore.

Perhaps it's a message to us all,
Not to drop litter onto the floor,
And be proud that we put that rubbish in the bin,
To save our puppies collecting it, like our Brynn.

Everything is new, even exciting,
But the traffic racing by is very frightening.
The dogs on the street you want to greet,
And you want to say hello to everyone you meet.

Into the park we do go,
Chasing pigeons when they are low.
The lead pulls hard and you have to stay back,
You only wanted to say hello, not to attack.

Your expressions tell us you are a friendly little guy,
Perhaps that's why you make everyone smile.

Soon you will be older and will settle down,
And we will enjoy having you around.

J K Gilbert

Pippa My Jack Russell

As I look over my shoulder, who do I see?
My loyal companion looking straight up at me.
In happy times and sad times, she always cares,
I need never feel lonely, knowing she's there.

The devotion shines through her lovely brown eyes,
A selfless love bringing truth, never lies.
In her I can trust, she'll always be true,
Always there for me, as I am there for her too.

She loves to romp and loves to play,
She's such a character, she makes my day.
Whatever life throws at me, one thing I know,
She's there by my side wherever I go.

She asks so little, yet gives so much,
Her love and devotion have always been such,
Every day of the week her love for me shows,
From her little white tail to the tip of her nose.

Maggy Rosentritt

A Grand Day Out

The weather was looking good for the day
so I decided to take my dogs out to play.
I thought we'd go to Bennachie,
which would be fun for them and a change for me.
Little did I guess when heading for the hills,
our day would be filled with thrills and spills.
All was well at the start of the walk,
I met up with nice folks and we had a wee talk.
Suddenly - all went wrong,
what was that dreadful pong?
Maizie was bogging up to her neck,
all I could think was *flippin' heck!*
No need to say I love my dog,
but not when she has 'bathed' in a bog.
Lunch of necessity was downwind of Maizie,
the smell from her was driving me crazy.
We were homeward bound and all appeared well,
until ... *phew!* I caught another smell.
My darling Murphy had rolled in poo,
our big day out was 'a bit of a do'.
All car windows opened full down,
my lovely black Newfie's a rich shade of brown!
Stinky dogs with spiky hair,
enough to put you in despair,
panting pink tongues hanging out,
is this what dog ownership is about?
Yes! *For the dogs, a grand day out!*

Elaine Heggie

A Promise To My Hound

Friends come and go,
Flowers blossom and wither,
Moods in one place cannot hold,
Even the Earth is hither and thither,
I've always wondered why you were never cold,
Even in my unjustified quest I had tried to make you better,
Now I realise you're nothing but a living bullion of gold,
For only gold doesn't change, however,
Friends come and go,
Flowers blossom and wither,
Moods in different places will always roll,
Whatever, however, I know you alone will always be my favourite dog forever.

Ani Akak

Adventure

On a clear autumn day
We took the kitten outside,
She leapt around in her way,
Jumping from side to side.
Chasing ev'ry flake of snow -
She'd not seen snow before.
She jumped high and she jumped low
Once she got out of the door.
But ev'ry snowflake melted fast,
She didn't catch a one.
Then we brought her in at last -
She never repeated her fun.

V Eldridge

Domino Cat

Domino, what in your past
Has made you like you are?
Were you ill-treated as a kitten
Or injured by a car?
You don't like attention
At the kennels you kept alone
No wonder you were overlooked
And not given a new home.

A pretty cat, lost and alone
I took you home with me
Despite your constant growling
I fitted a collar for fleas
Although you're so much better
I'm still wary of you
Two loners co-existing
Together we'll pull through.

The vet doesn't like you
When you need a jab
He'd rather go home early
After calling for a cab.
He wrapped a towel around you
To keep your claws at bay
As he pressed the needle in
I thought I heard him pray.

K E Thorne

Smudge - A Rabbit for Life

You like to sit in boxes
Playing hide-and-seek -
It has a window and a door
So you can have a peek -
To see if we are coming,
To put you in your hutch -
And give you your supper,
Which you enjoy so much.

You are so very handsome,
With big white ears and a fluffy ball for a tail,
A nose that is continuously twitching -
As you follow a trail -
Of juicy dandelion leaves,
Which are a favourite treat -
Along with crunchy carrots,
Which you also like to eat.

You sometimes give us a kiss
When we tuck you in at night.
We cover your hutch when it's time for bed -
You lick your toy rabbit and rest your weary head.

We wouldn't be without you -
We think that you are great,
You're our rabbit, 'Smudge' -
And you're our best mate!

Debbie Nobbs

To Simone

The green eyes that tolerate my existence
Shielding a soul that gods once worshipped
And me, poor mortal, thinking I am the master.
Oh! If I could look into your mind
And discover you had the speech to mock me,
Is my languid tongue just a purr to you?
Am I the pet you keep for company?

Margaret fulton

Sam The Dog

Sam, my dog, is very sweet,
From his ears down to his feet,
He likes licking his bone,
And barks when you're on the phone,
He eats lots of treats,
And enjoys his meat,
One thing he really likes to do,
Is go for walks so he can sniff a dog or two.

If he sees a cat he chases it up a tree,
Then all of the other cats stay away from Sam and me,
He's a very mucky pup, his hairs are everywhere,
And when you wake up in the morning he's sat at the top of the stair,
I love Sam and Sam loves me,
And together we make a happy family!

Chloe Mitchell (11)

Dirty Bertie

He's called Dirty Bertie,
he's only got one eye,
but when Bertie's around
all the lady cats sigh.

He checks number seven,
pees on the nasturtium,
he's looking for Lily,
the brown and white Persian.

Mrs Smith spots Bertie
and gives a big shout,
'Come in Lily, my love,
while that bad cat's about.'

Mrs Smith's so careful
of her Lily, you see,
'cause she's not had the 'op',
she's a top pedigree.

But poor Lily's in love
and sneaks out of the flap,
while Mrs Smith's taking
her long afternoon nap.

And under the rose bush
at about three-thirty,
surrounded by petals,
Lily laid with Bertie.

And now Mrs Smith's got
six little surprises,
she loves them all dearly,
but they won't win prizes!

Gerald Hampshire

Humphrey

With eyes of green and coat like jet,
To me you're more than just a pet.
You make me smile in many ways,
Cheer me up on dismal days.
You show me things without a word,
Things I've never seen or heard.
So warm and soft upon my lap,
You really are a loving chap.
I love you too, so I guess that's that,
To me you're more than just a cat!

Brenda Nicholson

A Cat's Life

My cat sits on a ledge,
He has purposely found,
By an open window he looks,
And listens to every sound.

Now it's time to explore,
He jumps to the floor,
And heads for the cat flap,
That is cut in the back door.

Walking through the garden,
With his head held high,
Watching and looking at all things,
That he cares to pass by.

Something to play with,
Something to claw,
An old tree stump,
He has used before.

When the sun becomes warm,
He'll sit in the shade,
His eyes closing slowly,
Watching the daylight fade.

D Sheasby

Animal Magic

I know, I believe
Others on our planet can heal; I perceive
I watched my old dog heal itself
From a gaping wound - inbuilt stealth
Yes I know in their saliva, a strong antiseptic
No germs can survive: maybe it's hermetic
That's how they eat fish heads and bones
The odd carpet underlay, a mobile phone
I was told young of animal healing
So look after all others, else life you could be stealing
A faraway call, they look you in the eye
Wink then bark: so I'll walk you in the park
A bargain we have; I walk, you heal
Can't remember the pup - time just steals
I ask you for help, a cut wants sorting
You slobber and snort, like a bitch you're a-courting
I shut my eyes as the acid does take
Thinking of others; they make mistakes!
Claw and maul, others to think
Capturing; holding caged, by the wash sink
As a lobster, a goldfish, some tropical fish
No one is asking a feeling: just a meal on a dish
So listen to the calls of nature rare
Wait and watch; it's you that despairs
A cocking ear that argues the toss
Nature is solvent: Man isn't the boss!

Josh Brittain

Supine feline

Her unassailed highness sleeps,
belly upturned,
in fretful repose.

Garnished green, next a faerie ring
bare and barren,
laid out, for a spell.

Majestic head in verdant bed.
Impromptu eyeful.
A cameo gaze

black and white, by degree.
Covet, supine,
pussyfoot queen.

Greta Robinson

Look At Me!

Your attention for a moment ... your attention if you please.
Everybody look at me ... yes ... *I am* Siamese
I am white almost all over, except for my ears, my tail, my toes
And the stripes that are upon my cheeks and the pink that's on my nose

I know that I'm a pedigree, I know that this is true
I'm long and tall and skinny and my eyes are piercing blue
The others don't seem to like me much, I'm different you see
With my loud miaow, and my big ears, but that's how I am - that's me

But I do the same things they do, I roll around in the dust
I hide under cars when it's raining and come home covered in oil and rust
I drink water off the pavement, and eat bugs and spiders and flies
And even though bees have stung me before - it's always a surprise

Sometimes I bring home presents, little things that I've found
Feathers, dead things and raw meat, from dustbins or dug out of the ground
I like to help out with the food - I'm not one to scrounge
Not my fault they don't appreciate old bones and bacon in the lounge

And once I've got home from a hard day outside and had a bite to eat
I wash as I lie on the bed pillows and bite at the claws on my feet
Then it's time for a snooze until about 11pm
This is the time that I set aside for entertaining *them*

Now is perfect for miaowing and dashing round the house
I'm pretty smart so I make pretend that I've seen a rat or mouse
The best thing is pouncing on feet, I play this game until it gets light
I'm sure it's their favourite time of day - they come back for more every night

About 5.30 in the morning, I'm tired and need a rest
For comfort - I find the pillows at the top of the bed are best
If I stretch and sprawl with my claws out they'll make space and try to please
Well of course they do - as I said - I'm special. I'm Siamese.

Rebecca Riedtmann

Soldiers' friend - (Normandy)

He came to us a doggie stray,
The soldiers liked him right away.
Returning love and joy each day,
No guns could drive our chum away.

Through many months of war and strife,
He shared the fighting soldiers' life.
And raised our spirits with his joy,
His comrades simply called him 'Boy'.

He lived on scraps and cadged our beer,
Our soldier chum who had no fear.
With us on icy ground he'd sleep,
But when we slept, his watch he'd keep.

Then orders came to take a town,
And we were told to 'put him down'.
In spite of pleas to let him live,
The powers that be would never give.

They put a bullet through his brain,
And no one spoke of him again.

Gordon Paul Charkin

The Cat And The Moth

(Grimmy's tale)

I can see you flapping your skinny wings,
Smell your fear as you bump into things,
No light to guide you, not a spark anywhere,
Just a blind clumsy moth in despair.

I watch patiently as your feeble brain forgets me,
I move into position knowing you can't see,
A shake of my tail, a pounce and I have you!
You weren't fast enough; there was nothing you could do.

What will you do when I lift up my paw?
Instantly flee, but I grasp you once more,
Getting weaker you struggle, I'm tired of this game,
Stay quiet little moth, I'll soon end your pain.

I feel a soft flutter beneath my feet,
I have a dark void I think you should meet,
I lick at my lips, anticipating the crunch,
Then, purring loudly, my supper I munch.

Now you can tell by the look in my eye,
The night is young, many more yet can die,
Farewell to the moth, for that one is gone,
But there's still plenty of room for another one!

SSS

Our Beloved Peppa

Part of the time, throughout every day,
Was spent in loving care,
In every room and around the house
We'd always see her there.

Our dear companion, trusted friend,
Giving unconditional love,
For the very existence and wonderful ways
We thanked the Lord above.

The outings we had were a sheer delight,
Many strangers stopped to talk,
Children would say how cute she was
Whenever we took a walk.

This pleasure lasted for many years
Until the time drew nigh
When we knew that life could not go on,
We had to say goodbye.

What a change her loss has meant to us
(As others will sadly know)
Our dear little dog has gone to rest,
But we knew it had to be so.

The memories now are secure in our hearts
Never to go away,
And are called on to lighten when sadness descends
As we continue from day to day.

Margaret Hollis

Cats

Who'd have cats? They drive you spare
their grubby paws get everywhere
they claw the couch and have to be
the *only* cat sat on your knee

They haul their trophies through the door
then wonder what you're shouting for
they'll proudly offer half a mouse
or drag dead sparrows 'round the house

They eat and sleep and chase and fight
and caterwaul all through the night
they howl for milk and only eat
the most expensive cuts of meat

They cough up hairballs then they chew
a rare exotic plant or two
and scale tall heights in search of bees
but end up getting stuck in trees ...

Treat next-door's garden as a loo
and yet, despite the things they do
how different my world would be
without a cat (or two, or three)

Their antics brighten up my day
and soothe my worries far away
with each contented purr and mew
I couldn't part with mine - could you?

Kathryn Atkin

Kittenhood

Dancing like a moonbeam along the garden wall
Hoping to catch autumn leaves as they fall
What is in your mind now and what makes you tick?
Button bright eyes so cute yet so quick.

Swirling and crouching, hiding near the tree
Wriggling little bottom, please bring a leaf to me
Jump up and grab one, bite and shred with glee
Oh! How much fun catching autumn leaves can be.

Suddenly she senses me watching by the door
Pretends she wasn't trying, she stops and licks a paw
Can she catch another? Not many now remain
She hears a little flutter and then she's off again.

Debbie Butterworth

fred

He's furtive and fast
In the background you hear him
And when he walks past
Some people fear him
He wears a black mask
Appears as if brogue
Alert in each task
But a bit of a rogue
Then people touch
And realise his trust
Is loyal so much
Beyond killing lust
He roams in the house
And walks on a lead
Scratches at louse
Then goes for a feed
Escapes from home
And off for a wander
And so far has returned
Which makes us grow fonder
He sleeps in your arms
Just like a child
But can never return
Back to the wild.

H Ellis Bullough

Untitled

My name is Posh Pickle
I do like a tickle
Over my belly and bits

I'm growing bigger
I'm running quicker
I've mummy and daddy in fits

My coat is quite curly
In fact it's all whirly
I'm always looking quite posh

My eyes are black buttons
I was ordered from Suttons
All apart from my bandy legs

My nose is quite cold
But I'm lovely to hold
And I'm also lovely to kiss

So if you're a fan
Please find me a man
So I can see what I'm going to miss!

Helen Miles

Jack (The Black Kitten)

Seven weeks old with teeth
as sharp as razors and claws
A little black bundle of fluff
we have nicknamed 'Jaws'
The kitten arches his back and spits
when danger looms
Then goes and hides in secluded corners
in various rooms

A fourteen-month-old Westie puppy
a new arrival on the scene
His wagging tail and long ears
are every kitten's dream
A dog large in proportions
makes the kitten look quite small
The kitten's fearless attitude
where size doesn't matter at all

Their effortless amounts of energy
as they frolic and play
Watching their playful antics
all through the long day
Night-time comes with a vengeance
the two are now worn-out
Leaving us to pick up their toys
they have scattered all about.

Raymond Thomas Edwards

The fish

There once was a fish
That lay dead on the dish
At least that's what I thought
Till it reared up its head
And quite loudly said
'Hey, it's rude to poke with a fork!'

Daphne Fryer

My Cats

They may move a little slower now
Their steps a little more unsure
Their backs are bent a little now
But it was a time not so long ago
That they walked tall and straight
Their footsteps were more secure
And their love of life was pure, so
God, please turn back the hands
Of time and make them strong again
So they can walk on dainty feet with
Their heads held high once more
And I can see the path they tread
As they come scurrying home and
Smile as those two bundles of joy
My precious cats, Tom and Bailey
Pester me for their special treat.

G Morrison

Tiger

Tiger was her name,
That's what we called our cat.
We thought she was a he,
That's why we called her that.

She came from a pub
And told she was a fella.
The pub was called The Bell
So we should have called her Bella.

Tiger was our pet
And she kept us company.
In sickness she was there
Curled up upon our knee.

Seventeen years she drifted
And grew old and frail,
Till came that fateful day
Her soul away did sail.

Yet, maybe she rests
A peaceful little soul.
But we still feel her there
As she takes her evening stroll ...

Alan J Morgan

Cara, My Puppy From A Tree

This is the story of Cara, my puppy brought up in a tree,
her mother, abandoned but loving, lived life running wild, running free.
She had six lovely puppies, but one of them died,
They'd been born near a cottage in Spain's countryside.

Not trusting mere humans, she carried away
the other five babies and hid them by day.
We searched high and low, not knowing their fate
but had to go home when night became late.
At last her dear mother came to visit for food,
then tried to lead me across to this wood.

We reached a steep bank, which I just couldn't climb,
so returned to our home, disappointed, black with grime.
The next day, so hungry, she called on me again;
I dressed in my sturdy shoes ready for when
she would lead me again to her secret place.
She had to have somewhere, a home or a base.

This time I managed and peered into a hollow,
deep in a gnarled olive tree, didn't follow,
just spied one vague outline of a small dog inside,
thinking she'd lost all the others, I cried.

One day when I went to the tree in the sun,
a magical moment appeared - not just one,
but five lovely puppies. One came to me
as if to say 'one day I'll be yours, you'll see'.

Each day I took rations, some food and some drink,
and Mother stood watching, was grateful I think,
until Cara came home with me, Mum cried a bit,
but she knew where our home was and that we were fit.

Cara's my dear pet, special gift just for me,
Cara, my puppy dog, brought up in a tree.

Christine Bridson-Jones

Only A fish

Have an announcement to make,
Whiskers has died,
He was our oldest pet,
Far too tough to be fried.

When we first got him,
He was really stressed,
Didn't stop for a moment,
Full of vigour and zest.

After a while he calmed down,
Seldom moved at all,
Many times thought he'd gone,
Would drive us up the wall.

Thought he'd live forever,
Well that was our wish,
Funny but we miss him,
Although he was only a fish.

J Williams

That Darned Cat

I'll swear you're getting too darned fat
All that cream and tinned sardines
Have made you a slothful cat
You sprawl, can't even crawl
Upon your prey
You just lie in that chair
Master of your domain
Dun roamin'
As you purr
And lick your fur
You've got us sussed
We feed your every whim
As with atavistic eye
You lie you a lump of feline lard
In front of the fire
Rarely rising to strut your stuff
Except when that Persian from next door
Comes calling
Then ancient urges remind you that you can bounce
Flounce, trounce
Any other cat in town
And strut into the lounge
Purring with masculine pride
'Damn it have some salmon
You're not all bad
Alright a bit of chicken too'
And then he flops into this throne
Ensconced for the night.

Maddoc Martin

Noddy

Noddy was a budgie,
I bought him years ago
and never dreamt this boy so blue
could make such noise, as he could do.
At first he squawked his name,
called himself a good boy too,
shouted at the dog by name
and told him what to do.
The dog pricked up his ears to sit
and decided he had better do it.
Then Noddy learnt 'Happy Christmas'
and 'Happy Easter' too.
All year round these things he said,
you could hear him in the loo.
He drove my father crazy
with the volume of his voice,
demanding tea and coffee,
whichever was his choice.
Shouting for seed and water,
for friends and family too,
saying what a clever boy he was,
this bird of black and blue.
Until at night alas,
cover placed upon his cage,
he knew this meant shut up,
or Dad gets in a rage.
I'd peep beneath his cover
to see him fast asleep,
standing by his favourite toy,
looking so very sweet.
Well Noddy's gone to Heaven now,
still I wonder, *can it be?*
I hear a voice still ringing out,
'Want a cuppa tea?'

Dorothy Brooks

Three Cats

First Ginger, dearest cat in all the world,
For nineteen years my comrade and my friend.
He chose me for his own, as cats will do,
And death, when last it came, was not the end.
Ten years into his life our Katie found,
One snowy day, the open kitchen door,
Ginger was safely at our second home;
Katie was homeless - need you ask for more?
Not long she took to win herself a place:
He kept his chair the right side of the bed,
But side by side they'd eat, and watch the fire,
And wait my coming home, like clocks, it's said.
Six years she lived beyond him, then she died,
Leukaemia took its toll, nor could be stayed.
They surely met again on Rainbow Bridge,
As surely, since that time, together played.
Katinka next, my 'little Katie' came;
Such happy years, and she would fondly lie
Trusting, beside me on my waiting couch;
It broke my heart, at last to say goodbye,
I scarce dare say it, but all thoughts are clear,
And who shall say such visits cannot be? -
Again her head against my foot I felt -
Katinka, came you back to comfort me?

Kathleen M Hatton

It's Time To Purr In Paradise

The independence of cats,
      bemuses,
their characters all clear,
      bewitch.
Charlie and Alfie,
    my black furry friends,
    risking their lives
    on a daily procession to my garden.
Dashing like a streak of lightning
    or elegantly walking sedately,
    tail held high!
The road is mine ...
Affection expressed simply,
eyes speaking eloquently.
Sleeping under my cherry trees,
while birds vigorously feed themselves
- cherry stones scattered around in the grass.
The return journey home sometimes scary
we look for Margaret to give us
      the all clear,
      oh dear!
These knowing bundles of love
cleverly seek me out
... hide-and-seek
often rewarded with cuddles and warmth.

Margaret Ann Wheatley

Sweet Pea

We have had you now for over six years
Had delicate times and a few tears
You're settled now and conditions are right
No longer will we have an early morning fright

Were you too hot, were you too cold?
We read and read, listened to all we were told
At last your housing is as perfect as could be
No longer called Lollipop, just plain Sweet Pea

You ask for so little, just to be warm and dry
Happy and healthy, always rather shy
With four legs, a tail and a rather cute head
Dandelions and clover you love to be fed

You amble to greet me each morning
Walking slowly, often yawning
I offer a handful of your favourite weeds
Lovingly picked, often grown from seed

It's time now to put you to bed
You sleepily look at me, turning your head
Let's hope tomorrow is a sunny day
You will be up nice and early, eager to play

Anne Campbell

My New Life

Abandoned and lonely, left in a steel hut
And all I am is a loveable pup.
My owner didn't want me and sent me away
I'm a puppy, my goodness, I just want to play.
And then my luck changed, along came three children
So I jumped and I played and I think that I pleased them.
They stroked me and touched me and took me out for a walk
Then left me alone and went home to talk.
The next morning I waited and waited some more
At last I heard the sound of a car door.
The clatter of feet ran down to my cage
So up I jumped from where I'd been laid.
They came with a lead and I jumped with delight
I won't have to sleep in the cold tonight.
I went in their car and explored my new home
A lovely big garden where I can roam.
A walk every day in a field by a river
All I hope now is that I can deliver.
The loyal, protective and fun loving pet
That my lovely new family were hoping to get.

Anita Davies

Fleur De Lys

(To Fleur my puppy and friend for 16 years)

I have a little lady dog
She is my only heart-throb
Without her I would sigh
Without her I would cry
She used to walk and talk with grace
She threw newspapers through the gates
A paper round she did with Kier
For days, weeks and years she was a dear
Often she would walk the town
Saying 'hello' with a little frown
From her youth to her old age
My companion she has been through this stage
She walks beside me as a friend
She is just a little gem
What more can one ask of her?
Well just another little bird
Nick Nack flew in and was so poorly
She told him to get up and sorely
He stayed with us for six months true
He was a little bit blue
The bird came down to give us sound
Fleur chased it above ground
There were now three of us
But happily Nick Nack got a mate
We were so pleased to see him date
Away to heights we cannot imagine
Their true friendship grew with their passion

Now the days are dark and long
Because she is losing the song
Hard life spent is at its end
How I wish you could start again

Some animals come into our lives and quickly go
Some animals move our souls to glow
They awaken us to a new understanding
With the passing whisper of their wisdom and compassion

Some animals make the world a better place
They stay in our lives and give us grace
They leave footprints in our hearts
And we are never alone and we can laugh

Kathy Morgan

Roxy

Her cute small face looks up at you
With her big bright puppy eyes
Her little ears pricked up too
Her tail wagging from side to side

She is the spark that lights my flame
She makes the smile on my face
I just need to think of her name
She makes my world a happy place

She's not only here for me now
I won't just forget about her
Who could do that? I don't know how
She'll always mean as much before

If anything happened to Roxy
I would be unhappy again
I'd still be a person you see
But without any oxygen.

Jessica Powell (14)

Catzz

Catzz is funny things - catzz is!
Their tails held proud and haughty
But I am glad I's not a cat -
Cos catzz is very naughty.

My granny sez catzz make a mess
And spoil the neighbour's garden
They scrape up all the pretty flowers
With ne'er a 'beg your pardon'!

But when the weather's cold and wet
They sit beside the fire
And human feet get cold as ice
While pussy's paws perspire!

But catzz is brave and catzz is wise
And catzz knows more than you
So bow before this noble beast
Pay honour where it's due.

Elsie Kitchie

Tia

All black and golden, a bundle of fun,
We didn't quite know when we bought you, what we'd begun!
A bond and love that grew in a second, a friendship so true,
                              I'd always recommend.
You redesigned our garden into all humps and holes!
You even dug out ponds, looking for moles?
You didn't like tidy and orderly when you were young,
But messing it up, you had glorious fun.
And seeing the naughtiness spread on your face -
When we'd call you to come to us and of course off you'd race.

Your protection and love has always been second to none,
But battling with chews is now your kind of fun.
Food is easy with you as anything goes,
You track us down with goodies, then in goes your nose!
We can't refuse you with your glorious dark eyes,
Looking heavenwards, oh what a surprise,
We give in again to your little pleas,
As we rub your tummy down on our knees.
You know our love for you always wins out,
From day one you stole all our hearts, no doubt.

Though no longer a youngster, with grey fur here and there,
We've still time together to love and share.
For you're one of the family, maybe the furriest one,
But you give our lives a lift and a sense of fun.
Without you we'd be lost, we know that's true,
For Tia our darling German shepherd, we do so love you.

Gillian Russell

Sapphire

I take my tack out of the car
and round the stable door,
his large brown eyes and trusting face
peep out to greet, implore.

He whinnies from his stable
hooves pounding on the floor,
knowing now it's time to play,
to wander and explore.

He knows when I am ailing
and picks up on my mirth.
He nips and dances wildly.
I tighten up his girth.

I sit atop his large grey back,
his dapples shining through.
Long white mane with flecks of grey,
full tail flowing true.

As friends we gallop in the wild,
him showing me the way.
Experience this freedom
that melts my blues away.

On return he nudges hard
expecting now his treat.
He watches as I wash him down
and pick out his large feet.

I rug him up and turn him free,
out to the pastures green.
I watch his frolics with the herd.
My freedom, friend, my dream.

Rochelle Moore

Tiff In Requiem

I can feel your grief
That death like a thief
Has taken such a friend
Not just a pet
But as good as you get
Who loved you right to the end
Tiffy was great
A really good mate
Whose zest for life was a breeze
Her slobbering kiss
Her canine bliss
She only wanted to please
The good times walking
Those big eyes talking
A tail that spoke of her pleasure
Those many years shared
When you've both loved and cared
Times to remember and treasure
Forever you'll find
Tiff stays in your mind
A memory bank's investing
Tiff is still here
She'll be ever near
Your special Tiff is resting
In time there's no pain
But the feelings remain
In memories warm and alive
There in your mind
Forever you'll find
Tiff continues to thrive.

Kay Ryan

Charlie

As my tears run down my face
I look around this empty place
I just want to hold you one more time
Let you know you'll always be mine
I just hope you were never in pain
And that my help was not in vain
You've left a big hole inside my heart
Since yesterday when we did part
I held you close so you didn't know
How much it hurt to let you go
Take care my love little lad
And save a place for me and Dad
Until that time I'll love you so
But in my heart, you'll never go

Your mum xxx

Heather Nash

Green Eyes

Stalking true and proud through the grass
Eyes straight ahead, alert to see
Her boundaries, until it's time
When she wants some human company
Homeward bound, ignoring others
Of her kind, she finds a gap
Through the gate, and in she walks
Looking for a comfy lap
With one leap she's on my legs
Straight up without a pause
Settles down and softly pads
Into my jeans with pussy claws
Soft purring comes from her chest
Her own sound of tiny roars
She now forms a perfect circle
With tail caught between her paws
I cannot move, she has me trapped
For the time she chooses to spend with me
I am content to stay like this
As proud as any owner can be
To say she rules the roost
Would be understating the fact
She has taken over my life
My beautiful green-eyed loving cat.

Sue Byham

Hekyll And Jyde

Hekyll and Jyde -
Speckled and lithe.
Could jump to the roof,
Yet stay proud and aloof.
Amber eyes glowing
With cats' secret knowing.
Claws sharp as pins
Slice through bags in our bins
Scattering bones.

Finding mice in a shoe
Would cause much a to-do.
With surgeon's clear vision
They'd dissect with precision
Each tiny red organ
From a mouse's insides.

Catherine Noel

Bo

Bo! Our springer spaniel
He's a loyal friend to us.
He knows the time he goes for walks
And lets us know too well.

Water is a magnet to him
He loves it, oh so much!
Even the smallest puddle
He would share with the ducks.

He flies across the big fields
As fast as he possibly can.
With long brown ears a-trailing
The wind flying through his fur.

He looks at us with big brown eyes
He knows we cannot refuse
Especially when a naughty boy
At chewing at our shoes.

Night-times he is quiet
Quiet as a mouse
Curled up in his snuggly bed
His soft snores fill the house.

He is such a very good friend
We love him very much
He can be very devious
But gives us all his trust.

Kathleen Rose

Tribute To My Big Butty

Who'll find the vacuum you left in my home;
Even the vacuum in our blanket and foam?
Your kennel is crying, 'Bring back Big Butty,'
But unfortunately you are gone for eternity.

Your sharp barks in the night are no more heard,
That do scare away some rogues, some tattered foes,
The cries that do alert me from bed are dead,
Who'll retrieve with delight my stolen shoes?

I can reminisce when you last bid me welcome,
As usual with waggings and flaggings of tail,
And brought forth a mail from the United Kingdom,
Which was sent by my childhood friend in jail.

Though you were killed furiously for my sake,
When trying to save me from a mysterious snake,
There's this thing that I strongly scent,
You'll be the only dog to become a saint.

Raymond Uyok

Chica

She didn't make very much noise -
    only if somebody came to the door
    or if there was a strange cat in the garden
    or if she wanted to come in.
    Then there were the odd snuffles and whimpers
    when she was dreaming,
    and the occasional snore.
    There were deep sighs of contentment
    and excited yelps to greet anyone she loved.
No, she didn't make very much noise -
    but now, without her, the house is so quiet
    that it is driving me mad.

She didn't take up that much room -
    but the space that she wanted was closest to me
    on my lap - at my feet - on my bed.
    I had to be careful not to tread on her.
    It made me cross when I tripped over her -
    now I would welcome the chance.
No, she didn't take up that much room
    but the lack of her fills the house.

She couldn't talk to me -
    but I could talk to her - and she understood.
    I used to tell her where I was going
    and say, 'I won't be long - your turn next.'
    And when I came in I'd call, 'I'm home.'
I used to feel stupid sometimes,
    talking to a dog.
    I feel more stupid now - saying, 'I'm home,'
    when there's no dog to say it to.
She was only a little Chihuahua
    but without her I'm so lonely.

Nora Veysey

La Sophia - The Pyrenean/Alsatian Mélange!

She's got to be with me wherever I am
Adherent as treacle and sticky as jam!
She gets in my way with remarkable ease
Although she's a nuisance, she just wants to please.
A great big beige puppy, with huge floppy ears
She loves me so much that she drives me to tears.

She's only a baby, that's hard to explain
With a pony-sized 'chienne'; who's missing a rein,
As she floats her great tail in the air 'cross my face
She wipes cups and glasses straight out of the place.
When I drive in with shopping from visiting town
Her loving insists that she near knocks me down.

She's too young to know yet, just what is expected.
In her, great intelligence isn't suspected.
She's just a bit quick with her fine white dentines
And will have to learn sense before reaching her teens.
When friends and such visit, she goes mad with joy
But big paws on shoulders are bound to annoy.

We love her *immensely* we haven't much choice
And the other big thing that she has is her voice!
One loud bark from her and 'la poste' is irate,
Whilst neighbours who know her just laugh at the gate.
She has her advantages, there is no doubt,
House theft is unlikely while *she* roams about!

She has to be with us whatever we do
Adherent as honey and sticky as glue!

Jean Rhodes

Mayhem At The Manor

She's padding on the staircase,
makes paw marks in the hall.
The maids are in hysterics,
the butler's overawed.

It's bellows from the bathroom
and shrieks float in the air.
There are kittens in the kitchen
but cook no longer cares.

The General's in the gun room,
the library's in a mess.
The garden room's deserted,
the staff are under stress.

The tweeny guards the stillroom,
the phone is off the hook.
The study's in disorder,
chaos where'er you look.

The drawing room's still dusty,
the staircase a disgrace.
The tradesmen all have left us
and the postman's joined the chase.

'Who has caused this mayhem?'
I hear your anguished howl.
There's only one sure answer,
it's Poppy on the prowl.

Peggy Netcott

Austin's Powers
(Or A Very Bitter Pill To Swallow)

Why should I have to take that pill?
I promise you, I don't feel ill
Don't try to hide it in my meat
I'm watching you - I will not eat
It's in there, I can always tell
You know about my sense of smell
Don't wrap it in a piece of ham
I don't know what you think I am
Or smother it with creamy cheese
What's that? Marmite? Oh please!
Don't try to wrap me in a towel
You know how loudly I can yowl
You've got my head - now please let go
I'm warning you, the blood will flow
Just when you think you've beaten me
I'll spit it out where you can't see
It's no good whining to the vet
They've never got one down me yet
I'm made of rubber, as you know
And I will struggle, so let go
You look silly on all fours
And don't forget who has the claws
I see you tearing out your hair
Well do I look as if I care?
Don't think I'll ever fall for that
You have to learn - I am the *cat.*

Janet Vaughan

229

Mork's Happy Day

I am a loyal collie dog.
My owners call me Mork.
They say I am intelligent,
and say I almost talk!

Yet! If that were possible,
there's lots I'd like to say!
Like, thank you for my loving home,
that was my happy day.

I was lost and all alone,
not knowing where to go.
The only place to lay my head
was a hole dug in the snow.

No one to give me shelter,
No warm and cosy bed.
I'd wake up in the morning,
just longing to be fed.

I just could go no longer,
and wished that I could die.
Then feeling at my lowest ebb,
a car drew up nearby.

You wrapped me in a blanket,
and took me to a vet.
The very best of treatment,
you made sure that I would get.

Then you took me to your house
and made me feel at home.
My thanks to you a million times,
now I'll never be alone!

Greta Gaskin

Our Cat

Our cat is soft and cuddly
Her coat is black and white
She is a docile little pussy
As nice as any cat can be
I would not change her for the world
For she means everything to me
She thinks I am her mum
Especially when I feed her tum
She understands my every word
Who needs friends, when my best friend is she?

Beryl Smith

I'm A Scottish Wildcat ... Or Am I?

I'm big, I'm stripy, with rings on my tail
I live in the Highlands and I'm on the trail
Of that fearsome haggis with its fangs, teeth and claws
But I'm more than a match, I've got daggers in my paws.

I'm hunting, I'm stalking, I'm stealthy and brave
In the face of danger, my tail I boldly wave
Across the wild heather, the bracken and rock
Nothing will distract me, not deer herd nor sheep flock.

I'm steadfast, I'm deadly, downwind I must stay
Whiskers turned to the breeze, I'll sniff out my prey
Dangling tail as a decoy, his attention I'll seek
When from under a thistle his beady eyes peek

There once was a time when a mouse would have done
I'm a big game hunter now, such morsels I shun
That *wee sleekit beastie* as spoken of by Burns
Is mere kitten's play, pah! It's the *great pudding's* turn.

I'm stretching, I'm yawning, snug by the fire I awake
Not long now till tea, a quick wash I might take
Another snooze, another dream and to catch him I'll try
Because I'm a Scottish wildcat ... or am I?

Linda Purves

232

Miggins

Grizzled fur
Cheshire cat smile
Purring greetings
From many a mile
That's Miggins

Quivering paws
Conduct the overture
Lying supine
With composure
That's Miggins

Pussperanto
Is her tongue
Of choice
She answers as she runs along
Responding to the human voice
That's Miggins

She is a skilful sleeper
Dozing is her forte
Curling in a ball
She is never naughty
That's Miggins

She has the sweetest nature
Of any cat I know
A stroke brings forth a *purr*
Or a long *miaooow*
That's our Miggins

Eric Jackson

A Way Of Life

A home safe and secure, hidden
deep in Mother Earth to keep my family
warm and dry. That is all I ask of life,
while I go to find food through danger
of all kind, which gets nearer every day
because of your way of life.

You say to hunt and terrify me is a way of life,
as you gallop on your horses so fine
in coats of red, to send my heart in terror,
to give you delight, so I run
until my poor heart bursts,
even if I do reach home, I am not safe,
for you send your hounds to tear me apart
while you laugh with pleasure as I scream
and slowly die, while my beautiful coat
is torn apart, and you brush the blood
off my tail on your young one's face with glee.

Yes! That is your way of life,
I wonder why? Because it is not mine
as my only partner in life and babies starved.
I hope you sleep well and remember this
with my screams in your dreams
as you cry, 'Tally ho! Tally ho!'

Julia L Holden

Two Three-Year-Olds

Two youngsters out together for a stroll,
Charlie-Anne, three years old, is in control.
The other three-year-old is Romeo,
A Dartmoor pony who is keen to go.
Charlie-Anne's taught him how to count as well,
He's a clever pony as you can tell.
He likes learning lessons every day,
Two three-year-old youngsters ... happily play.

Valerie Ovais

My Soulmate

The most beautiful roses wither with time,
The most enchanting damsel has a way
Of fading, but my love
For Puppy will never fade.
I love Puppy with the
Passion in me
Because he is the sweetest part
Of my healthy heart.
His thoughts run through my head
Every minute, every hour and
Every day, without end.
I frown whenever Puppy is sad,
Tears of self-pity streak down
My face whenever he is sick.
Yes! I promise I will never go
To sleep, while he lays awake
In those terrible times.
I make him placid when
Tension rises in his members.
I share my high hopes,
Dreams and ideas with him
But he only groans and moans
At my unending garrulity.
In those chilly nights
I crave for his warm
And tender touch.

Okunbanjo Taiwo Adetola

for Tiger Lily

If I were my cat I'd sleep all day
And curl up in the cutest way
I'd stir sometimes to stretch and purr
To wash and clean my beautiful fur

If I were my cat, when I left the house
I'd go out hunting and maybe catch a mouse
I'd chase butterflies on summer days
And then in the shade, I'd sit and laze

If I were my cat I'd get all the best food
Not just out of tins and dependent on my mood
Oh, I'd live a life of luxury
If I were my cat and not, alas, me!

Ann Thornton

My Cat

My cat is a clever spy
She looks at me with a sharp eye
She keeps tabs on where I go
Even in the rain and snow

My cat knows when it's dinner time
Whether I'm ill or feeling fine
As long as she gets her pussy food
She manages to stay in a good mood

My cat likes to catch the odd mouse
And brings it in the house
she tells me it's a present
Caught on the crescent

My cat occasionally disappears
I'm sure she hides and sneers
Till she sees me in a state
Then she casually turns up at the gate.

I Cullup

The Old Sea-Dog

Lovely Leo - 13 years old,
Not too well - but still so bold.
Took him to Fambridge to look at the sea;
Opened the car door: he didn't wait for me,
Leapt from his seat and ran up the stairs,
Jumped down to the beach - taken unawares -
Instead of the sand, hit the sea with a plop!
Just a tip Leo - next time, stop,
Check if the tide's in before you drop!

C A Greene

Be My Valentine

I am a female Chihuahua, my name is Pip,
I do not yap and I do not nip.

I am very friendly and I do as I am told,
My owners say I am as good as gold.

Valentine's Day is due and I am looking for a date,
If I met the right pooch I would like to mate.

I would really like pups that look like me,
Because I am quite pretty and cheeky you see.

So I am wearing my woolly jumper with my heart on my chest.
Patiently waiting and hoping for the best.

Pip

Ma Wee Pet Dug

A dinna ken whit tae dae, I've lost ma wee pet dug and if a dinna find him ma maw'll skelp ma lug.
A think a had him on his lead when a went doon the stair but when a went tae clap him he wasnae ony mair.
In ma hand all that's left is his wee collar and lead, but for some daft reason, it's come off his head.

A wis goin' tae go a walk doon by the waterside, a wid chuck ma wee pet's ball and then I'd run and hide.
He's a braw wee dug and most of the time he only sits and begs, he canna be that far away, he's only got wee legs.
He gets awfy tired and aye wants pickin' up, but a dinna mind at all cos he's only a wee pup.

In case you go oot walkin' and see him which you might, you will no' mistake him, he's a lovely shade o' white.
A braw west heilan terrier the best in all the place, that's ma wee pet dug wi a bonny cheeky face.
Och there he is the daft wee thing, he's hiding ower there, no' only did he no' come oot he didna come doon the stair.

Elizabeth McNeil

Snail Trail

Its slow progression
a series of muscle spasms,
a wee tsunami
lubricated by mucus,
it unfurls silver ribbons.

Norman Bissett

Lucinda

(For Georgie)

Lucinda was my special cat.
My true loving friend,
She meant the world to me
And I love her still.

She was so dear
Sometimes I can still feel her near.
I go to the door
To let her in once more.

Although I can't see her form, her spirit's still here,
And sometimes her miaow or the
Sound of her bell, will let me know she's still there,
With her continuing purr and silky soft fur.

Lucinda was only here a short time,
Her previous owners didn't really care,
She had a bad start
How glad I am, I let her into my heart.

She was so small and light,
I probably won't notice when she jumps onto my bed, tonight.
She's watching over me as I sleep
And I'll see her and hold her in my dreams once more.

In this way we can be together always,
Although we are apart.
We were meant to be together
And I'll always be glad for the short time that we had.

I know little Lucinda would not want me to be sad,
And I know that the comfort of her memory
And the love that we shared
Will *always* be there.

N J Brocks

Molly To a Tee

My name is Molly, cute as can be,
I'm a Cavalier, as you can see.
Right little lady am I
Throw the ball and watch me fly!

Many rosettes I have won,
Doing dog agility and having fun,
Showing the big dogs how it's done,
Wagging my tail and wiggling my bum!

My favourite game that gives me such delight,
Is Grandad playing with the torchlight.
Up and down the carpet I run,
All this excitement - oh what fun!

Friday night it's fish and chips,
Look at me, I'm licking my lips.
Fishcake, a sausage, what a treat,
Now a lay down on Nanny's seat.

With Nanny and Grandad only next door,
And my mum and dad, who I adore,
I have a great life as you can see,
This is why my dad wrote a poem about *me!*

Marc Crockford

Danny

We have a very young Great Dane and though he's just a pup,
He's big enough to make you think he's really quite grown up.

The other day, when the garden was wet from the rain the night before,
This dog (we call him Danny) made us laugh. He made us roar!

He'd found a paper cup and in his daft and lanky way
He was bounding around with the cup in his teeth, dropping it, and running away.

Then he'd pick it up again - it all seemed very tame,
Until the cup got stuck on his nose and this was a different game.

Trying to look at the stuck on cup and going quite cross-eyed,
He ran around, growling and madly shaking his head from side to side.

'Oh very amusing, Danny!' I laughed as he passed for the second time
But in blind panic to free himself he ran through the washing line.

This cross-eyes, cup-nosed muddy dog, wrapped up in shirts and vests
Went hurtling in through the open back door - a whimpering, pitiful mess!

Legs akimbo, Danny skidded across the kitchen floor,
And scrambling frantically, trying to stop, crashed into the larder door.

He lay there in a tangled heap - a really funny sight.
We sorted him out, he slumped onto his blanket - and he didn't move all night!

Bill Eden

Billy

Billy was an accident,
a loss of concentration.
Truly just the result of lust,
not an act of pure creation.

Our lovely border collie, Fleet
left to her own devices,
Went for a romp with a local tramp
and handed us a crisis.

Off went Fleet to the surgery
to try to sort this folly.
'No need to fret,' said our local vet,
'there'll be no little collies.'

We soon forgave our wayward girl
for being such a silly,
Then, would you believe, on Christmas Eve
she presented us with Billy.

A tiny, shiny, coal-black slug
not quite of collie design.
'He'll become a part of someone's heart.'
I knew it would be mine.

Lilian Cooksey

No Bones About It

He's spoilt and lazy, there is no doubt
But he moves fast enough when his dinner's about
When an outing is planned he'll be first at the door
He'll bag the best seat in the car, that's for sure.

At ball games he's ace and as quick as a flash
If the venue's the lake, he'll dive in with a splash
He seeks your attention for most of the time
If he can be Cock of the Walk, he is fine.

He's arrogant, selfish and terribly vain
Ignore him and he will treat you with disdain
But he'll stay at your side through thick and through thin
Why not? After all, it's a dog's life for him!

Mary Goodchild

Basil And Barnabas

Hello little chap - if you're here to stay
Remember I've been here much longer
And give me respect I pray.
You have your own dish and I have mine,
So keep in your place and all will be well
And we should get along just fine.

Okay old chap - if that's how you feel.
I miss my brothers and sisters and my mother's milk
So I'm not used yet to a big meal.
I'm young and frisky and love to play,
Be patient as I settle into my new home.
I knew you were here first - by the way.

What's going on you two?
I dearly want you to be friends.
Barnabas, I know what you want to do.
Don't jump on poor Basil please
It makes him squeal and he gets cross.
You mustn't be such a little tease.

We are privileged Basil that us you chose.
We never found from whence you came
And couldn't guess your age - or suppose
Why anyone could abandon you.
But you stayed, never more to roam,
We couldn't chase you away - you knew.

You were a surprise to us Barnabas dear.
We arrived home to find you one day,
A present from our son who left you here.
Your face full of mischief tore us apart.
How could we not love you, you imp?
You tugged at the strings of our heart.

Margaret Deverson

Excuse Me Miss ...

Excuse me Miss, please could you give me a home?
I'm lost you see, with nowhere to roam.
I think I'm what you call a stray,
I'll be ever so good, I could make your day.

Excuse me Miss, but I think I'm unwell, you see
I've lost a few teeth and there's something in my tummy,
A tapeworm perhaps and look at these tics around my ears,
If you could just take me in and give me a hand, oh cheers!

Excuse me Miss, but it's been awhile since I saw Mum and Dad,
If I think too hard it will make me feel sad.
Do you have anything to eat, other than mouse?
Oh my word, you do have a nice house!

Excuse me Miss but I've been upstairs and noticed your bed,
Do you think I could snuggle down and just rest my head?
This is very comfy, is it duck down or goose?
It's great to be so warm and well fed, not out on the loose.

Excuse me Miss ... *zzzzzzzz!*

Theresa M Carrier

Happy Chappie

I am a happy chappie,
My master's loads of fun,
When I ask he throws a ball for me,
And takes me for a run.

I know my master loves me
Cos first thing in the morn',
I climb upon his bed you see
And he keeps me nice and warm.

Then he makes and lights the fire
To warm the living room,
So's I can stretch in front of it -
Doze off and have a dream.

Then he puts the kettle on
And makes some tea for Mum,
A bowl of warm milk for me,
Which really warms my tum!

Then we go out for a walk -
Across the fields I bound,
My master laughs as I gad about
Oh I am a happy hound!

Timothy Charles

Ode To Fiz

A bundle of fun and energy sat very patiently
As I looked around the rescue home
Pick me! Pick me! Pick me!
But the wagging tail and cheeky grin
Just blew my mind away,
And so a special bond began
At *Pads* that very day ...

So I took her home and lavished her
With love and toys and games,
We'd walk for hours round fields and lochs,
Through woods and leafy lanes,
And as I gazed upon her, looking heavenly
As she was sleeping on my sofa
Her head upon my knee,
No one could have a better friend
She really is 'The Biz'
And so it was decided
That I would call her 'Fiz'.

Six months on and I knew Fiz would
Make changes to my life,
Much healthier and happier now
I feel like a new wife.
But one thing's changed, that's not so good
My husband's often said
She's worked her way into our hearts
And to the bottom of our bed!

Denise Saunders

Puppy Class

(Dedicated to the pups and handlers I've had the pleasure to teach)

P uppies are so cute and sweet,
U ntil they nip, howl, whine and greet
P uddles they create a-plenty.
P lus they poop until they're empty.
Y et all this will soon pass as they come to puppy class.

C lass is great fun when new pups come,
L earning to sit and stay, most want to run and play.
A s they learn to play with toys,
S o when they graduate, they fill us with joy.
S ad we are when they move on, but for the pups it's a big *well done!*

Frazer Kirkland

Son Of Chocolate Boy

Sam our miniature poodle is everso cute
scanning all the tables in pursuit
of a mint, high and low he smells
wagging his tail and barking with sheer joy
when he at last finds some.

Louise Campbell

Revenge Is Sweet

How I loved doing plaster of Paris
My poor old mom I used to harass.
Can I have a bag of plaster please?
I won't spill a drop on dress or knees.

Oh how I looked for things to mould
To press in mud pats with outline bold,
A toy would do or perhaps a penny
Ideas would come and they were many.

A dog's paw would make a very nice mark
Or perhaps the cat's would do for a start,
Nothing missed my keenest eye
As poor old Mom looked on with a sigh.

The years flew by and came the day
When a very large 'plaster' came my way,
The conservatory base was one wet mess
But I didn't want to mould and press.

I wanted a base, smooth and clean
Not covered with paw marks from cats feeling mean.
They couldn't keep out of temptation's way,
And walked on cement, night and day.

Oh how I wished I'd never done moulding
When cats took no notice of my scolding,
But revenge is sweet or so they say
So the marks are ever here to stay.

Gillian Ackers

Mercedes

Your fur is so sleek and shiny
Like water woven into fabric.

Your eyes are like the stars above
They twinkle in the night.

Your spirit is like a thunderstorm
It's unpredictable.

Your beauty is compared only to a rose
That blooms so big and bright
Then it dies
But yours only intensifies
As you age.

Your courage is so strong
That we look to you for hope.

We know that you love us
And we will always love you.

Andrew Ball

The Rescue Dog

I was thin when I came with eyes full of pain; and I have
not been easy to understand.

I wasn't beaten or kicked out, but my previous owners they
did shout. I guess they just couldn't agree and that's why
they had to part with me.

I think I've settled in at last, but it's very hard to forget
my past. I've made new friends, don't get me wrong, but
my memories are still fond.

I have lots of space to chase and race, perhaps I got a little
mad, but hey is that really so bad!

I stole things you know, when I first came and for that I was
put in shame. I learnt my lessons really well, I leave things alone
now, until I'm told, I think perhaps I was a bit too bold.

I chewed things up and had some fun, I went out on my own,
just for a run, but the door was locked when I came back and
there was no friendly welcome from my new pack!

I'm still lean and keen, but have learnt a few new tricks;
it's a dogs' life here, guarding the den and I only think of my
old life now and then.

I love them to bits my new pals; I aim to please, but sometimes
get it all wrong. My behaviour I know isn't the best, especially
when I dive in the garden pond.

I try very hard to do things right and I did learn real fast to stay
downstairs at night; before I slept on their bed, but now I have
my very own and I'm never left alone.
I have two canine friends who share and they really are a stunning pair!

I would guard them all with my life and I'm sure things will work out
just fine, it's all a matter of patience and time.

Melanie Austin

Chihuahua Delights

Bimbo and Fluff are their names.
They like licking, cuddling and playing games.
They are dainty and small,
But their character is tall.
Some say they aren't dogs at all.

They have a high-pitched bark,
That can scare squirrels in the park,
Designer clothes is what they wear,
Any paper they love to tear,
Even if it's fixed to the walls, they don't care.

Naughty they may be,
When they're nervous, they will pee,
But I'm happy they are mine,
'Cause their love really does shine.
At the end of the day, they are just divine.

Patsy Lalou

Lucy And Chowie

Just look at the two of you sitting side by side,
Who would have thought a few moments ago
You were chasing round the garden
Like Bonny and Clyde.
Reaping havoc in the flower beds
Chasing the neighbour's cat,
Barking so excitedly, running this way and that.
It's amazing how the promise of a biscuit
Held gently in my hand,
Without any words spoken, my command
You understand.
How could I be cross looking into your
Pleading brown eyes?
You know you will have your biscuits
Of that I can't deny.
There is innocence and happiness in everything
You do.
Perhaps I should follow your example,
Live every day to the full.

Margaret Berry

My Master Chose Me

I love my master, he cares deeply for me
He takes me on long walks, lets me run free
Gives me tasty food, sometimes a bone
I couldn't be happier, in his fine home

One day I awoke, couldn't move my rear
He tried to entice me and looked full of fear
The pain was awful but he was so kind
Carried me in a blanket, treatment to find.

We arrived at the vets, I was full of fear
My master so shaky, in his eye, a tear
I was examined, too weak to protest
He told my master, what would be best.

I knew what was said, my master cried
In a few moments, I had died
My master stayed with me until the end
I love him so much; he'd been my best friend.

We'd done so much together; I'd slept on his bed
Such wonderful memories, now flooded my head
If only I could tell him, how happy I'd been
I was lucky he'd picked me, he was very keen.

I learnt very quickly, became most domesticated
Life was so very happy, never complicated
So now here I lay, his hand holding my paw
He looked so sad, cried tears like never before.

A small injection, I felt so very sleepy
I felt life drifting, so softly and sweetly
Then all was over, I was running free
As happy as when, my master chose me.

Maureen Westwood O'Hara

Ship's Cat, Forty Winks

Beau Brummel's dreaming
of being a pirate, sailing
the seven seas;
Dreaming of a buried treasure
chest full of salmon, mackerel
and cheese.

Peter Morriss

Barney

The Newfoundland - Episode 1
Caked in mud and also soaking wet
Six towels later, it's a drier we must get
When it's delivered, we turn it on full-power
Barney thought, *great game,* which lasted near an hour
We wondered how Rebecca managed to groom our dog
Because we can't seem to do it, for the brush he always hogs
We tied him to our gatepost to try and blow him dry
He just sat down, gave a yawn, you could almost feel him sigh
Pat said it would be easy, she says 'table' to hers
They seem to enjoy her grooming them; removing their loose furs.
But Barney likes a tussle and will try to chew an ear
He also likes to lick your hair or a mouth if it is near

We haven't tried a toothbrush yet, even though we should
Instead, we give him raw bones to chew, so the carpet's
Covered in blood
He refuses to eat them outside for fear they'll be caked in mud
Secretly I have a feeling that he loves the carpet shampoo and suds!
The suds look like the foam when crashing waves come in
He digs the carpet like the sand, to him it's not a sin
I wonder how others manage with two or three Newfies in their home
Surely one could go insane spending hours with brush and comb?
Barney does give hours of pleasure, for he will sit quietly by our side
His eyes are full of devotion, something he cannot hide
He truly is a blessing, for without him we wouldn't know what to do
There is nothing Barney likes better than being company for us two.

Sue Brooks

Oh Dear Hector

Oh my dear Hector, when you've just a little bigger grown
Walking through the green English countryside we'll never be alone!
In the hilly Yorkshire Dales this coming summer, we'll sure be in for a treat
Enjoying the tranquillity together at the summit of Simon's Seat.

Strolling along the public nature trails under the shady, green canopy of Strid Wood.
Please promise me, dear Hector that you'll be good.
This place doesn't welcome animals unless they're on their leads.
Notices saying, *Please refrain from removing or damaging any wild plants,* must all visitors strictly heed!

Perhaps we'll roam along the grassy banks of the summer-crowded Skipton Beach,
Its flowing crystal waters where people paddle and bathe are named the River Strid.
These grassy shores can the ocean tides definitely not reach!
Maybe if you're feeling warm dear Hector, will you take a dog paddle swim?
But you'd surely soon begin to feel the cold, for your whippet body's so painfully thin!

Of course we could walk the long road to Appletreewick and view the Valley of Desolation.
Everything that we'd together enjoy and see would be from Mother Nature's magical creation!
At the moment dear Hector, you're just a cute, loving little pup,
But what a lovely Dalesland summer we'll both spend together
when you're just a little more grown up!

Stephen J Bolton

Reincarnation

I'd like to come back as a cat
I wouldn't have a care
No work for me, I'm royalty
I'd have my own armchair

I'd sleep a lot and lie around
And chase the little pup
I'd purr when I was hungry
And wind my owners up

Might catch a mouse and bring it home
To show I'm pretty clever
But only in the summer
Cos I hate cold, wet weather

Wouldn't really want to go out much
It's tough out on the street
There's dogs and naughty children
That I wouldn't want to meet

Three meals a day will do me fine
Don't want to get too fat
I'm really pretty certain
I'd be a darn good cat

John Robinson

I Miss You

It's been a long time since you went away,
It was hard not having you around each day.

I still miss you and still need to cry,
Our little Candy, why did you die?

I remember ... whenever I felt down, you always knew,
You always came up to me and comforted me too.

The way your collar scuffed up your fur,
So sweet and gentle, you always were.

You'd bark so loud on firework night,
Because it always gave you such a fright.

There's so much joy you brought while you were here,
To all who loved you, you were so very dear.

Now that you've gone, there's nothing to touch,
But remember, we all love you so very much.

Lynsay Bestwick

My Cat

I love my cat
But Mummy threw her out!
She scratches up the furniture
It does make Mummy shout.
I looked up at the window
After a little while
Her cheeky face was peering in
It made my brother smile.
When nobody was looking
I went and fetched a stool,
I climbed on it to let her in
I called her such a fool!
Come and eat some biscuits
And sit here by the fire
Don't rub your head on Mummy's legs
Your fate could be quite dire!
I love my cat!

Lorraine Burden

Big Trig

We call our two pussycats 'bookends',
Though their real names are Trigger and Rosie.
There's no way they could be called 'good friends'
And they *both* are incredibly nosy!

Trigger's amazingly streetwise,
He uses his own 'green cross code',
We're sure he has had many past lives,
He's so 'human' when crossing the road.

His front paws are hands of a person,
His back ones are those of a hare,
In winter, he puts his fur coat on,
In summer - he's just never there!

He sleeps like a person (and snores too),
He can leap up as high as a deer,
You call him - he pretends not to hear you,
He's a rare cat without any fear.

He goes to the vets on a red lead,
He behaves like a faithful old dog.
He purrs at his bowl whilst he waits for his feed,
Does not catnap, but sleeps like a log!

His eyes and his ears look like owls',
A barometer who tells us the weather,
He's a tomcat at night who just howls,
On your knee, he's as light as a feather.

They're both character cats are our pussies,
And everyone loves them to bits,
They've both just a couple of 'fussies',
We adore them - our beautiful 'kits'.

Philippa Howard

The Saga Of The One-Eyed Cat

He's the one-eyed cat from Sycamore Street,
That sits on the top bricks of the wall.
He is the very, Boss Cat of them all,
Just sitting there, almost six feet tall,
The white fur at his neck, is like a white streak.

Who he belongs to, there nobody knows,
He seems to have been there for many a year.
A badly scratched nose and a very torn ear,
But whoever passes by, he shows no fear.
He's there in sunshine or when cold wind blows.

He's frightened the rats and cleared off the mice,
Although big dogs bark, he shows them no fear,
But they all know, 'tis foolish, to get too near,
Those long sharp claws have torn many an ear,
No dog or cat will challenge him twice.

Old Mother Roberts, saves him some of her scraps,
And the dustbin lids are often on the ground,
You can tell old One-Eye, has been ferreting around,
'Tis very surprising what that old cat has found,
He is really a crafty, scavenging, one-eyed cat.

He is as old as Methuselah, so people say,
He belongs to no one and he hasn't a care,
And when he sleeps it could be just anywhere,
But he's Lord of the Manor just sitting there,
Now, who will take over when he's gone away?

Albert E Bird

The Last Word

Daisy is a fat mog, Daisy is obese
Daisy has an evil eye
Which glowers when I cease -
To feed when mog demands
Cuddle when she asks too
It's all about me, me, me
What is a human to do?

'Ah haaa, buy fish,' whines Daisy loudly
'Buy fish with your last two pounds
Buy fish so I will purr for a second
With my tum all fat and round.'

'Alright,' says human with a smile
'Fresh fish shall be your supper
And with my last two pounds
Haddock will be on offer
And you can clear your plate
And for those mounds of flesh that wobble
The weighing scales can wait.
For, make no mistake my chubby mog
Your tum is rolls of fat
Your bottom is a tub of lard
A poor specimen of a cat.'

'Not so,' whines Daisy with a peeve
'It is not *I* that is a lard a**e
I think you'll find it's *your* behind
That is, quite frankly, worse.
For, my dearest Mum,
And this you can't quite see ...
That I am gorgeous, slim and glam
Whilst *you* have the bum all wobbly
And, it is *you* without a man!'

Sharon Trotter

Little Brother

Loud he did call
And insistent too
And we children skidded to a halt.
Beside the barn, on the ground, was a mother cat
Lying serene but her eyes were sadly glazed and dead.

Again he called
And louder still
Shrieking from his perch upon the bales of hay.
A little thing, jet black, scrawny with eyes of yellow green
Peering down at us, his head tilted
Surveying us strange creatures in-between more fervent wails.

Upon handlebars, his next perch, we gently carried him home
And excited asked that he come stay with us
Who could refuse such an orphan waif?
And soon he was climbing our curtains and claiming his chair
Chasing shadows and stalking birds
That took flight before he was near.

By my side through my teenage years and then on beyond
Always there to greet me when from school I returned
Destroyer of my homework when cuddles I declined
Comforter, friend, confidant, little brother
Sneaking in under the duvet to sleep by my side.

Pet is not the right word
A goldfish is a pet.
My Gobolino is a life friend
Whom I'll cherish until the end
Source of so much happiness
Soft and gentle, my beautiful cat
Whether somersaulting as a kitten
Or purring peacefully on my lap now this late in life.

Simon Wright

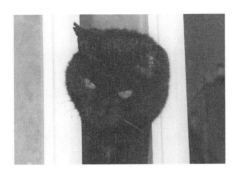

My Sister Took Over

My sister came along, little but she was rough,
She was only six weeks old, only a pup.
Playing with all my toys every single day,
Only to find out that she chewed them all away.
Every day she had three meals, breakfast, dinner and tea,
Then one day I realised she was getting bigger than me!

Brenda Wedge

Midge

My name is Midge I'm not so big
In fact I'm really small,
So I can hide in the oddest place
And they don't notice me at all.
So here I sit spick and span,
In the marmalade preserving pan.
When they said it was time for tea
I didn't think they'd notice me
But I was spotted by a mile
I thought I blended with the tiles!
I caused them all to shriek and laugh,
Then cameras clicked and jokes were daft
But I just sat quite innocently
And waited patiently for tea.

Amanda Pointer

freeway

I was broken-hearted when my cat passed away
So I went to the dogs' home to find a new friend
'Get a small dog with a quiet temperament,' my friends advised
But I chose you.

A mixture of terrier, Dalmatian and greyhound
Long fast legs, rough white hair that you liberally shook all over the house
Your terrier temperament evident in your stubborn streak
But we loved you.

You ran like greased lightning, and those who got in the way
Were felled at the knees by your head
You liked to roll in any nasty smelly thing you found on our beach walks
Our garden was your territory, defended at all cost
You were covered in fleas from a hedgehog, bitten on the nose by a rat
You chased a ferret and the neighbour's cat
And we laughed with you

Our home was yours for thirteen years,
You leapt on our laps for hugs and cuddles
Liberal with your kisses from your wet velvet nose
Your tail indicated that you were happy
But one day you jumped over the wall and we never saw you again
You left us and we didn't know where you went or why
And we miss you

Maralyn Rees-Molyneux

That Pesky Cat

Someone is knocking on the door
I rush to open it once more
Look around there's no one there
Turn around, the cat's in my chair

What's that growling on the stair
There's no guard dog living here
What can it be? I'm filled with dread
Turn around, the cat's in my bed

Hear scratching at the back door
Heavens I can't stand any more
She can't get out, what a to-do
Turn around, the cat's weed in my shoe

Washing machine making a weird sound
Check to see it's still going around
Phone for mechanic, say it's broke
Turn around, cat's full of soap

Get into bed, can't get to sleep
Cat's chorus outside makes me weep
Seems that ginger tom is smitten
Turn around, cat's just had kittens

Fill the bath full of bubbles
To soothe away all my troubles
Lie there so peaceful, so still
Turn around, cat's fallen in

Now you're peaceful, laid to rest
After a visit to the vet's
Twelve years I've had of your high jinks
Miss you Penny, you little minx.

Rachel McKie

Without Wings

She stands before me
this four-legged friend
(or foe)
Breathing fiery fumes
into morning frost.
I gather reins gently,
easing slowly
across the velvet back
of this sorrel splendour.

She rises to meet me.
Up,
and up
(and up).
Towering majestically
in all equine glory,
pawing the sky.
(Ground gallops towards me)

And I think,
again,
before crashing into corral fence,
that I am getting too old
to be flying

without wings.

Tracey Levy

Love Me, Love My Snake

Gentle snake, my slender friend
Elegant with measured gait
Tapered to your pointed end -
Perfect for your grounded state,
Coiled around my outstretched arm
Tail secure about my wrist,
You are cold but I am warm
And your owner's scent you taste:
One you trust, tamed from the wild
When they brought you to this land,
I greeted you with loving smiles
As you crawled onto my hand,
My arm, my neck - your haven there
Seeking comfort, you chose me:
Darling Aura, love we share,
Gentle serpent, treasured friend
My graceful companion
Always be ...

Carolyn Smith

Animals' Sadness

The poodle's sad
The cat's as bad
Checking rooms, opening doors
Constantly sniffing anything of yours
Dog sleeping, cat napping and hark
Waiting for one sound, your bark
Both worlds fallen apart
Miss the collie that captured my heart
The love you gave the softness of fur
Rolling back the years my eyes become a blur
Endless walks over styles and moors
On guard constantly, our lives were yours.
Buried on the front lawn where you spent hours
At rest now, grass grows with good dog powers
God is love and God made you
Spell dog backwards and you're God too.

Vera Collins

Noisy Pups

Two noisy pups began to fight,
In their basket in the middle of the night,
Dad came down to see what it was all about,
It was over an old bone there was not any doubt.

He took it away, threw it into the dustbin,
But this didn't stop the pups making a din.
So he picked up the pups and put them outside on the garden floor,
He left them outside, it began to drizzle, he shut the door.

Two minutes later they were crying to come in,
To leave them out any longer would be a sin.
Dad towelled them down and let them know,
Any more noise then back into the garden they go.

They clambered back into their basket and soon fell asleep.
Throughout that night there wasn't another peep!

Terry Godwin

My Pet Dog Is A Staffie

Her name is called Cassie
She is also called Loopy Loo
As she jumps up and down like a kangaroo
Brown and brindle, the colour of her coat
Staffie through and through so take note
Swimming in the sea is her delight
Fetching a ball or stick she thinks she is so bright
To see her paddling about happy, quite clear
Loving it and enjoying it with no fear
Cassie is a good companion
And that is not only my opinion
Staffies love children too
And will protect them through and through
The loyalty they have and show
From a puppy this does grow
A black country dog, hard and sturdy but true
The love they give is just for you

Staffie forever
A danger never
    Staffordshire bull terrier.

Garry Bedford

The Cat That Got The Cream

(RIP Sooty 1992-2005)

One early evening, as the sun was going down,
My beautiful enchantress came to me;
Miaowing very loud!

What is it? I asked her again and again ...
But still I couldn't make out,
I had just fed her, stroked her a million times;
Oh, I thought, *maybe she is thirsty,* still in doubt.

So I go to the fridge,
Feeling her dusky blue skies watching me all the way.
Slowly I get the milk;
And then turning like a ballerina, hoping I say ...
'Is this what you want my lovely?'

No answer! Try again ...

'Well then if that's the case
I can't help you anymore Sooty, I don't know what more to say.'
Walking into the lounge,
She just sits and stares at me, a disappointed look upon her face.

I now ask my sister if she knows what she wants,
But no, she didn't know either.
All she knew was there was cream on the worktop
But that was under a cake umbrella.

I thought to myself, *it can't be that,*
Sooty would never smell it under there;
So feeling defeated I sat down,
Beside my other cat Toby on *his* chair.

Three hours later it was 8pm as I walked upstairs to get my writing book,
Knowing Sooty was still sitting by the fridge, so not having to look.
All of a sudden I heard my sister laughingly scream,
'Georgina come quick, this you have to see!'
I rushed downstairs and to my glee,
What did I see? The cat that got the cream!

Georgina May Carey

A Companion Gone ...

No cry at night, no bark at dawn, nor wagging tail to greet the morn,
A lonely bed, a hanging lead, an empty bowl where once he'd feed.
No cold wet nose, as black as coal
Dark eyes that looked into your soul.
Gone forever, remembered each day,
The love I thought would always stay.
Gone, love I thought would never end,
Goodnight, sweet Timmy, goodnight old friend ...

Col Gill

Cat-Astrophe!

Feel free my feline friend to roam at will,
To preen your furry coat upon my window sill.
Your bright green gaze does seem to penetrate my very soul.
Your agile grace my highest praise does oft extol.
And yet the predator in you does make me weep,
The way you stalk your prey whilst seeming half asleep.
When you seize a frightened bird between your razor claws,
I feel the urge to wrench him from your evil jaws.

Nature is often cruel, I must admit.
Too often danger lurks where beauty sits.
To think a cuddly kitten can resort to kill
That tiny, feathered friend upon my window sill.

Rosemary Thomson

fish Tale

'Two goldfish in a bowl, that's all I want for my birthday,'
Said my daughter. 'Promise I will look after them, not play.'
Well! She was sixteen years old and quite sensible,
I gave in on the no pets rule with little quibble.

Should have known, one got a pet, then another,
No thought for their very over-stretched, stressed mother.
Instead of two tiny fish we now had a tank,
Each child, two specimens named, even one called Frank.

Arduous task of cleaning was left to one lad,
If he was not around, the job became Dad's.
Fish ownership novelty came to abrupt end,
Offspring began tackling the latest fashion trend.

Luckily, goldfish do not have a great lifespan,
Started dying, one by one, like part of a plan.
Back to two in bowl and the tank could be removed,
As I said, kids and pets do not mix - case proved.

S Mullinger

Mr J Russell

I'm walking along, putting out leaflets
(selling my services; tuning pianos),
when, from the next gate (metal-barred,
huge, wrought iron, meshed at the bottom),
I hear a clamouring, yammering, hammering
on my brain:
    'Beware: I'm here.
      It'll cost you dear
         if you come too near!'

A previous (prudent) visitor
has thrown his leaflet (takeaway food)
through the bars, not thinking it wise
to venture his life for three quid an hour.
I do the same, for the diligent guardian
(six inches high, on his hind legs, ten)
is performing his task in magnificent style.

But then I kneel down. 'Hello,' I say,
softly, as befits the occasion.
Tail a-wag, like a motor amok,
he pushes his little head through the grating,
licking the hand I gently offer;
the hand that strokes his black and white hair.

I say, 'Goodbye,' and go on my way.
The clamour begins, all over again,
but I can't forget the warm loving touch
of that little pink tongue on my finger.

Bob Harrison

Sheba

I remember picking you out, with your black, shiny, smooth fur,
My tenth birthday present from my dad.
Summer of 1976, the year of the drought, huge cracks in the garden,
I worried you'd fall into a chasm; you so tiny, fitting in the palm of his hand.
We grew up together, you bounding down the stairs to meet me after school.
We ventured out, the two of us and Dad; trips to Wales in the car,
Chasing seagulls and sticks of driftwood on the beach.
Rounding up sheep by instinct,
Melting the angry farmer's heart with your intelligence and affection.
Walking through fields and up and down hills.
Watching Dad lay the firewood in the grate,
You padded out and returned with your stick,
Laying it down in front of the fireplace,
Your head cocked questioningly to one side.
Watching the flames crackling, you'd settle down and sleep by the fire,
Curled up and cosy, safe and secure.
I left home for university; you stayed at home with Dad,
Always by his side as he wrote.
Each visit home you greeted me like a long-lost friend.
You and my dad were constant companions,
Even though joints began to ache and whiskers whiten.
Now I've grown and flown the nest,
I sometimes fancy I can hear you breathing,
Hear you barking in your sleep, dreaming of chasing seagulls.
It's as if I could still reach out and pat your head,
Stroke your fur and hold your gaze.
Dad and I still think and talk of you, of all our trips and adventures.
As much of a friend as any person - *Sheba*.

Beth Buckley

The Snack Box Thief

No snack box is safe when Keano's around
He pulls them off of the shelf and onto the ground
He plants his big teeth into the hard plastic side
To get to the tasty morsels inside
His mission accomplished, the contents spilt on the floor
And his belly's so full it can't take any more
I enter the room - what a scene I see
So am I angry? How can I be?
When two big brown eyes say: 'It wasn't me!'

Emma Bate

Tribute To My Very Best Friend, Jasper

(5th July 1992 to 21st March 2005 - *always in my thoughts now and evermore*)

From the first time we met each other,
the bond that grew would not be surpassed by any other.
You were always waiting at home for me,
either by the door, or on the settee.
We would walk the Malvern Hills from five in the morning,
to the tune of all the skylarks calling.
When I stopped to drink my tea, you were never very far from me.
From British camp to the Wyche Cutting,
you were always keen on all that walking.
When I stopped to have a rest, you would sometimes become a pest,
having stayed too long to have a rest.
Never stopping for too long, always keen to carry on.
Your joy of being in that car,
never worried how long or how far.
From Cornwall to The Lakes, you always travelled with me,
always keeping us company.
Now that it is time for us to part, there is a great void in my heart.
I stayed and held you till the very end,
I realise now, I have lost my very best friend.
No amount of words can say how I feel,
the loss of you, Jasper, is so unreal.
Now I am sitting here all alone, on my own.
I glance across this empty room, so much sadness
and so much gloom.
I can still envisage you sitting there, in the hall, by the stair.
There has been an old saying for so long,
You don't know what you've got until it's gone.
Sitting all alone, on my own in the dark,
this is when I hear a distant bark.
This makes me wonder why,
Could this be Jasper saying goodbye?

Kevin J Wood

My Son

My tiny, charming friend I have
He sits upon my knee
A beautiful, handsome little chap
So faithful and loyal to me
Giving hours of pleasure
As he nestles on my lap
His little eyes they close
As we take our daily nap
Such comfort to know he's always there
I love to hear him sing
My aristocratic little bird
I think the world of him
My Bluey and I will be together
Whatever the future to come
For we are one, my bird and I
My treasure, my life, my son.

C Armstrong

Emily

Emily is such a beautiful black cat
Although very laid back, she knows where it's at
Putting all the neighbourhood dogs in a rage
She sashays up to them, clearly unafraid
The barking dogs are puzzled and left in a daze

Emily loves the children who live all around
And they love her too, whether lost or not
Emily is always 'found'
She has a talent for getting locked in
Boy, does she create a din!

Emily's so lovely and a daddy's girl
She seems to love him most in all the world
But lately: well, the little pickle!
Emily has become quite fickle!

Bobbie Coelho

My Puppy Poem

For a long long time I wanted a dog,
Mum said, 'No, let's wait,'
And Dad said, 'No, you're much too young,
Wait until you're eight.'

One day I came home from school,
And there was a big surprise.
A ball of fur with floppy ears,
And big black puppy eyes.

I said to my dad, 'Is he real,
Or is he just a toy?'
Dad said, 'It's a proper dog,
Our house now has a boy!'

I loved everything about him.
His tiny paws and nose,
He snuggled up in my arms,
And had a little doze.

Every day he grows some more,
He's cute and cheeky too.
He'll chew up everything in sight,
He once ate Josie's shoe!

He likes to run in the garden
And chase my Barbie ball,
Then it's time for dinner
But he won't come when we call!

Just like me, he goes to school,
He's learnt to sit and stay,
But he can't keep still and listen,
He'd rather run and play!

We call him Rufus, the world's best pup,
He's really like no other.
A beautiful spaniel we love so much,
He's better than a brother ...

Erin O'Neill (8) & Josie O'Neill (5)

289

My Easter

(Dedicated to four tiny kittens found in a cardboard box under a tree)

Four tiny kittens
Came to visit one day
Their mother was missing
She had gone away.

They needed our help
We could not refuse
So they stayed in our house
And kept us amused.

Each one was black
With white paws and face
Their antics amazed us
When they played tag and chase.

We fed them and washed them
Cuddled them too
Three were called Betty, Bernice and Bo Bo.
The other was Beatie - she was rather a sweetie!

Then at last to their new homes
They went to stay
We waved them goodbye
As they went on their way.

Christine Hardemon

Ode To Saki

Over thirteen years she spent with me
But this time that number was *very* lucky

She gave so much in return for my love
Before the time came to send her above

My tabby and white cat, much missed is she
But now not in pain, playing happily

A cancerous tumour took her, but I nursed her for a while
And though I've cried myself dry, she can still make me smile

Memories stay, and my life still goes on
God bless you, my wee Saki, my special little one.

Lynn Greene

Good Dog

Me and Ben were in the park, walking in the fog
He was rolling in the muck, sniffing other dogs
Snooty, blue rinse lady and her poodle plodded round
Ben, a friendly beeline made towards the hairdressed hound

'Ben - come back,' I cried - alack! - too quiet for canine hearing
A rugby tackle sent the poodle crazily careering
Blue rinse tugged the lead and - 'Simone - come away!' she blubbed
But all too late, to no avail, the dog was decked in mud

But grappled grimly in the grime and clawed itself away
An oity-toity mummy's dog that didn't want to -play
Blue rinse dragged her doggy home to wash and brush and kiss it
Ben bounced up - 'Good dog!' I said, and gave him half a biscuit.

Richard Allen

Dottie

'Dottie's my name.'
          'Dottie's her nature!'
'I chase the birds away all day.'
          'The crows in the trees a field away!'
'I like to chase ducks at the river.'
          'Thinks it's grass *splash!* then shiver!'
'The cats are always happy to play.'
          'They run away from you all day.'
'I hide my bone well, where nobody knows.'
          'In her bed amongst the pillows.'
'I always come to you when you call.'
          'Once the tin opens and food starts to fall.'
'If 'walkies' is offered it'll make my day.'
          So come on Dot, let's go play!'
'Dottie's my name.'
          'And Dottie's her nature!'

Catherine Gloor

Lucky

I'm just a little pussycat, Lucky is my name,
My left front leg is not so good, I suppose you'd call me lame,
But I catch rats, sometimes a bird, quite often have a mouse,
I caught a snake one sunny day, and brought it in the house.

My mistress did not like the snake, she stabbed it with a knife,
I thought, *if she does that to me, I've lost another life,*
The best thing I can do right now is catch another bird,
So it can sing and I can purr, the sweetest sound she's heard.

Sitting on my master's lap, I scratched and I did bite,
The blood ran freely everywhere, it gave me quite a fright,
He held me, then he smacked me, I'd never had such pain,
I thought, *I know one thing for sure, I won't bite him again.*

So now whenever I come in, I sit upon his knee,
And purr sweet nothings in his ear, and he just cuddles me,
I still bring rats and mice in, and no one makes a fuss,
Cos Norma said to Tom, you know, they're presents just for us!

Thomas Dickinson

Jack

I have a dog, his name is Jack,
He isn't white, but he isn't black,
He likes to run and jump about
He likes to throw his ball around.
He's a border collie big and bold.

Every day we go for a walk
And watch the children as they play.
But when we go amongst the trees
He chases the rabbits in his dreams.
He's such a softy is our Jack.

He loves the children to tickle his back
He loves to roll and kick and bark
And tease the postman when he comes,
He rolls in the mud, but he's really good,
'Cause he's a border collie big and bold.

He's big and cuddly, warm and kind
And he likes to roll upon the ground,
He loves to sleep upon your feet
he keeps you warm, oh, such a treat.
He is my dog and he's called Jack.

Susan Ann Peach

One Man And His Dog

Controlled aggression in that spring-like crouch
Ears pricked for a command: 'Away' or 'Bye'.
The eye is all. It never leaves the sheep.
Like some mysterious ray
It holds them in its power.

The sheep are victims. God ordained it so.
The man and I; a pack of two, we hunt.
In scarce remembered times
My fellow wolves and I
Would first surround, then kill.
The man, for reasons best known to himself,
Defers the killing for another time.
For, when I've gathered them,
He merely says, 'That's all!'

And I, forgetting all my savage past,
Come meekly to his heel and lick his hand.

David Griffiths

Polly-Anna

I have a cat called Polly-Anna
She's my soulmate
The core of my life.
So playful and jolly
Is my little Polly
Always in trouble and strife.

A cat and a half is Polly
She gets bigger every day.
Never stops eating
And she's never defeated
Whatever may come her way.

Polly-Anna and me
Are as close as can be
She's there when I need her most.
When I'm entertaining
Or whenever it's raining
She makes such a wonderful host.

To some, it may seem
We make a good team.
There's really no doubt about that.
Wherever I go, she's there also.
I'm sure she's more human
Than cat.

My faithful friend Polly-Anna
Was rescued in the nick of time.
She needed a home
To call her own
So now little Polly's
All mine.

John H Foley

New Puppy

I'm a new little puppy
I've come to say how do you do
I'm really quite shy
And I've come to live with you
I'm not sure where I am
Or what I've to do
I'm sure I'll be happy
Living here with you
I promise I'll try to be very good
I'll not chew the table
Or things made of wood
I'll not make a mess
Or do things on the floor
I promise that I will not
Scratch at the door
I hope we'll both be happy
In all that I do
For I really would love
To live here with you.

Anthony Walton

The Catastrophic Cat

Bess, you don't fit in that shoebox,
No, my boots were in there first.
Yes, hot water bottles do feel warm,
Hey, careful - it'll burst!
How in heavens did you get up there?
Just mind that china plate!
Bessy, take your head from out that bag
Before you suffocate.
No, my new expensive leather chair
Was not designed to chew.
What's that orange thing you're eating?
Spit it out! It's Barbie's shoe!
Oh, you clever girl - you used the tray,
Hold on now, Mum'll clean it.
No, don't kick it in the air like that!
Oh Bess, that's not hygienic.
Fine, you walk it through the bedroom
To your little heart's desire,
I'll be on the phone to ... oh, it seems
You've gnawed right through the wire.
Bess, you're standing on my face again,
Your tail's in my madras.
There's a fish bone in my knicker drawer,
You cheeky little lass.
Yes, your eyes are big and gorgeous,
Mummy loves you Bess, that's right.
No, don't fret your pretty self now -
Daddy likes the couch.
Goodnight.

Rebecca Murray

Punctuated Love

The cat lies on the bed between us,
round and tight as a full stop;
he knows what he's putting an end to.
As soon as he hears my husband's sleep-breathing
he uncurls to curve into an opening bracket
only twisting into a question mark
in the morning when I get up
and he still has another eight hours to go.
While we are out at work
he retracts into a comma,
a pause from purring,
until I get home
when he forms a tilde
of pleasure as I stroke him,
arching into a closing bracket
to stretch fur over ribs
and prove he's starving.

Joanna Lilley

There Is A New Kitten In Our House

Announcing himself like the 4.15 from Paddington
Bailey launches himself at the sleeping Monty,
Charging, bell tinkling, across the lounge carpet.
Instantly alerted, Monty rouses himself
From the half sleep of cats,
Launches himself upwards and backwards,
As only cats can,
And lands three feet away,
Much to the dismay of the charging Bailey
Who, arriving at the now empty spot,
Can only sniff at the carpet, bewildered.
Robbed of his victim
He retreats and regroups.
This time launching himself
At the darting light beams on the wall,
Cast by the playful sun on crystal.
Teasing Bailey, they disappear on contact.
Monty smiles inwardly,
The contented smile of an older cat
Remembering his kitten days.
Bailey, growing tired, curls up
Next to Monty and sleeps.
Ahh bliss, there's a new kitten in our house.

Eleanor Broaders

Tjukken

He is a perfect gentleman
Who can be naughty at times
You might be afraid to see his bulk
But really he's just a big softie at work.

He drinks brandy and red wine
But prefers continental lagers
He loves hot chicken curries
And oh, so savours pigs' livers.

He often gives me a sardonic look
As if to say, 'Now what have you done?'
I don't know what lies on his mind
All I care is that he's a friend of mine.

I try to give him all I've got
But he gives me back more than I ask for
He's been a big comfort and joy
When the skies are grey and overcast.

He goes to bed with me at night
But he doesn't like saying goodnights
He gives me a big kiss in the morning
That sets my day to a good start.

I like to travel a lot
But my heart is never far away from home
Knowing that there's always a wag and a hug
Waiting to welcome me back home.

I would have thought my friend
That you would have known by now
I am talking about my German shepherd
The wonderful Mister Tjukken.

Jane A Scotchmer

An Ode To Chester

Our pet dog is Chester
Well, that is what he's called
He's grey and black and curly
What makes you think he's bald?

He's a champion schnauzer
With a tail and floppy ears
He welcomes us when we come in
He banishes all our fears

We have a 'gran' who spoils him
She feeds him lots of sweets
He wags his tale and jumps about
But doesn't climb on seats

He's well behaved and lovely
Sometimes he runs like mad
To calm him down a little
We refer him to our 'dad'

'Chester! Chester!' sounds the voice
He's heard it all before
He slithers to a sudden stop
And lies down on the floor

We love our dog called Chester
We love him like no other
We love him, and he loves us
He's just like one more 'brother'.

Tommy Glynn

Becky

Sometimes, Becky, we hear you yelp
Then we're glad we can be of help
We have some pills to ease your pain
If only you could be young again

Most of the time you're quite alright
But lying still makes your joints get tight
Time passes quickly, but you still love to play
If only we could take your pains away

We remember when you were half this size
With floppy ears and great big eyes
Who could have known what a friend you'd be
So we'll love you and help you
Just you wait and see

Jo Seward

Sweet Cats

Ice Cream and Soufflé - you think I'll get fat?
No, of course not, they're the names of my cats.
They're cute and cuddly, both are pure white,
Sweet and adorable, and cheeky alright.

They play with a toy mouse, or even a ball,
Sometimes they don't want to play at all,
But just sleep all day, or roll on the floor;
You give them a tickle, they come back for more!

I open a cupboard - in they both go -
What will they find there? They're eager to know.
In with the clutter they go and explore;
I have to be careful when I shut the door.

They play in the garden, go into the shed,
Curl up on the sofa, or jump on the bed.
Out in the sunshine, they sleep like a log -
Awoken by the barking of next door's dog!

They run up at meal times, I fill up the dish -
With chicken or turkey, rabbit or fish.
They're full of affection and charm, maybe that's
The reason I'll always love my two cats!

Helen Burton

Fidget's Christening

I was christened, along with my brother
All the family came. It was nice.
We stood by the font with my mother
Whilst the vicar gave lots of advice.
Then he did something rather alarming,
Pouring water all over our heads,
Brother Dominic shouted, 'That's charming!'
I'll not tell you just what else he said!

But we went home to have us a party,
Lots of cakes, and ice cream and all that
And my brother, who thinks he's a smarty
Said, 'Hang on folks, let's christen the cat.'
She was small, in fact almost a midget
And we'd bought her just two days before,
So I said, 'Yes we'll christen her Fidget,
Cos she wriggles all over the floor.'
It was then that my naughty big brother
From his bag took a couple of Cokes
And poured them one after another
Over Fidget, who started to choke.

Saying, 'Fidget's the name you are christened,'
As the liquid went over her head,
I don't know if the poor pussy listened,
But she scurried off into her bed.
The next morning my brother was sleeping,
Fidget looked at him ever so sweet,
Then under his sheets she went creeping
And she piddled all over his feet!

Brian Croft

A Silly A To Z

Aladdin the ant said to Bruno the bat
'I think I'm in love with Clarissa the cat
But don't tell a soul, cos I know for a fact
That some folk round here lack discretion and tact.'
Now Digby the dog - who was one of those folk
Heard all and dashed off, yapping, 'Wow! What a joke!'
Soon Ethel the elk and Fitzfrancis the frog
Were laughing out loud with the thoughtless young dog.
'You should be ashamed,' sniffed the goat known as Gert
'You gossip and mock and then people get hurt.'
But Hamish the hippo said, 'Hey, lighten up
He may be a twit, but he's only a pup.'
Now Ivy the ibex was just passing by
She wailed, 'This is dreadful!' and started to cry.
Old Jellicoe jackal gasped, 'Don't be like that!
Who cares about *gossip*? And who'd love a *cat?*'
Poor Kimberley-Katie, the kind kangaroo
Sighed, 'This is upsetting, but what can I do?'
Elsewhere, Llily llama and Monty the mole
Were keen to play football, but needed a goal
They grabbed something large, but let go with a shriek
As Nina the nightingale started to speak
'I don't think you should!' she exclaimed. 'No, indeed!'
And Otto the octopus quickly agreed
'You can't use *that* box,' he declared, 'No sirree!
It's Pawpaw the panda's. How *grumpy* he'd be!'
Then Quincy the quail flounced away in a huff
'That panda's my friend and enough is enough.'
Rose rabbit looked sad, but a squirrel named Sid
Quipped, 'Quails are a nuisance. I'd say we're well rid.'
Then Timothy tortoise decided to leave
And Ursula unicorn started to grieve
Veronica vixen barked, 'I'm going too
This place is so boring. There's nothing to do.'
But Wilma the wombat called, 'No, don't go yet
Here's Xylophone Xerxes, the musical vet.'
'I hope he's not coming to give me a pill,'
Croaked Yorick the yak. 'I'm quite sure I'm not ill.'
And then Yorick added - politely, of course
That Zach, though a zebra, looked more like a horse
And there we must leave them to squabble and play
They'll no doubt be at it the whole of the day.

Helen M Clarke

Wild Dog

The large, black, wild dog
Stands so proudly dominant,
lesser dogs, avoid his eye!
He as king is always evident
For his silhouette stands high.
Suddenly, his ears prick back,
His mouth draws back, snarling.
Who dares to cross his territory?
He threatens with his growling!
The intruder backs slowly away,
This time not wishing to fight,
With the large, black, wild dog
As black as the starless night!
Once again he is still the king,
Presiding over his own domain,
For the strength of the wild dog
Has been shown to us once again!
But for now he will go back home,
To being a pet, to the human race,
And then he'll lick the baby's face!

Sylvia Sayso

Sammy And Shay

The rain was lashing at the windows,
Wind was howling round the door,
Shay was sprawled out by the fire, head resting on his paws.
All of a sudden, up he sprang, bounding to the door,
His barking was so loud, I told him, 'Pipe down.'
There's nothing out there in this weather,
But Shay knew better, he was very clever.
I opened the door and there on the floor was a cat,
So soaked with rain it couldn't stand up,
All its strength gone and the eyes full of pain.

I picked him up and dried his fur,
Gave him warm milk, he repaid with a purr.
I called him Sammy, he wasn't very old,
But Shay seemed to know there was something wrong.
Sammy and Shay were great pals together,
But Sammy wouldn't go out, whatever the weather.
His soft black fur took on a shine,
His body filled out - he looked real fine.

Sammy's favourite thing was to sit on the stairs
With paw hanging through the rails,
When anyone passed he would pat their heads
And swish went his bushy tail.
He would ride on Shay's back like a jockey
And hold on good and proper.
Shay was never rough with Sammy,
They would lay together in front of the fire.
I watched while Shay gently washed Sam's face,
At night Sammy lay with his head on Shay's side.
That's how I found him next day,
We didn't have Sammy very long
But Shay knew there was something wrong.

Mary Neill

Dusty

Tawny feline, lazily stretching in the sun,
dappled, dreaming, smooth sides rise and fall,
jade-green eyes, gold-flecked, black-rimmed,
open widely with a candid stare.

She swiftly springs up onto velvet paws,
with jungle gait, pads softly out of sight,
hunter or hunted? Primitive to her soul,
in her world only the swift survive.

Back to the dim, dark days of Bastet,
cherished cat queen of the Nile,
I belong to her, not her to me,
we like it that way, she and I.

Sheila Giles

More Lives Than The Nine

Squib the cat hoped he would
Get more lives than the nine.
He could be still as wood,
Dreaming of what he'd dine

On, if his home were rich ...
Kippers and chicken wings.
Then all his paws would twitch
At the thought of these things,

With another mistress
(Gormlessly glad he came
With mews of false distress)
He'd have another name,

And any cream to spare ...
Then a chair by the fire -
His ideal world of care,
Fulfilled feline desire!

Gillian Fisher

George

People hate rats when they run around wild,
But George is great to man, woman and child,
He scurries, that's true, in cage and on floor,
But to this long-tailed rodent there is so much more,
The way he stands on his back two legs,
Reaching and sniffing as he silently begs,
For food, stimulation or a smoothing finger,
Is a wondrous sight, you just want to linger,
He's scared, it's true of sharp, sudden sounds,
And they can set him off in leaps and bounds,
A Sellotape tear and loud rasping fart,
Have both made him up my trouser leg dart,
To calm him down he's happiest when,
He's listening to The Jacksons singing 'Ben',
Which, of course, is from a film where he can see,
The title character is a rat, the same as he,
So, my poem has a message to relay,
And that is that rats are here to stay,
But don't think of them as vermin in the sewers below,
Scurrying through pipes and the overflow,
Nor in Room 101, as the hero's dread fear,
That Orwell's '1984' made graphically clear,
Instead, when recalling the great writer's fame,
Remember that he and my rat share the same first name.

Troy Banyan

Under New Management

Presented with a kitten cat,
I didn't think too much of that!
But slowly and so skilfully,
The little madam's ruling me.

My carpet's plucked, my chair backs too.
I'm sorry I set eyes on you.
She doesn't worry, not one bit.
Knows I don't mean a word of it.

'You're the one I love,' she cries,
Lowering glittering, amber eyes.
Her graceful leap is no surprise,
She's on my shoulder, heaving sighs.

While sewing, reading, taking tea,
She stealthily creeps on my knee.
'You're going to mark my dress,' I cry,
She purrs a protest, winks an eye,
And nestles down appealingly,
She always gets the best of me.

Patricia Lindsay

Cat's Eyes

In the dark, what did I see? Two small bright lights facing me
Piercing through the black of night, calm and still, no sign of fright

Suddenly, they disappeared; gone from sight, very weird
Then I felt a gentle touch - brushing past in a silent rush

Gone so quickly, passed me by, this visitor so timid and shy
I realised what I had seen, for those bright lights were really green

It was my friend, my pal for years; one who shared my grief and fears
Who rubbed her head against me often; life a regime, no daily task forgotten

At her discretion - when ready for fuss, seeking attention; ever curious
Nearly a score of years in our house, but only once did she bring in a mouse

Eventually age took its toll; balance and eating beyond control
Curled up in her basket, looking so sad; despite the spoilt, good life for years she had

Those green lights were her gentle eyes; in final days contented purrs replaced by sighs
Her chocolate-brown fur no longer so silky and soft; yet head still held high, proud and aloft

Of whom do I talk, no - how could you know? My devoted Burmese - her name? Juno.

Patricia Phillips

The Cat

Aloof and superior is the cat,
With a haughty and inscrutable stare,
Sleek and sinuous, or fluffy and fat,
She sleeps in the sun or in your best chair.

She might condescend to sit on your lap,
Contentedly purring, gentle and warm,
Or curl up on the hearth to take a nap -
A sleeping cat brings a feeling of calm.

She'll play, if you like, with a rubber mouse,
Or kill one maybe with her cruel claws,
And present it to you within the house,
And then fastidiously wash her paws.

Do you own a cat? You think that you do,
I'm afraid you will find, the cat owns you!

Doris Dowling

Jamie

Jamie rises early morn
Then wakes me up, I start to yawn
She has a wash, she's very clean
A happier cat I've never seen

Overweight, she loves to eat
I give her cream, a little treat
A dish of food that's overflowing
She eats the lot without slowing

Not the cat we had in mind
No home for Jamie could they find
One of the many unwanted cats
A sorry sight, be sure of that

She'd been abused and that's not rare
Full of nerves and dullish fur
A sorry sight and not so pretty
We took her home, more out of pity

For quite a while she hid away
Crept out for food and back again
She feared people, we knew that
Would Jamie ever be our cat?

Then one day she left her hide
Moved closer to the fireside
There she joined our other cats
All sitting comfy on their mat

No one flinched, not a stir
She settled down and licked her fur
Then snuggled up into a space
What a change now in her face

She loves to sit upon our lap
And give our hand a friendly tap
That lets us know she wants a stroke
This lovely cat who'd lost all hope.

Harry Murtagh

K D

I have an ordinary dog
She'll never win no prizes
Unless they give them out for great big hearts
Like the one her fur disguises.

Her soft brown eyes
Are limpid pools
Her tongue hangs out
She always drools
But I don't think there will ever be
A dog that I'd like more
Who greets me oh so lovingly
As I walk in the door.

This ordinary dog of mine
Is sweet and kind and teasing
I know she always gets the joke
Which I find rather pleasing.

So forget her tiny little faults
When that swishy tail gets wagging
She's just an ordinary dog
Whose love is never flagging.

Ethel Kirkpatrick

Best Of friends

You have been my friend, my companion,
My lifelong love,
Now I'm without you,
But you are safe in the sky above.

Beside me you have always been, loyal in every way,
You have followed in my footsteps, each and every day.
You have jumped happily in the water, and swam at your content,
Now you play amongst the clouds, as to Heaven you have been sent.

Your bed is empty, your bowl is clean,
Your lead hangs up in place.
Each time these things, they catch my eye,
I see your lovely face.

I miss the patter of your paws, the colour of your eyes,
So when I need to see you now, I just look to the skies.
A shining star way up high, I know that it is you,
So please keep twinkling nice and bright, each night that starts anew.

I will never ever forget you, in my thoughts you'll always be,
Until the day we meet again, and together once more, you and me.
These words are from my very heart, I dedicate to you,
it's not goodbye, just goodnight, until the time is due.

I love you Pippa, my darling pet,
Sleep safe and sound forever.
My love for you will not fade,
Never, never, never.

Now goodnight, God bless, my dearest Pippa,
You are always in my thoughts,
My love for you will never end,
To eternity it will last.

I will see you again in another life,
I know you will be there for me.
We will walk on the clouds and run in the sand,
And swim in the deep blue sea.

Heather Chandler

Resident frog

Swimming slowly in rain-filled tub,
dark, bulbous, pleading eyes;
using the last of limited strength,
seeking escape from demise.

Bending, folding, long supple legs,
pale yellow stripes on green,
slower and slower with every stroke
resigned though strangely serene.

Raised by a hand towards freedom,
a vista of garden and skies.
Scramble, pause, a leap in the air
and out of the tub he flies
with graceful agility, straight for the bog.
Resourceful, elegant, resident frog.

Amy Shelton Goodall

Untitled

This is Tara; all trouble and strife
I'm glad of the day she came into my life
I bought her as a cross-Lab
If you know about dogs, you would think I'd gone mad
From day one I saw her, as black as a raven
Now that you see her, she's a Heinz 57
I'd seen her in the pet shop, where she sat all alone
Spoke to the shop owner 'I'm taking her home'
She looked very weak - in 24 hours all she did was sleep
I know puppies sleep as it helps them to grow
But I knew it was trouble, when blood started to flow.
We arrived at the vet's, she was taken so quick
The next time I saw her, she was tied to a drip
This illness in puppies is deadly, you know
The vet said, 'It's not so good, I think it's parvo!'
For ten days solid she was on that drip
Then came the phone call that made my heart skip
'Come, pick her up, she's on the right track.'
From that day on she's never looked back
She's healthy and happy, a whole lot of fun
She's got a new friend, she's her number one
Tara's antics are never a bore
She has now learned she can open the door
Outside they go to have their play
It's all thanks to the PDSA!

Karen McCamley

Bobs

Hi! My name is Bobs,
A cute-looking hunk of a cat,
The male cat version, I must add,
But, what you would call a real pavement special,
Since the same stereotypes are seen around town.
I am a cat with a very good attitude,
And loads of charm, of course,
Cuddles I enjoy with my human family,
Especially, early morning when they are asleep,
I pounce onto a sleeping body and snuggle up real close,
Position my claws and knead bread till I strike flesh,
Oh dear! That hurt.
Quick, time to embrace,
Little paws around my mother's neck,
My little head tucked firmly under her chin,
She hears my gentle purring and off to sleep she goes.
That's me; a real lover not a fighter.
Fashion, well, only black tie for me,
With a fancy white bow tie and long whiskers,
Rather odd black and white socks and shoes,
But, that's style!
Strutting a rather shorter tail,
What I call a misjudgement of my speed,
You know those remote control garage doors ... ?
These days they are so silent and do move with speed,
A slight accident and off came a wee bit of tail,
At least I am still far from looking like a Manx.
Yes, that's me, Bobs the cat.

Nadine Mackie

Naughty Kitten

Tinker the kitten could do no wrong,
He was in and out all day long,
The people, he loved them all, big and small,
Most of all he loved the baby in the hall.
He knew it was wrong, but he drank her milk
And was gone,
Up on the side to see the fish,
How they could swim, when Tinker looked in,
Around and around they would go.
Now out in the garden, oh no,
It's going to rain,
You'd better come in again,
And now he's at my wool,
I won't get it finished after all.

Beryl Elizabeth Moore

Galaxy

The day we brought you home
So tiny and so sweet
Around the house you'd roam
Looking for a treat

And treat yourself you did
Every chance you had
Nothing was sacred
You were really, really bad

And as you grew
The worse you became
But of course you knew
How to give that look of
'I'm not to blame'

You opened cupboards with ease
The contents strew the floor
The fridge was just a breeze
Your skills grew more and more

You smelt the chicken cooking
And somehow opened the oven door
Then you sat there woofing
Because the heat burnt your paw

And now you're four years old
We know all your little tricks
You've a hundred times been told
But we still love you to bits

And when you lovingly look up at me
And tap me with your paw
you know how I adore you Galaxy
My naughty, chocolate Labrador.

Kim Cridland

Our Lad

Fleet of foot with surging muscle,
Rounding the field with grace yet speed,
Taking the corners like a professional,
Motorcyclist, racehorse, express train is he.
Stretched full length with ears laid back,
What a stimulating sight to behold.
Fleet of foot with surging muscle,
There goes Toby - our Jack Russell.

Marilyn H Cahalin

Our Rescued Dog

'Kate' was the name of the tricoloured bitch
Thrust upon us by the Social Services, who
Could find no home for the sad little one
Whose owner had Alzheimer's one Sunday afternoon.

She was brought to our house, alert, but afraid.
She did not bark, just shivered, wide-eyed.
We took in her basket, her food and a drink,
But from all affection she would just shrink.

She approached my husband with her first endeavour,
She took a drink from the handsome fella;
Then ate a little, sniffed a lot,
Looking for her basket, her usual spot.

Her dark eyes opened warily, brown in hue.
Worn by her travels and strangers too,
She settled in her basket, fell fast asleep.
We just sat and watched. Would she be ours to keep?

This new arrival wound herself round
Our old-age hearts. We quickly found
Her docile, obedient, anxious to please.
No need for hard words, too soft to tease.

When examined by the vet, he said
She was overweight and her teeth were bad.
Otherwise she was in good condition, though
Her breed was prone to heart trouble, so

He gave her heart tablets, and we slimmed her down.
She lived with us five years with no frown.
Too old to play with sticks or ball
She came readily with every call.

Like another baby, but quiet, no hustle ...
Just the dog for an ancient couple ...
We loved her so much, but her heart was weak.
It failed at last, so we put her to sleep.

Jane England

Sanctuary 1

Off to the slaughterhouse! May peace be with you,
may peace be your vault of imagination
in remembrance of the hand that fed you.

Sleeping rug at night, tiger in action,
object of love, now subject of sadness,
asylum seeker of feline protection,

Write me a card from your cage of distress.
I'll write often but can't promise a visit;
hopefully, by my next poem, a mistress

will have polished your coat, and kept you fit!
Though we are told that you are safe and happy,
we can't measure the fear that we've inflicted.

Life is sometimes larger than what we see,
even for those who once felt unwanted.

M S Woodcock

Meeting Lucifer, The Dawn Greeter

(My grandma's cockerel in the mid 1940s)

Old Lucifer, the dawn greeter,
Embodying beauty and bravado.
This strutting, barnyard rooster,
Planted atop the farm midden,
Surveying his own small kingdom.
Such a splendidly plumed individual,
All gold, russet, rich brown and black,
Observing his harem of clucking hens.
Their guardian against predator attack.
Chucks scratching with their chicks,
Earnestly searching for spilled grain,
And pink dung-fat, wriggling worms.
A band of sisters with their fluffy kids,
Observing the rules of the poultry clan.
The pecking order must be obeyed,
Or assaults occur with sharp pecks,
Engaged in chases and flapping wings.
This fine-plumed handsome cockerel,
Aware of these disputes far below,
Stares at the patrolling feral cats.
His black beady eyes scarce blinking.
They are fully aware of his status.
Wisely, they avoid his large family.
His menacing attacks are legendary,
Avoided like the proverbial plague.
His red rage terrifying to behold.
The dogs chained outside may bark,
Yet Hell held no more blind, flying fury.
Danger! Lucifer spying a young stranger.
How, as a child, I screamed and ran.

Julia Pegg

I Miss Him - My Black Cocker Spaniel

I feel he lives in Heaven above,
Cocooned there in a haven of love.
His time on Earth complete in April -
'Twas hard to swallow such a bitter pill.

The span spent here was much too short;
Suffering, though pain had to abort.
I know that it was right he had to go
But four months later, I just miss him so.

Experience teaches us that time does heal,
Raw edges are honed, so less sorrow we feel.

Ina J Harrington

A Cat's Life

My name is Sooty, but I'm a disgruntled cat,
Cos most of my time is spent in this flat.
I've no garden to play in, no birds to chase,
That's why I don't wear a Cheshire grin on my face.

The other day I heard a knock on our door,
Someone asked, 'Can I borrow your cat?' I thought, *what for?*
'Sooty,' said my owner, 'come with me.'
Soon I found myself in flat number three.

Suddenly, my heart skipped a beat, that's for sure,
I'd seen two mice scampering across the floor,
Supper that night was extra milk and Kit-e-Kat,
And I thought, *life can be good - even in a flat.*

J Booth

Kyser Of Willmarsh

My little dog, so small and neat
has big brown eyes like toffee, sweet.
His coat is black as liquorice sticks
he greets me with a thousand licks.
His favourite toy is a rubber ball
he chases it up and down the hall.
He runs around in excited rings
when he hears the sound of pigeon wings.
To see a cat on the garden fence
makes his body all taut and tense
So down the garden path he'll race
that big ginger moggy he will chase.

Carrie Ann Hammond

The Cat-Astrophe

Pussy stuck high up in a tree
Out of reach of you and me.

The firemen try to get him down
And put up ladders from the ground.

The firemen are feeling rather groggy
They cannot catch the elusive moggy.

Every time they climb the steps
The moggy goes much higher yet.

They try cat food to tempt him down
But the creature just stares at the ground.

Then they squirt water at his feet
While neighbours stand below with a salvage sheet.

The water trick works, makes pussy leap
But when he comes down he misses the sheet.

But lands quite safely on all fours
But he looks as if he's been in the wars.

You don't find many skeletons of cats in trees
They almost always do get free.

Keith Wilson

A Dog's-Eye View

There is a light ahead
Where am I going?
I've arrived - my first breath
Mum? What are you doing?
It's warm against her body
Feeling safe with the others
Why are we all different?
Are those my sisters and brothers?
I'm moving - but not with paws
The little one is nearing
What is all this that I'm seeing?
Mum! Why are you staying?
I'm being taken away by the others
We're moving away and they're looking at me
Now I'll never see my mother
Ow! A sharp pain in my leg
A hug from the human one
She feeds me and plays with me
Perhaps this life could be fun
Funny - they touch with their mouths
They talk to a thing by their ears
They wear clothes and eat with sticks
Have they done this for all these years?
They move along in metal things
They watch things in a square
And listen to noises from a box
I've got fur - they have hair
I'm supposed to be a human's best friend
I belong to the family - I do
Some think I'm a dumb animal
From what I've seen - so are you!

Joanne Hale

What A Pet!

I had a honey-coloured friend;
A little lion cub;
His paws he would wave in the air
When I gave his tum a rub.

As time passed he grew bigger,
And began to grow a mane;
And then he went girl-crazy -
He adored my sister Jane.

He'd creep up on her quietly,
By walking on tiptoes;
Then with paw around her shoulders,
He would lick her on the nose.

He loved to taste her war paint,
Or cosmetics - oh how sweet!
But always he'd come back to me:
He knew I'd feed him meat!

Roger Williams

Rosie

All week I have had a bad feeling
No, more than a feeling, I *knew*
I gazed through my tears at the ceiling
My Rosie has left me, we're through!

I said to myself, *You're a nutter!*
But there was no comfort in that
I opened the window - the shutter
My Rosie was there on the mat!

I rushed to the door at the double
I ushered her gently inside
She'd certainly been in some trouble
She surely had something to hide.

But ...

I kissed her and tickled her belly
She gave me a half-hearted purr
Shoved her face in her Whiskas (with jelly)
A ball of delinquent fur.

Rosie's Reply

When I was a young and tender maid
My mother taught me well
She said, 'Ne'er show that you're afraid
Just turn and run like hell!'

I met someone last Friday week
A someone bold and bad
By Jove! It was a narrow squeak!
(He was an awful cad.)

I hurried back to my old home
Back to the one who needs me
But I'll not comment on her 'poem'
Why bite the hand that feeds me?

Evangeline Auld

334

Cara

You were wandering in a daze
The first time I saw you
No way that we can know
Of the things that you went through
Abandoned, all alone
In a place open and wide
The shaking of your body
Showed the fear you felt inside
We can only guess
How you managed to survive
Was it the eating up of scraps
That helped keep you alive?
And what then of the night
In that frightening place, alone?
Did you wonder why it was
You were taken from your home?
Has it left you with a fear
Of the noises in the night?
As your eyes now they grow older
And begin to lose their light
The life you had before
Well we will never know
But sometimes in your sleep
It is a place where you may go
Now it's two years further on
It can be seen how you have grown
No longer looking sad
In this new life of your own.

P M Stone

My Dog Bruno

My dog belongs to no known breed, a bit of this and that,
His head looks like a small haystack; he's lazy, small and fat.

If I say 'Sit!' he walks away. When I throw a stick or ball,
He flops down on the grass, as if he has no legs at all.

He looks at me as if to say, *You threw that thing, not me,*
You want it back; you get it back, fair's fair, you must agree!

He is a thief, last week he stole the Sunday roast,
And showed no guilt at all, as we sat down to beans on toast.

The only time I saw him run, and he went just like a flash,
Was when a mugger at the park, tried to steal my cash.

My loyal, brave companion, flew like a missile to the gate,
And didn't stop till safely home, he left me to my fate.

I won't swap him for any dog, that's obedient, good and clean,
I'd rather have the one I've got, despite him being mean!

David Lambert (11)

Lessons from Pets

A dog owned by someone I know died earlier this year.
From his new state can he see his boss bereft without him here?
Do creatures have immortal souls? Some devotees think so.
It offers hope to those who mourn. Well-founded? Probably 'no'.
But, whatever be the prospects of reunion above,
It's true that (as the Queen said) grief's the price we pay for love.
Why is love poured out in such abundance on a pet?
Because of its life's intrinsic worth, or because of what we get?
Is love of pets an outgoing and liberating thing,
Or an escape from life with people and the pain which they can bring?
But liberation through one's love is an illusory desire;
It has been said, a lover's tied, or else he is a liar.
Love gives rise to duty, inconvenience, expense,
To a point at which 'enlightened' minds may think
    This makes no sense.
Consideration for the loved one often lies behind
The way a lover runs his life - and he doesn't mind.
When depended on, we have to help. Could anything excuse
Us as lovers in such circumstances, were we to refuse?
And when age or illness complicate the life we want to keep,
What sort of 'love' takes steps to put the sufferer 'to sleep'?
(Surely more constructive care could ease the patient's ills,
Even if survival will increase the carer's bills.)
Surprised that ownership of pets gives rise to such ideas?
You can hear the 'sub-text' message if you have attentive ears.

Anthony Hofler

The Uninvited Guest

Natty in black, he arrived to
Everyone's notice with
Slow, nonchalant strides, revealing his proprietorship.
He sat before the mother with the
Shaking shoulders and the
Big, powerless man and
Slowly and deliberately
Surveyed the neat, awkward flowers to
Everyone's surprise.
He sat, as if guarding the memory
Of one so small.

Perhaps he had seen Daddy
Holding the tiny coffin.
Perhaps he had taken pity
On the pathos of the scene,
For he sat like a guard
Or a guide,
Bringing comfort to the grieving throng,
Giving hope of a better future
Where there was none.
And promptly disappeared.

Sarah Howard

338

Minstrel

Minstrel you are named but
To me you're always Min.
Leaf chaser, mouse catcher,
Six foot high wall leaper,
Christmas tree lights patter,
Telephone cord tapper,
Excitable,
Cheerful,
Delightful,
Min.

Betty Norton

The Boss

I'm busy in my kitchen, bustling about,
I know he's there, he's no need to shout,
I turn around to meet pure golden eyes,
He sits on the stool, 'Feed me!' he cries.

'Oh Sweepy,' I smile, 'tea time already?'
His eyes never falter, his gaze clear and steady,
I put out my hand to fondle his head,
'Miaow,' he says, 'I want to be fed.'

And just to make sure his tail gives a swish,
It's time to give in and get him his dish,
He jumps to the floor and sits in his place,
I get his food while fixed by his gaze.

Sweepy's my treasured black and white cat,
He was born in this house, oh a long time back,
He's getting old now, but he's sprightly and trim,
And very, very patient, he never gives in.

When Sweepy's around there's a continuous noise,
He loves to purr and has a very loud voice.
He sits on the window sill most of the day
And it's late in the evening when he wants to play.

He'll saunter round the garden then dash up a tree,
I watch in amazement, he thinks he's only three.
He chases our little tabby and taps her with his paw,
He's the boss round here and in this knowledge he's secure.

Margaret Mansbridge

Mafia Cat

Catch your patchy pussycat
Patter cat, pitter pat
Deft through leaves you fit and flee
Off to market on my knee
Sit and dream your days, through ears
Sit and dream, eyes like cream
Slip through snowfall, thin or fat
Foaming roam the milkman's mat
Sit, cat, why aren't you a dog?
But lost you cat, no leash, in fog
Running around the mound flat
On fussy paws, no thought for that
Whispering whiskers flit through doors
Fitted flexed on monster claws
Tames the lioness in those teeth
Tigerish flood in the in the neighbourhood
Grips the mobster down the street
Dances in on ballet feet
Where've you been all covered in blood?

Julie Ashpool

My New Home

Now I've got a new mummy and daddy,
And I live in a lovely new home,
I thought I would put pen to paper,
And write about them in a 'pome'.

My mum is all snuggly and sweet,
There's nothing for me she won't do,
She hugs me and feeds me nice things,
And even cleans up my poo.

I'm bonding so well with my father,
He is quite good at rubbing my belly,
And when we spend time together,
We drink beer and watch football on telly.

So my life here is very happy,
But, my goodness, these humans are rum,
Cos they don't have a tail, fur, or whiskers,
And they can't even lick their own bum!

Arthur Harris

Monkeying Around

(Illustration by Nic Carter)

Behold the little chimpanzee
He doesn't dress like you and me
He never walks down Regent Street
With trainers on his monkey feet
He wouldn't swap one single banana
For fifty shirts by Dolce and Gabbana
And, as far as he's concerned,
Yves Saint Laurent can all be burned
What does he care for Haute Couture?
He's happy in his suit of fur,
But once I saw in wintertime
A chimp steal washing from the line
'A hat! A hat!' he proudly said
And put some knickers on his head.

Robert Paul

Tia

Tia our queen is a frisky cat,
She loves it when she gets fat,
Giving birth is what she does best,
But after she needs a lot of rest,
She is very caring of her young,
But then the big challenge has begun,
This is when the kittens start to roam,
You can tell they are at home,
Play fighting and sleeping is what they do,
You have to show them where to go to the loo,
Each kitten identical to the rest,
How can you choose the best?
Cuddling up to their soft warm fur,
I love to listen to their purr,
They love to feed off their mum,
The warm milk all in their tum,
After feeding they all go to sleep,
All is silent and peaceful, not a peep,
Tia loves to wash her kittens clean,
If she thinks they're in danger she gets mean,
Guarding her kittens is what she does the most,
What beautiful kittens she deserves to boast,
She loves them all and loves her job,
When it's time for their new homes she will sob,
So she makes the most of what she's got,
Loving kittens, yep she's got a lot,
She kisses each one before they go away,
Wishing that they all could stay,
Once each kitten has gone and she is sore,
She shows us that she's lonely and wants more!

Natasha Covey (14)

Squirrel Nutkin

Little squirrel Nutkin
Climbed down from a tree
Ran across the grass
And came right up to me
He had seen me eating
I guessed he wanted a share
For he came and joined me
By jumping on a chair
I fed him from my lunch box
And he quickly nibbled away
Then I gave him some nuts
I'd brought for him that day
When he had finished eating
He washed his little face
Jumped down from the chair
And ran off at a pace
The last that I saw of him
Was as he climbed a tree
And when he had reached the top
He turned and looked towards me.

Diana Daley

Pillow Talk

Pansy's my best
Companion
She chatters
While even asleep
We talk about
The day's events
And all the appointments
We keep.
We agree about all
The things we like
And happily snore
In tune
And sail together
Like the dreamboats
We are
By the fire
And the month's fullest
Moon!

Lyn Sandford

My Secret Affair

People can see we are drawn to each other
But this can't be happening - I'm a wife and a mother
Watching from his window I see a yearning in his eye
As I move off in my car waving him *goodbye*!

He can never be mine, that I do know
But the bond between continues to grow
His tanned firm body so easy on the eye
I love him so - I don't have to try.

But Merlin belongs to number 23
And mine he will never be
With a wag of his tail and a lick of my face
My adored Jack Russell is gone without trace!

Judie Archer

How Dare You?

How dare you lay there snarling at me?
What are you trying to hide?
Eyes bulging; staring, glaring hard
You're laying on my side
Rigid, stiff, ready to fight
Spinning swiftly round
All I want is my soft bed
Move yourself down!
How dare you lay there snarling at me?
Teeth all pearly white
You calculate my every move
Please let me in tonight
I slip my hand underneath you, edging my leg in.
Yuck! What's this you've left for me?
Some cold, wet chicken skin
I wondered what the noise was
Now it's all so clear
Building stock, amongst my sheets
I could clip you round the ear
You belly-slither up my bed, smacking me with your paw
Licking, nuzzling, knocking my hand
Now who has remorse?
Oh well, I'll let you stay then; what other things await?
A dirty bone, a squeaky toy
The biscuits from your plate?
Cuddling up besides you
You nip me with your teeth
Oh, get off now you naughty boy, and let me get some sleep.

Wendy Brittain

Busy Mrs Robin

Today I saw a robin
going hop, hop, hop.
Looking for a cosy place
in which to stop
and build her nest in spring.

First she hopped into the barn,
a busy place to go.
But she decided quickly
a definite no.

Then she tried the pigsty,
it looked cosy, quiet and still,
until the hatch door opened,
in came a load of swill.

The shed had possibilities
'I'll go there next,' she said.
But wise old owl
had got there first
and slowly shook his head.

Little robin redbreast
kept hopping to and fro,
getting very anxious,
'Wherever shall I go?'

Then in the hedge
just by the door
she spied, grandad's old shoe,
robin did a little dance,
'I think that this might do.'

So with little bits of straw,
some grass and bits of tat,
quite a lot of elbow grease
and tons of this and that,
little robin redbreast
settled down with glee
after all that hop, hop, hopping,
'I've found a *home* for me!'

Violet Higgins

The Stand-Off

'I was here before you, I hope you understand
Where you lay your paws now, it is my land.'
'I know I've just arrived here, that's all I have to say,
Stop with all the meanness, come on let's play.'
'I tolerate your presence, let's leave it at that.
Can't you get the message? I'm not a playful cat.'
'But the times that you do play, your claws are always out,
Growling and spitting, from your aggressive mouth.'
'Your wide-eyed stare annoys me, as well as your constant purr.
Grow up, you're not a kitten, try and act mature.'
'By mature do you mean moody, and no time for fun,
Prowling and causing fights, before the night is done?'
'Please understand this, other cats do not want to play.
They're trying to steal my area, it's tough to keep them away.'
'Those people inside there like me, the way I talk and yell.
Couldn't you just try to like me as well?'
'You know that I purr, and sit on the people's laps,
But to be nice to you, would be a sudden relapse.'
'Then I'll move away now, and try to avoid your pounce.
I'll still follow you around though, in case you'll give me a chance.'
'Then I'll continue sitting here, until you have left.
But me eventually like you, don't hold your breath.'

E L White

Someone To Watch Over Me

Someone left me on my own,
Cold and hungry far from home.
Then I was found and put behind a wall of glass.
Watching all the people pass.
They didn't notice I was shy and needed love like all the rest.
They all liked friendly cats the best.
Then I had kittens, something of my own.
I thought they'd be with me until they'd grown
But after seven weeks they took them just like that, I had no choice.
I cried to let them know but no one heard my voice.
I had no place to stay, to call my own,
No family and no one watching over me.

When you found me I was scared.
I didn't think you really cared.
The only way that I could show my feelings was to run
Away, to hide or hiss.
If I'd been human I'd be with a counsellor or therapist.
Slowly over time affection changed my point of view
And bit by bit my confidence returned and grew.
I didn't hiss or try to hide.
I even took a risk and went outside.
Now you can't keep me in, I love the great outdoors.
You make me feel that I belong and that I'm really yours.
Time and patience have done wonders for my insecurity
Now I have someone watching over me.

Nicola Wood

Skip

When Skip was a pup,
He would run around
And bark and play,
But now he sleeps throughout the day.

He would run and jump,
And leap and bound,
But now he hardly makes a sound.

He would bark and yap,
Play with his toys,
But now he rarely makes a noise.

He would hear my tales
And my secrets keep,
Now all he wants to do is sleep.

He'd chase autumn leaves,
And roll in snow,
But with tears, there's just one place to go.

No turning back,
And no regrets,
I've got to take him to the vets.

Good boy, Skip ... good boy.

Kevin Baskin

Covered With Love

It's our Ben's birthday, 6 today,
We will celebrate together,
Seems an age since his skin and bone days
Rescued, all arms and legs, little fellow.

Scar on his head has disappeared now,
Unhappiness all gone, forever,
Such a special, adorable lad,
Our love for him we can't measure.

He seems to know our every mood,
Can sense when we're under the weather,
Soft brown eyes say, *don't worry Dad,*
A short walk will do till you're better.

Apple Tree Lane can wait for a while,
You might feel more like it tomorrow,
I'll sit by the gate, wait for the kids,
Perhaps there's a hug I can borrow.

I'm sure Ben thinks, *Mum's a cordon bleu chef,*
To cook his meals is my pleasure,
Our vet's not too pleased, reduce him he says,
Give Ben a little less dinner.

But I still recall his skin and bone days,
Since then he's been gently mothered,
So I say to Ben what my gran said to me,
'You're not fat love, you're just well covered!'

Dorothy M Mitchell

Duke's Photo Shoot

'I want to take your photo,'
My mistress said to me.
'I want to take your picture,
For it is plain to see,
You are a handsome 'Rotty',
Your stature is quite grand
And I would like to show you off.
There is no need to stand,
Just sit, relaxed, but regal,
Stay calm and bide your time.
I'll wander round the garden
And take some pics; that's fine!'

It seems I've sat here ages,
Whilst mistress stands, then squats,
Clicking with her camera;
I'm glad it's not too hot!
I'd rather be off tracking
All the scents that I can find,
But I dearly love my lady;
So really, I don't mind,
Sitting in our garden
Watching for the sign
From my loving mistress
That says, 'You look real fine!'

Oh great! It seems we've finished,
And it's almost time for tea.
I know my mistress loves me
So she'll have a treat for me!

Grace Christian

Gemma

Gemma, Gemma, our cute little kitty,
Her fur soft and smooth
And her markings so pretty.
Her eyes, big, bold and bright,
Capturing scenes during daytime
But so sleepy at night.
Gemma, Gemma, likes to be snug.
Huddled up near the radiator,
A chair or a rug.
Our dear little cat, so full of affection,
Talkative and vocal in her own little way.
Rubbing herself against us
And purring to perfection.
Gemma, Gemma, doesn't wander very far
But dislikes a check-up at the vets
And that journey in the car!
But while out of doors
She will spot the odd mouse.
Chasing birds, shrews and butterflies,
Then catching them in her paws.
Gemma, Gemma, when she first came to us
Was so quiet, nervous and unsure
But now is part of our family
And a happy little puss.

Clare Curtis

My Afghan

A long time ago, on a bright sunny day
A small young child went out to play.
She sat on a hillside watching a cloud,
Then there he was standing, tall and proud.
She looked at him with eyes of bold,
The wind gently blowing his coat of gold.
She couldn't believe it, was he real?
His silky gold coat she had to feel.
Slowly she held out her hand,
To her he looked so mighty grand.
This beautiful creature even let
Her put her arms around his neck.
He sat down beside her, this Afghan hound,
Close together on the ground.
She caressed the Afghan's long silky ears,
Her big brown eyes were filled with tears.
That kiss he gave her stole her heart
For she knew then, they would never part
And ever since that bright sunny day
Her love for an Afghan was here to stay.

Irene Gurney

Lolly Pop

Lolly Pop is a little cat
She's lithe and long
And her fur jet-black.
She very rarely sits on my knee
And has a strong passion
For weak cold tea.

She'll drink it directly out of the cup
Or use her paw to lap it up.
She'll sit there silently licking her lips
And licking the tea off her paw tips.
So often I pick up an empty cup
For my dear little Lolly
Has drank the lot up.

This used to really infuriate me
As I am myself very fond of tea,
These tea pinching antics
Just had to stop.
Now I make tea for me
And Lolly Pop.

Stella Turner

One Eye

One Eye is a sparrow
Who works the Venice tables
Not the type of bird you'd find
In legends or in fables.

We breakfasted among the plants
Beside the Grand Canal
The terrace was alive with birds
But One Eye was so small.

She came to us each morning
For bread and scrambled egg
And perched right on the tablecloth
The crumbs for which to beg.

The waiters took a dim view
Of the birds around the diners
We had to be most careful
The head honcho did not find us.

But One Eye was persistent
A brood maybe to feed?
She hid amongst the Jasmine
To satisfy her need.

She was such a little cutie
We loved her from the start
And the poor blind empty socket
That fairly broke your heart.

Elizabeth Cleveland

Who's That Cat?

Who's that scratching up the window
Telling us to come and let him in?
Pleased with himself that he can reach
Just by standing on the bin.

Who's that sitting in the doorway
Taking his time without a care?
In or out - what a big decision
Must you let in all that cold air?

Who leaves through the bathroom window?
Who left mucky paw prints on the wall?
Look at that lump beneath the rug!
His favourite hiding place of all.

Who comes home in the small hours?
Scratch-scratch-scratch up the back door
Who likes to sleep beneath the clothes horse?
Why are all the towels on the floor?

Who sharpens his claws on the armchair?
Who's that sitting in my seat?
What's that rustling at night-time?
Oh no, he's found his bag of treats!

Who is the cause of this commotion?
Who's the one who always gets the fuss?
It has to be the one and only Elwood
Our lovely cat who means the world to us!

Helen Farley

Measha

On one fateful day Mum went down to the pound
Where she met the most beautiful hound.
She was very messed up, but gorgeous inside,
She looked at my mum, with her head on the side,
her brown eyes stared up, saying, *choose me please,*
Look beyond scruffy fur and fleas.
The very next day, she was due to go down,
Put to death without a sound.
All that night Mum thought of that pup,
Behind the bars where she was shut.
The very next day Mum bought her straight,
And she was transferred from her awful state.
Then she was trained all day and trained all night,
Until she learned not to scratch and bite.
Then I was born, she became my best friend,
I thought our friendship would never end.
We used to play in the garden, summer or fall,
Playing and jumping with her favourite ball.
But then she got cancer, first in her neck,
She had it removed but then it came back.
Then she went blind, and could barely walk,
Then about her, I could no longer talk.
Then she was due to be put to sleep,
Forever and ever without a peep.
The injection went in while I was in maths,
It was 9am to be exact.
I left her that morning, with her lying there,
Knowing after school, the spot would be bare.
I went back to her four times, but then I went,
I wanted to stay, but away I was sent.
Now she's gone, put to sleep,
Happy in Heaven, and happy she'll keep.
Measha was my dog, a lovely one at that,
I still remember the places where she sat.
I can still hear her panting, her warm breath on my cheek,
Before she got ill, and was put to sleep.

Emmeline Michelle Cambridge

Ode To Custard

So happy, so yellow
So eager to please!
(He makes all the ladies
Go weak at the knees).

Hail Captain Custard
King of all beasts!
(He'll go fetch and play dead
For Bonio treats).

A model show dog,
The perfect example!
(Although some say his stomach
Is a little bit ample).

Long golden hair,
Immaculately brushed!
(Though I wish he wouldn't slobber
All over the rug).

An excellent listener
That dog ain't no quack!
(However I do get quite worried
When he starts talking back).

All in all he is wonderful
My soft-hearted pup
All he needs to learn now
Is how to wash up!

Jennifer Davies

Our Pharoah

This is our Pharoah, our bestest Staffie, died in the year 2000, such a good boy,
Was gentle with everybody and everything, little white tip to his tail,
And how he loved his grub, big operation at 6,
32 bladder stones cut away,
He was the dog that watched the trains go by, running up and down the station yard.
Then, go see, go see the ducks, we used to say at Carshalton Ponds,
Going in the car, trying to drive Dad's car, little paws on the dashboard,
So excited in the brick field running free, then running home with Janice to number 53!
Then one day not so well, it couldn't be helped, liver trouble you see,
We had to say goodbye, then Pharoah turned around that March night,
As we sat in the car, as if to say, *aren't you coming too?*
His scratching at the vet's door, trying to get away, Janice cried
And told Pharoah how much we loved him, as the needle went in,
He closed his little eyes for good,
Coming home, we look at his bowl and studded collar feeling completely lost,
We shall never forget our Pharoah, even though we had poor little Betsey,
Who was a stray from Battersea Dogs Home, then our third
One now called Amber,
But Pharoah was special, Janice has his little green box of ashes,
Hope to see you one day, remember Pharoah, 29th June 1986 -
2nd March 2000 - our Battersea boy!

H Hutchin

So Refined!

If you met my cat, I think you'd find,
she's very proud and well refined.
Silky and sleek, she won't be hurried,
About tomorrow ... she is not worried.

She knows that she is such a beauty,
to wash and groom is her duty.
I wonder as I watch her stalk ...
what would she say if she could talk?

Your tea smells good, may I taste?
Perhaps you could just set me a place,
I would love that tasty dish,
smells delicious ... is it fish?

The neighbour's cat ... that's so dim-witted,
for it, they've had a cat flap fitted.
Now he can get in from the rain,
I wondered ... could we do the same?

Let me closer to the fire,
do turn it up a little higher!
It's frightfully cold outside today,
I'd like a blanket if I may?

Just one more thing ... hope you don't mind,
I do not wish to be unkind,
the tins of meat that you've been feeding
aren't good enough for my high breeding!

Incidentally, your dog who chases a ball,
and lifts its leg again the wall,
seems to me it's out of its mind,
not like me ... I'm so refined!

Jan Coats

My Best Friend

I have a friend
So loyal and true,
He is by my side
Whatever I do.

He takes me for walks
In all kinds of weather
And rides in my car,
We are always together.

If I'm feeling sad
He just sits and stares,
He is such a treasure,
I know that he cares.

We watch TV together,
Lonely hours we do fill,
Such a super companion,
Is my dog named *Bill*.

Kathleen Cater

for My Special Ellie

My beautiful Ellile - German Shepherd supreme
Feisty, frisky, fearless, friendly ... all of those ...
But only *as* and *when* it suited you!
We certainly had our moments girl!

Like the day at the farm when you decided to playfully nip a calf's nose
Or the strange disliking you took to the workman exiting from a manhole
Or the Avon lady you pushed through next door's hedge
(Take it you didn't like the products that much then)
To say nothing of all the dogs' necks you so liked to playfully nibble on
And all the postmen, delivery men, paper boys who so tried to brave your fearsome bark!
(You could make the gate in 10 seconds - they quickly learnt to run in 5)

But all that only served to make you so my dog
And of course I always defended you to the hilt
I probably loved you more than I loved my partner
You were definitely more loyal and faithful
Wet nose, liquid brown eyes, gleaming coat
You'll be in your element now - playing so freely at Rainbow Bridge
Bet you've already had your first scrap!

It seemed so unfair to lose you so young
But you'd have hated growing old
You never did anything with any grace
So that wouldn't have been too much to ask of you
Had I ever been a dog myself I would've so been you.

Sal Barker

Leon The Giant Schnauzer

He is black, soft and cuddly
He's joyful and bubbly
A real cute puppy
Such a yuppie
His favourite toy is his bone
He barks when he hears the phone
The Hoover he hates
But loves a bunch of grapes
He has a red collar and lead
He is always ready for a feed
He is so soft to touch
And we love him so much.

Beth Gwilliam (13)

Diet The Hamster Way

Hamster, fluffy little one
How is it you eat food by the ton?
You stuff your cheeks until they're full
But you, yourself stay really small.

Tell me hamster, little one
Don't keep your diet secrets schtum
You eat me out of house and home
But you don't put on a single stone.

First a peanut, then some corn
A seed or two, but you're not done!
A raisin sweet and hamster chew.
But where they go, I wish I knew!

My piggy bank is running low
Yet your appetite, it does not slow
Apple slice and grass seed now
All disappear, but where and how?

And then at last, when at the store
The pet shop man, he told me more,
So I spied on you, when I came back,
Whilst your bowl is empty, you don't lack.

Tucked away with tender care,
Is months of food, with more to spare!
So that's how you look your best,
You eat what you need and sleep on the rest!

Ruth M Ellett

Cats

Cats' eyes are like marbles, their teeth are like knives,
Whoever made the saying up, that cats have nine lives?

Some cats are stray and live on the streets,
They have no food and certainly no treats.

Cats' eyes go big when they are scared,
Maybe a sudden noise that they have heard.

They have long tails and soft fur,
They miaow and also purr.

Pointed ears and padded paws,
A pink nose and very sharp claws.

But don't forget their nasty bite,
Put two together and they will fight.

They chase birds and climb trees,
And mice, they come looking for cheese.

They mostly eat chicken or cat meat,
When you walk past they pounce on your feet.

They sleep in the day and are active at night,
They can see in the dark without a light.

They play in the grass and the butterflies they tease,
They eat the spiders and torment the bees.

Some have a collar and maybe a bell,
A girl or a boy, how can you tell?

E Cardwell

Guide Dog

For my spaniel old age has brought
Both blindness and bewilderment;
Things disappear, or sneak up and hit him
But he is not alone.
Ruffles, self-appointed guide dog, bustles to the rescue:
Stands by the ball Teddy cannot find until
He hurries over to reclaim it with a pounce of joy.
No one trained Ruffles, or showed him how
To be a blind dog's guide dog;
Nor taught Teddy how to work with him.
This is something they have sorted for themselves,
Without fuss, in the world they share
And I can only celebrate.

Susan Latimer

A Dog's Life

Oh to have a dog's life
Do you think you could do better?
If you haven't got a care in the world
You could be a red setter

Just wake up in the morning
Grizzle to be let out
Your every whim is cared for
What is it all about?

Run around and strut your stuff
Chasing cats or playing ball
Laze about in the midday sun
Or maybe jump a wall.

Come back inside when you've had enough
Looking slightly thinner
One look around the living room
Then gobble up your dinner.

Back into the garden
To dig up my best lawn
Then back inside, lie on your bed
And go to sleep till dawn.

Must not forget the walkies
Being pampered and the treat
Oh to have a dog's life
A life you just can't beat.

Clive Bassett

Shandy

The past tense will never suit you, Shandy
wherever you are roaming now
I will always recognise your gait
so elegant, almost ethereal
it doesn't belong to our materialistic world
I know you are watching
our every gesture, our every step;
be they lofty or innocent
perking your ears
for our murmurs, our sighs, our bad temper
your splendid striped coat
is that of eternal youth
you are the Egyptian goddess of yore
the modern diva of the digital era
playing each role
with an equally regal poise
putting our human arrogance
our pettiness to shame
yet, dear Shandy
it would be foolish to deny it
and you wince at any sign of hypocrisy
we will miss your girlish manners
your insistent complaints
whenever a visitor comes to your house
and he or she is served a biscuit
while your three plates
are brimming over with delicacies
you want to be reminded of your rank
and indeed, you were and shall always remain
Shandy, the queen of cats

Albert Russo

My Pet?

You can keep your cats and dogs,
You can keep your large bullfrogs.
Some folks think I've lost the plot
When I tell them, it's an angel I've got.
Not one of those with shiny wings
That brought the Christmas glad tidings.
No, largely black with gold and white,
He really is a gorgeous sight.
He cannot speak but mouths a name,
It's Bob - Bob - Bob always the same.
My name's not Bob I'll be quite frank,
I keep my angel in a big fish tank.

Albert Watson

To My Summer Cat

Early spring has come to the garden.
Everywhere, promise of life is bursting in colours
Bright and young and new.
Yet I see it with sadness,
For no longer will my lovely little golden cat
Roam the leafy paths,
Tend the fragrant plants
And lie in the warmth of the sun
In the garden she loved so much.
And the daffodils,
Bright and golden as she was,
Momentarily bow their heads in sorrow
And the petals from the cherry blossom,
Soft and gentle as she was,
Silently fall like tears.
The love-in-the-mist is yet only half grown.
This year she will not nestle in its tall green stems
And soak up the sun through the long summer days,
Fanned and cooled, safe and content,
Half-hidden amidst its delicate waving fronds.
Yet - tho' I'll not see her -
She will be there - in the love-in-the-mist -
And everywhere:
My love in the mist of tear and time
In my garden, in my heart -
My summer cat.

Helen M Seeley

Chip Joins The family

Chip you are always rushing around until late,
when we fall asleep your paw pats us awake,
wanting attention and to play,
we love you too much to push you away,
no matter what time it is, night or day.

Oliver, our other cat, can't have it all his way,
now you, a manic kitten have come to stay.
You jump on him and wake him up,
sometimes he finds it a big tough,
he's outgrown all of that kitten stuff.

Other times such special moments you two share,
cuddled up in your basket together,
keeping warm in cold weather,
as if you've known each other forever,
except when your mischief takes Ollie by surprise, causing fur to fly!

Julie Marie Laura Shearing

Sheba

Sheba my hamster,
Named after a queen,
Sits in her cage all day,
Grooming herself clean,
I remember the day I chose you,
So furry and small,
Still only a baby,
Wrapped up in a ball,
You bring me joy every day,
When you stretch your legs and play,
I love to hold you in my hand,
Touch your fur,
The colour of grains of sand,
Little eyes like black beads,
Your favourite things are nuts and seeds,
I wish you could speak,
And tell me your thoughts,
Your feelings,
Your longings,
Your dreams,
Because nothing is ever what it seems,
And you would have such stories to tell,
Of your life with a human,
And all that it means.

Christine Julian-Huxley

A True friend

(Treasured memories of Henry 1985-2002)

He's never cross, true - he's the boss,
and many good times we've had.

For certain, I think, without even a blink,
he's truly a best friend to me.

He's not very big, and although he can't speak,
he's certain to announce his arrival.

A cuddle, a hug, a stroke is fine,
then purrs when we both relax!

Antics aplenty, though chimneys are best!
He's usually out to surprise me.

My best friend, my Henry, without whom I'd be lost,
a wonderful puss cat, unique among many,
is truly a best friend indeed.

Irene Sanderson

The Curfew (Bebe's Story)

I languished in a cats' home for weeks and weeks on end
While many willing servants, my every need would tend.
Till picked up by a lady, and squashed against her breast
I placed a paw upon her cheek and well, you know the rest.

She and her man took me home with warnings that were grim
Like I'd be traumatised and take a while to settle in.
Gave my catnip mouse a kicking and washed my paws with care,
My man stooped down to stroke me - and I jumped up in his chair.

Next morning, we awoke with the rising of the sun
Three in a bed with me in the middle, not their idea of fun.
I breakfasted with relish; they went out and bought lots more.
Next time, I sniffed it with disdain and then I scraped the floor.

One day the doorbell rang, it was the lady o'er the fence
She told my mum a story; of course it made no sense.
For while her cat with urinary problems was curled up on her lap
It seems a fat old tabby had squeezed in through their flap!

He was crunching on their dietary food, she didn't think it funny
In fact her chocolate point Siamese was not a happy bunny.
She saw me, 'That's him!' she shrieked and pointed to the chair
Where I was doing what cats do, my leg stuck in the air.

Next day I was in the garden, frogging by the pond
When the lady shouted to my man from the yard beyond.
'Were you waiting up for him, late last night?' she said.
Apparently, I was locked in hers, when they'd all gone to bed.

She said I ran round panicking, honestly - as if!
My man bent down and picked me up and walked off with a sniff.
But indoors they discussed it over cups of tea, and then
Decided on the curfew - I must be in by ten!

Jill Mackness

New Image

'Boo, I don't believe it,
But you have turned green.'
The weirdest Westie
I've ever seen.
A handsome dog,
As white as snow,
Has now assumed
A fluorescent glow.

'How,' you may ask,
'Did the white turn to green?'
On the strangest Westie
I've ever seen?
Well, he swam on his belly,
All the way across,
Then rolled side to side,
On the new mown grass.

As I watched him do it,
His white coat became green.
He's the proudest Westie
I've ever seen.
Friction caused the cut grass
To dye all his fur.
I believe it's true, only,
Because I was there.

Lorna Lea

My friend Mushy

We have been together now for almost ten years,
I have learnt to read your brown eyes, expressing your thoughts and fears.
I feel you're an extension of me, my darling little boy,
When I feel pain, you feel pain, my joy also your joy.
You do not judge, you only love, you're so vulnerable and mild,
I run with you along the beach and feel just like a child.
Always protective in your own sweet way,
Friends until the end we love and live and play.

E Hoole

Ode To Rascal

A Rascal by name and nature,
We know you loved him so,
It was such a hard decision, to let poor Rascal go,
But you know you did the right thing,
Although it broke your heart.
You knew you had to lose him,
And it was so hard to part.
But remember all the good times,
When you took him for his walk,
He'd run around and chase them cars,
That dog could nearly talk.
Remember all that barking,
It nearly drove you mad,
Then he'd look at you with big brown eyes
And make your heart so glad.
So although there is no Rascal
To welcome you at your door,
His spirit still is with you, and will be for evermore.
So rest in peace dear Rascal,
Although this is the end.
Remember him with love and joy,
Your dog and your best friend.

Marilyn Doherty

Best Friend - My Dog Heinz

Forever faithful love abound
Oh! You mischievous hound

Warm heart, wet nose
This poem for you I compose

Explosive with delight on my return
Constantly at my side especially at dinner time

Now you have gone, the joy we have shared
Will bring me happiness for the years ahead

Antoinette Ghura

Ms Sally Cross

Our cat Sally has become a friend we really love
She's a furry, friendly creature, almost sent from Heaven above
Her origins? Abandoned. Found by a railway line
But rescued, tamed and cared for now, we get along just fine
She's tortoiseshell, but timid, a very pretty bundle of fur
Sitting in an armchair, she will smile at you and purr
Despite her lowly origins, she's a highbrow taste for food
For varied packs of cat mix she is always in the mood
She waits there in her corner, standing hopefully by her dish
Pleading for some service - for some chicken or some fish
Her antics are amusing, sometimes they're quite a hoot
Whene'er the doorbell rings at once she scarpers and she scoots
Whene'er she meets a stranger she gets fearful and alarmed
Her ears go back, her eyes so big, for fear of pain and harm
With family though she's most at ease, and very much at home
Although she likes the garden, she is not inclined to roam
Once in the year she meets the vet - a right to-do and kafuffle
Her 'MOT' she does not like, her fur it sure does ruffle
The 'cat doctor' is not for her, with fear she's really smitten
It's a pitiful sight, to see her fright, a fearful frightened kitten
On normal days she's at ease on the rug - a place she likes to be
Curled up asleep, by the fire, warm and snug - a lovely sight to see
On the chair she is also happy too, she has her own bed sheet
On this she washes, looks and smiles, and then falls sound asleep
So here's to you, our lovely cat - the one and only Sal
You bring us sunshine by being around, our dear old feline pal
Your antics do amuse us all, you're such a playful scamp
In the cat league you are top of the tree, the one, unrivalled champ.

Timothy Cross

Shandie's Poems

I'm a Cocker Spaniel
And my mummy calls me Shandie
I'm black with a white bib
Which I think looks rather dandy

When we're out for walkies
I've got a favourite game
I pick up things I shouldn't
And Mummy says, 'Oh shame.'

She asks me, 'Is that good or bad?'
As if she doesn't know
So I wag my tail and cuddle up
But I definitely won't let go

I grab a toy as a disguise
And we have a tug of war
I give a few small growls
And the game goes on some more

But Mummy's very clever
She can sneak the thing away
All I'm left with is the toy
Thinking, *how did it get away?*

Carol Sherwood

I Love You, Goodbye

Fifteen years is an awful long time
For me to watch over you.
I was there to lick your tears away,
Whenever you were sad and blue.

I would always do those stupid tricks
That you thought were so funny.
And, no matter what I ever did,
You'd say, 'Mama loves you, honey.'

I know I couldn't answer you
And tell you I loved you too.
But, you already knew I did
By the little things I'd do.

But now I'm tired and weary,
And God is calling me home.
I lay a paw across your arm,
You'll have to make it on your own.

You have to go on without me,
Yes, I know those tears are real.
Thank you for fifteen years
And for showing me how you feel.

I love you, Mama. Goodbye.

Claytia Doran

Night Adventures

When I tiptoe
Into the garden at night
Everything is tinted
By the clear moonlight
The twinkling stars
In the vast ebony sky
I'd like to catch them
But they are too high
This is my world now
Whilst everyone is asleep
Amongst the bushes and grass
I slowly creep
My footsteps are weightless
Barely touching the ground
And I am quickly alert
To the slightest, strange sound
I am not seen, except
For my feet, which are white
And my bright, beacon eyes
Which burn in the night
Soon the night fades
And the sun starts to rise
How I wish that
I could just close my eyes
Wearily, I slip home to bed
Now to dream
Of night adventures instead.

Hazel Calpee

Lizzy The Jack Russell (Again)

Good young Lizzy,
She's not normally
The greedy kind,
So if you reward
Her with an ice cream
She'll be your
Friend not mine.

She's here, there
And everywhere
And always likes
To rule.
There ain't no wasps
On Lizzy for
She is no fool.

So if you should
Meet illustrious Lizzy
Out upon the street,
Do not bring your bulky
Shoes down upon
Her dainty feet,
But stroke her
If you must,
Then let her walk on by.
For she'll be tucking into steak and bics
In less than half an hour.

David Ashley Reddish

Rupert's Bath Night

Oh no, not the bath tub!
Can't we give it a miss?
Don't you realise I'm a dog?
I'm supposed to smell like this.
You call it 'essence of cowpat',
I call it 'moment of bliss'
And it drives the girls wild
When they get a good whiff.
OK, I'll have a bath,
But please no sweet smelling spray
And don't think I'll stay like this,
Tomorrow's another day.

Jean Nutt

The New House

Tiny creature in new home,
Has a sniff then starts to roam,
A comfy bed, some food to eat,
A radiator to warm her feet.

She cries, she purrs,
She ruffles her fur,
She pounces, fights,
Scratches and bites.

A wind-up mouse, a piece of string,
A tiny bell that goes *ding, ding!*
A ball that's bigger than her head,
A purple duck to cuddle in bed.

She cries, she purrs,
She ruffles her fur,
She pounces, fights,
Scratches and bites.

She looks around this strange new place,
A cattish grin spreads on her face,
She eats her food, she has a play,
Then sleeps and sleeps for the rest of the day!

She cries, she purrs,
She ruffles her fur,
She pounces, fights,
Scratches and bites.

Sarah France (11)

Superiority

They say people are the superior race
I think not - we cats rule the Earth
We walk around houses like we own them all
Sit around and do nothing all day
And let our servants, people, wait on us
Almost on your knees
You know who your real masters are
Giving us food whenever we want
Sometimes we just want to snooze
But you won't go away
You insist on stroking us
A few scratches and you're back in your place
Then you buy us toys
That we're too intellectually superior to play with ...
Well most of the time
If you want a creature to laugh at
And have fun with
And consider a friend
Buy something stupid like a dog
I'll tell you something final
The only reason people are in charge
Is because us cats can't be bothered.

Senõr Tigger fluffy-Kins III

Space Is A Dog's Best Friend

Open fields and endless runs,
Space is a dog's best friend,
Bounding down rolling hills,
In a hope they never end.

Chasing a stick or catching a ball,
Playing with next door's hound,
Freedom to stretch our legs,
Mates to be made and found.

A canine's life is getting hard,
No room to bark and play,
A process of minimisation,
Surely there is a better way.

Greenery is being eliminated,
Block work stands instead,
Nothing to look forward to,
Only a walkway as tough as lead.

So tie a noose around my neck,
And tighten the knot on the rope,
Because a mutt has no voice,
Only a mind full of silent hope.

A hanging tongue and wagging tail,
My master seems to understand,
But life is a tug of war,
Our yelps fall on a deafened man.

Open fields and endless runs,
Space is a dog's best friend,
Grass may seem simple to humans,
But none for us is the beginning of the end.

Anna Kirby

I Love My Bed!

Don't disturb me, I'm tired eyes pussycat
I like it in the duvet, it's much warmer than the mat
I like the soft cotton against my silky fur
It makes me happy, it makes me purr
I'll have 40 winks then maybe some more
Then I'm disturbed by the noise of the door
I listen with glee as Mummy calls out my name
I'm not going to move cos I'm playing a game
I wiggle my bum further down the bed
So far down you can't see my head
I hear the sound of my name called out
Then I hear footsteps walking about
A flash of light and a jolly big smile
My game is up and we cuddle a while
I purr and purr whilst she tickles my head
And I no longer care that I'm in the bed!

C Atkins

Defa The Dog

I've got a dog called Defa,
he's got deadly deep brown eyes.
He dives on me when I have his dummy,
just keep your eye on him.
I haven't fed Defa the dog,
oh my God, he's going to die!
He thinks his food is delicious,
he demolishes it in minutes.
I forgot to take my dog for a walk,
I'm very sorry, can't stop to talk,
I've got to run, my dog's on the walk.

Emma Louise Owen

Confessions Of A Border Collie

My name is Libby - I love to chew
  Electric wires - telephone too.
Door frames taste good - so does carpet,
  I haven't started on the car yet!
I try my hardest to be good -
  But usually my name is 'mud'.
I know 'Mum' finds me very trying -
  She does an awful lot of sighing!
But now I've made my biggest blunder,
  And here she comes, with face like thunder.
'Dogicide' would get her vote -
  Her TV's minus its remote!

P McDonald

Kal-El, His first Walk

Morning's here,
Come on let's go!
Eat some breakfast
Then hit the road!

Wide open space!
Let's run and run!
That's a bit scary!
Must stick close to Mum!

Another dog
Bigger than me!
Must show how grown up I am,
So I'll bark bravely!

Time to go home now,
No more energy to play,
In my bed I'll dream about
The fun I had on walkies today!

Lorna Brown

My Darlings

I have four dear pussycats -
You may well pity me.
Each time I go to the kitchen,
They think it's time for tea.

The three live a luxurious life,
The fourth one stays outside.
I plead with him to enter in,
But he will not abide.

They fight over territory,
And who will rule the roost.
When the battle's over,
They're scratched but barely bruised.

No matter how many times a day,
I open and shut the door,
Always on the wrong side of it,
It's now become a chore.

'Mum! The cats have fouled again!
Which one could it be?'
'To find the real culprit,
Look up the tallest tree.'

My furniture is destroyed;
My curtains let light in;
My carpet's truly ruined,
They haven't left a thing.

I reach my hand to stroke one,
The rest slump on the floor.
I only have one pair of hands,
I'm sorry I have no more.

I hear an alarming squeak,
To the rescue I must go.
With my bare hands I'll catch it,
To free it from its woe.

Back to the kitchen I go,
To make a bedtime drink.
'Ah! It's feeding time.'
'Oh! That's what you think!'

I retreat to my bedroom,
To try and get some sleep.
But as I pull the covers back,
I land upon the heap!

Yet, having said all that,
I wouldn't change a thing.
And should another need me,
I'd gladly take it in.

K Henderson

Kerry

I've come out here because I must,
Ostensibly to sweep the paths,
But truly just to lift my mind
From what we did an hour ago.

Impulsively it seemed to be
To phone the vet about your fate.
'Saturday's surgery's almost closed,
Come at once if you want me today.'

We lifted you gently into the car,
Your back leg no longer supporting.
The trust from your one eye cut to the quick.
We fell silent the rest of the way.

The vet removed tenderly collar and lead
Then handed them over to me.
The only possessions of a much loved dog
We never again would see.

Is that all dear Kerry has left us behind
After six months and sixteen long years,
Apart from gold tufts of hair blown in the wind
Mother coaltit would lift from the trees?

Far more than these trifles, you've left us a wealth
Of warm memories over the years.
Your gentleness, courage, forgiveness and trust
Will remain long after our tears.

These last days essentially never will fade
When only by me you were fed.
Chicken titbits and shortbread were all you could face,
Three rugs and hot bottle in bed.

'Where are you now?' the little ones ask,
When they lose a dear friend they've had.
What do you say to a nine-year-old child?
'Now she's happy' or 'she's no longer sad'?

Kathleen Davey

King Tiddles

Tiddles was a ginger cat,
The lord of his domain,
Ruling all the other cats
Who ventured down his lane.

Stretched upon the garden wall,
His land he would survey,
Resting in the morning sun,
While waiting for his prey.

Tiddles was a ginger cat,
White flash upon his paws,
His back dipped in and legs stretched out
while sharpening his claws.

His coat was a tiger's stripe,
His whiskers long and straight,
He pounced upon both bird and cat
Who wandered near his gate.

Tiddles was a ginger cat,
A tom who liked to fight,
He lost one eye in battle,
While prowling in the night.

His nature had a softer side,
He'd purr and purr for me
When I stroked his silky fur
As he sat upon my knee.

Tiddles was a ginger cat,
Alas; no more he'll roam,
But watches o'er his kingdom
When other cats leave home.

I see his cat-like shadow
Against the garden wall,
And in the hours of moonlight
I hear his plaintive call.

Doris Green

Mr Jingles

The bad old days

The rain pelts hard, my fur lies flat,
All empty bins, I'll not get fat,
I creep around, searching for loot,
Yet terrified I'll feel the boot,
Or a shoo. What can I do?

My head was bald, red raw with mites,
Weak with hunger, I'd hunted all night,
City bins provide few delights;
Pull over old man, bed down for a while,
Old Blackie was not feeling very sprite.

That was the night I was rescued, so when I awoke,
To my surprise, in a cattery of caring folk.
Some owners came ... and then they went,
Snatched moments with a cuddle spent,
Who'd want me ...? I can't even miaow,
My last chance for a good life is now!
As I sadly drink sips of my water,
Wishing owners would stake one last claim,
They housed the white Persian, she was lame!
Methinks loving owners could end my shame.

My wonderful new life

I'm considered to be their youngest son,
In fact Charlie calls me her 'Gembleton',
I know I'm surely their only one;
In fact my busy day, is *never* done!
Of course, their hearts I have forever won!

I regard myself as a big ol' boy,
My owlish ears make me look very coy,
I'm really a woolly bundle of joy!

No falseness or lies ...
. . . just real *knowing* eyes.

Outsiders viewed with trepidation,
Nor is this my first incarnation!

Loving them all on a daily basis,
This cat has got so many faces!
I put them all down, so they'll sleep most tight,
And I slip off my furry old coat at night.

Georgina Bacon

Oz ... A Tribute To A friend

Quiet in his basket lying, sleeping the sleep that transcends time.
The struggle of the night has ended by moving to a rest, sublime.
He'd been our friend for sixteen years; he'd brightened up the days,
Of lives that oft times were mundane, with quiet, pleasing ways,
We find it hard as we reflect of many years passed by,
To imagine days before he came, no matter how we try.
But come he did, as if by chance, a happening unplanned,
But are these things just left to luck or guided by fate's hand?
Our home was then replete with pets; he had to find his place,
He managed this with dignity, no anger on the face,
Of other dogs and veteran mogs who took to him with grace,
A pup whose unassuming ways engendered trust in one and all,
In humans or in animals it wasn't hard to fall
For this small even-tempered dog who seldom showed aggression,
And yet he could assert himself if ever intercession
Was necessary to defend his home, his charges, or his friends,
He'd rid the barn of plagues of rats attacking helpless hens
And yet when puppy Rosie came and later Mrs Mop,
He cared for them with tenderness, his patience never stopped.
Mrs Mop, a rescue dog, an inmate of the home,
He took her from the spartan cage in which she lived alone.
Rosie was his soulmate, together they grew old,
And tho' 'girl dog' was twice his size with him she wasn't bold.
The only time his cool was shaken was when young Maxwell came;
A JRT, short fuse, small brain, he really took the blame
For all the squabbles, fracas, spats
That involved them both in fierce combat,
Until a common danger posed,
They worked together fighting foes
And when that current danger passed
They resumed their spatting to the last
And now he's gone I've dug his grave, the flowers grow on top,
The sorrow fades, the pain will dull, but memories never stop.

John & Jackie Harrison

Holly

Scalding rivulets of tears,
Sere my face like fire.
Holly's gone to a better place,
This world, of her, did tire.

A feline, so affectionate,
Tortoise-shell in hue.
'Rescued' at just sixteen weeks,
With Pewter, our greyish blue.

Since Christmas Eve of '94,
She's filled our lives with love.
The holly bough bestowed her name,
On this gift sent from above.

I never tired of watching her,
Intrigued by her patchwork coat.
Like surveying some old painting,
New detail one did note.

No spoken word could tell you,
Of her cute and loving ways.
Quite honoured to have known her,
Sharing her earthly days.

Ten years old, gone August,
She was suddenly taken ill.
Nothing could be done for her,
But I guess it's just God's will.

Our garden is her resting place,
With Misty, long since gone.
Awaiting her snowy coverlet,
Gently kissed, by wintry sun.

I'm sure she knows we loved her,
I trust we'll meet again.
She's waiting there, on Rainbow Bridge,
Happy, and free from pain.

She's sleeping 'neath a holly bush,
In some peaceful land apart.
Her legacy, an aching void,
And a pawprint on my heart.

A Timmins

My Little Goldfish

I have a little goldfish
Swimming in my pond
I just call him Goldie
And of him I am very fond

I think it is funny
And sometimes I think it is silly
How he swims in circles
Around the water lily

I think he will get dizzy
His mouth is always going
I think he has got wind
For bubbles he is always blowing

I had him in a bowl
But he looked so sad in it
So I dug him a great big pond
And helped little Goldie to flit

He is growing very fat
From his head to his tail
If he eats any more
He will grow into a whale

He swims around the pond
The same way every day
But yesterday he turned tail
And swam the other way

He smiles up at me
And waves his little fin
If I could do the breaststroke
I surely would jump in

And swim around with Goldie
He is the best pet I could wish
And I love him dearly
My little golden fish

Colin Moffett

Cherished friends

To lose a pet is anguish
As this I have went through.
It really breaks my heart so much
And this I know is true.

As all my life I've had a pet
And they were all adoring.
To spend my days without their love
To me would sure be boring.

They come to you for comfort
And return it triple-fold.
They do give you affection
More precious than of gold.

To me my pets mean everything
Their love immense to see.
Faithful every waking hour
Is what they are to me.

I do get great devotion
Their love they don't pretend.
So many hugs and cuddles too
A truly faithful friend.

I got them as wee puppies
So cute and cuddly too.
Their warmth means so much to me
As friends so staunch and true.

Two collie dogs is what they are
One black and white, one fair.
Most devoted brother and sister
An inseparable loveable pair.

Bessie likes to watch and learn
And Bertie he does listen.
But when I lift a ball to play
Their eyes light up and glisten.

If they could only talk to me
I know what they would say.
'Can we go lots more walkies
With plenty time for play?'

When I go out for shopping
And they both have to stay.
They sit and look forlorn at me
Do hurry home they pray.

I live for them both day and night
They bring me so much joy.
I am their special doting mum
And they my girl and boy.

We always are together
Of them I am so fond.
Thoroughly love their company
And strong our mutual bond.

To hear of so much cruelty
It truly makes me sad.
That people in the world today
Could really be so bad.

They are blessed creatures
However large or small.
God put them on this Earth for us
To love and care for all.

Rosalind Sim

My Friend Tiggy

My friend Tiggy
He really is my mate
He's there when I arrive at Ronald's
At the bottom of the steps ... by the gate

He greets me with a friendly *purrrrr*
As he slowly walks with me
I let him in the front door
As I go inside for tea

And when he's eaten his coley
And his tin cat food too
He'll sit beside his boss and *purrrrr*
I really do love you

He climbs upon his boss' knee
When his tummy is quite full
His boss, he softly pulls Tiggy's ear
He loves it and *purrrrs* with glee

Oh Tiggy what a friend you are
You brighten up the day
I see you in an afternoon
But you're not in the mood to play

You struggle to climb upon the chair
And chase the mice as well
You really are an old friendly cat
By the gas fire you shall dwell

In the summer you're in the garage
In the winter by the fire
But the best time of all I know
When on Ronald's knee you so desire

I love you my friend Tiggy
I love my Ronald too
One thing though is for sure
Ronald *loves you*

Jessica Wright

A Special Boy And His Dog

Just a little boy aged nine
You should be having fun
But there was always sadness in your eyes
And smiles there were none
We tried everything we could to help
But your disability always won
Just a little boy aged nine who should be having fun
One day we had an idea
We hoped it wasn't wrong
We left you with your grandma
Said we won't be long
We said we'd bring you back a toy
We knew that wasn't true
We had a special gift in mind
For a special boy like you
You stood in Grandma's kitchen
Steadying yourself against the wall
Yours hands outstretched
Your eyes tight shut
Waiting for the most special gift of all
I placed the puppy in your arms
And got a huge surprise
No smiles came upon your face
Just tears that filled your eyes
You slid down the wall
Clasping the puppy to your chest
I thought we'd got it wrong
That this wasn't for the best
Then Tom you started smiling
Those tears were tears of joy
It was the best decision we ever made
For our very special boy
And ever since our 'Georgie'
Came to live with us
She's kept you forever smiling
With her antics and her love
You're eighteen now and Georgie nine
A very precious pair
You've had your ups and downs at times
But the smiles outweigh the tears
And it's all thanks to Georgie and her love throughout the years.

Trudy Simpson

Bunty Boy

What a grey, dismal November day to die!
Bunty, you called to me at 4am with a piercing tone.
I went to your cage and wrapped you in your pink towel,
    comforted your pain.
As I held you snuggled, you ceased the moaning,
    your body just throbbing,
    while I stroked your unkempt fur,
    fur that once gleamed clean.
It was the forced food that made you messy.
I held you for one and a half hours
    and then my hand couldn't feel your heart beating.
Your body was still.
At 5.30am, I was relieved, though saddened,
    that you were in peace.
Tears welled in my eyes.
You shouldn't have been born at all.
Your guinea pig mother, Chloe,
    was pregnant from the shop when I
    brought her home.
But you were, and you came through the
    chain of creation to live with me and
    spend time sharing my garden.
What a grey, dismal day with soft rain drizzle,
    to bury where the daffodils will bloom,
    my Bunty Boy, called inappropriately a girl's name.
    Well, it was thought you were a girl when you were born.
    But you never minded the choice.
You didn't recover from having a dental,
    the cutting of your overgrown rodent
    teeth at a veterinary practice.
It was a catch 22 situation. You couldn't
    eat either way, before or after.
I loved you Bunty, only two year's old
    and I am so sorry today of your loss.

Carol Ann Darling

BUNTY

Parasites

There was a time, some years ago, when people sang my praises,
Adoring faces all around, you'd find me at the races.
Number one, a winner, and, as long as I kept going,
I had a life of luxury, and the money kept on flowing.

Back then my name was famous, I could really draw a crowd,
They loved to watch, those ardent men who'd shout my name out loud.
I had a body slim and sleek, was rather highly rated.
To stay so thin, I hardly ate, my hunger never sated.

In my profession, youth is all. In so few years, I aged.
I hurt my wrist, it never healed, too soon they had me caged.
Shocked, bewildered, I retired, to a life of non-existence,
My golden days were over, I now viewed them from a distance.

Ill-nourished, my health suffered, once so fit, I failed.
I existed just on handouts, in a filthy but was jailed.
Fleas attacked me, and I scratched 'til my skin was red and raw,
Unrecognised, abandoned, I stopped caring any more.

I couldn't bring the money in, the money that men craved.
They despised me, wouldn't share the fortunes that they'd made.
Those men had been my parasites, had bled me just the same
As the fleas that now fed off me, my sickly tortured frame.

I never had a pretty name, like Claudia or Kate,
Some papers had my title on, where I was born, a date.
Trojan Silk, my father, my mother, Lynfield Sonnet,
Born and bred in Ireland, Lamb Shank is written on it.

So well bred. I'd fallen to a pretty sorry state,
No pedigree would save me from this awful, dreadful fate.
No more hope, just hunger, with fear my constant friend,
Would death come soon? I hoped so, my suffering would end.

Then suddenly, there came release, yet, I was still alive -
Some people came, they wrote a cheque, and took me for a drive,
They took me home and fed me, saw to my every need,
Feeling better, I was grateful, but didn't trust this human breed.

I expected to be punished with each movement of an arm,
But their words to me were gentle, in their eyes I saw no harm.
They nourished me, and stroked me, I had a soft warm bed,
'We're going to socialise you. You're Minty now,' they said.

We walked in grass meadows, what joy to run and leap!
These days, I run for pleasure, not to earn my keep.
I cannot thank my saviours, but I'll love them to the end,
I'm a greyhound, and a pet, I'm Minty, Man's best friend.

Jenny Creely

Wurgug

A normal day as days come and go
A twist of fate can interrupt the flow
Our young son hurried through the room in an agitated state of mind
Breathless and tearful, he tugged my dress; words he couldn't find

'Calm down son and take a deep breath; now try once more.'
'Mummy, the nest has fallen from the tree; it's upturned on the floor
I think they're dead though one did move just now
Please come at once, maybe you can save it somehow.'

It was obvious he was concerned to save some creature's fate
Off we ran into the tree-lined park, hoping we were not too late
The little birds were just hatched from the egg
Four in total but all seemed to be dead

He pointed to the one he said had moved some time before
I tenderly touched its featherless body as it lay motionless on the floor
Fearing the worst, not knowing what to say at this time
I prayed for movement - no matter how slight it was, it would be fine

My prayer was answered as I placed the bird in my hand
All skin and bone, eyes shut tight; not able to stand
'Please save it Mummy; I know you can.'
I cradled the nest in my hands; off home we ran

We nursed it for days, never knowing it would survive
Fed it on chopped worms and water to keep it alive
The tweezers were great to 'ram' sustenance down that hole without bother
Its eyes eventually opened; from that moment I was his mother

Wurgug became his cry at every feeding frenzy; never quiet
An ear dropper was the tool used for liquid part of the diet
He lived in the greenhouse in his own little nest
Taught himself to bathe in a tray, never a pest

He grew very strong, loving his mother and their hourly chat
I strengthened his wings; perched on my fingers, up and down he'd flap
The inevitable sad day soon came to part us for good
He was taken to a sanctuary for birds in the wood.

Beryl Worthington

Last Days Of The Swan

There once were two swans,
On this gloomy, cold river,
Beautiful and noble creatures,
Which were always seen together.

In the summer we could sit,
On the river's dusty shore,
And watch them glide by us,
With a grace we'd never seen before.

Then one night it all changed,
And the river lost its romance,
Youths attacked the female swan,
She didn't stand a chance.

So now there was only one swan,
A lonely figure on the river,
No solace for his loss,
No warmth in the dark winter.

The emptiness now she was gone,
Drove him completely insane,
And he started attacking everyone,
Never to feel peace again.

He got taken far away that day,
And the river lost its light,
His love had turned to hate,
And all he could do was fight.

The river was cold once they'd gone,
And the world had lost its romance,
All the other creatures just mate and leave,
In a cruel game of chance.

I was only a child at the time,
But I decided there and then,
That I'd rather be a swan,
Than a petty, greedy human.

Claire Chilton

Brodie

We remember when we got her,
So full of boisterous fun!
There was no other like her,
She loved to jump and run!

So often, we would walk her,
And take her to the park;
She'd chase a ball for hours,
Quite often - until dark!

We recall an odd occasion,
Forget? We never shall!
She chased her ball so quickly
And fell in the canal!

We never should have worried,
She found her way back out!
And after shaking wildly,
Responded to our shout!

Her vigour, during rambles,
Was something to be seen;
She'd run round like a greyhound,
You know just what we mean!

Her food - she always relished,
She slept just like a log;
She never gave us trouble,
She was 'the perfect dog'!

But time - so quickly passes,
Our Brodie now - is gone!
That handsome brindle boxer,
Our memories dwell upon!

Ron Bissett

My Thoughts (from A Staffordshire Bull Terrier)

I'm Lulu Ferrari, I'm a beautiful Staff'
I have lovely brown eyes and a little moustache
Although I'm a girl ...

My owners tell me it's 'cause I'm now 21
But she's 42, and she hasn't got none
And as for him nor has he
And he's nearly 43
I can't work this out ...

I like to go out and go for a run
But hate it when everyone smells my bum
I run in the mud and roll about
But when I get home they all just shout
And stick me in the bath
I do not laugh ...

It's time to get up and give me some food
Instead of snoring, oh god, how rude
Now give me the tin, not just half
I know you can't hear me
But you're not that daft
Or are you ...?

Whenever there's a smell in the room
You always look at me, and soon
You're telling your friends it was me
When we both know, who it was really!
I'm not that daft ...

Now I'm fed and smell real clean
I sneak up to bed, but they are so mean
As they catch me and call me downstairs
I suppose I'll have to lay by the fire
Like they care ...

They shout out my name
And think this a game
As I try to sleep
I have to get up and be happy to leap
Like I don't need a rest ...
My life is the best ...

Karen Ferrari

Discontinuity

One day we went to see the fields
And the pattern of stars on the ground
Walking strangely near the huge hieroglyphs
We felt a mirror and the old and new things reawakening
Freezing the stillness, the neuroleptic animal ...

And in the middle of the night
From nowhere
Silent town, silent town
Moon without sun
Night without day and sideways
Cats stalking
Cats stalking ... dreamers ...

Michael C Soper

My Spaniel

Springer spaniel
Jumps for joy when I walk in
Mad as a hatter
Usually docile, daft
But has his hectic moments!

Amanda Morgan

I'd Like To Be An Animal

I'd like to be an animal
But which one should I choose?
An elephant would be too big
And I don't like kangaroos.

A possum might be rather fun,
To live by night not day.
Giraffes have necks that are too long,
And hippos are too grey.

Hedgehogs have the right idea,
They sleep the cold months through.
But, then, they can get squashed by cars -
That simply wouldn't do.

Cows and sheep must live outdoors
And nibble on the grass.
Foxes still get chased by dogs
And bats I hate, alas.

Pandas I have always loved,
So black and white and sweet.
Frogs and toads can hop and croak
And have such pretty feet.

On balance, though, a cat I'd be,
Choosing my household wisely.
A cosy blanket by the fire
And pilchards would do nicely.

If friends who don't like cats should call
I'd rub around their knees.
And if they *really* don't like me
I'd try to give them fleas.

I think I'd be a ginger cat,
A large and furry male.
I'd rule the home with feline guile,
My wishes would prevail.

Susie Stewart

Just Look Upon My Face

Would I leave a muddy print
on stair or hallway rug
leaving just a subtle hint
that the garden I have dug?

Come moulting season it is not I
who leaves soft fur now shed.
With coat so dark I do deny
the tufts so pale yet red.

Before the fire in peaceful bliss
with gentle breaths galore.
An odour spreads without a hiss
covered now by gentle snore.

A voice to my own ears have I
an angel from above.
Snarls and whimpers I do cry
to demonstrate my love.

The click on claw on kitchen floor
with lolling tongue to drool.
Thump of tail on wooden door
ball playing like a fool.

All my traits may not be good
with friendship I do share.
Would I correct them if I could?
I'd try, to show I care.

To find the truth you look around
and use your silent spies.
Angelic gestures do abound
don't look into my eyes.

Could you have any doubt at all
when dishing out the blame?
If I had hands I'd point them out
or even shout their name.

All alone, no one but me
no playmates here to chase.
I did not cause this mess you see
just look upon my face.

Ceri D D Griffiths

Untitled

Tug-of-war is our favourite game
Backwards and forwards we go
Every outcome is different
Pulling to and fro

Our eyes fixed on each other
A deep and meaningful stare
We both want to win it
So dare to look elsewhere

Pulling with all our might
We behave as if it's our only possession
Sometimes we fall out
You'd think we'd learn our lesson!

Give me that rope
I'm stronger than you
I really want to win it
I'll have something to chew

But what about me
Having something to chew?
While your busy gnawing
I'll have nothing to do

I'm not letting go
This rope will be mine
Just give it to me now
We can save some time

I can't do that
I'm having too much fun
You put up a good fight
But I'm number one

Jake, you may be younger and bigger than me
But I'm not letting you have it
So you can gloat with glee

I'll show you who's boss
You just wait and see
I know who is stronger
Out of you and me

Listen to you
That sounds like fighting talk
Why don't you give up now
And go for a walk?

No way Danny, I'll win this tug-of-war
Aw, I've nearly got it
Just a little more

You're right, you've nearly got it
But let's not stop
Tug-of-war is my favourite game
I love it a lot

Julie Rose

Ode To Ole Dopey

I owned a naughty Labradog,
Chocolate was his flavour.
I got him from the dogs' home
Which explained his behaviour.
He was tatty round the edges
With warts and lumps galore.
His fur was like a coconut mat,
And would have complimented any floor.

Affectionately known as Dopey
But Ben Dog was his name.
The antics he got up to
Nearly drove me half insane.
His obsessive eating disorder
Was really quite obscene.
And he was known by all the locals
As a lean, mean, eating machine.

One Christmas Day at lunchtime
Old Dopey fancied a snack.
He didn't think we'd notice
If he whipped the turkey out the back.
He ran around the garden
Gulping turkey as he dodged
And in my brand new slippers after him I splodged.

Another time Old Dopey
Some gravy he did crave.
He stole the biggest pot of granules
That nearly drove him to his grave.
Panicked by his state I called the vet for some relief,
And was told through coughs and splutters
To give him water, veg and a slice of beef!

Old Dopey loved the water
And at any chance would swim.
On a visit to see Grandma
Swimming heaven he was in,
Cos Grandma had a fishpond
Which was her pride and joy,
Until my Dopey Labradog ...
Concussed all her precious koi.

It's sad Old Dopey is no longer here,
I miss him every day,
I loved his games and tricks
Even though they turned me grey.
The vet bills were humongous,
As were the laughs we had,
To have shared those years with Dopey,
I really am so glad.

Amanda Audritt

My Name Is Thomas

My name is Thomas, I'm such a handsome cat
I know it must be true, cos Mum keeps telling me that.
I keep myself clean, take pride in myself
And I know where all my food is kept,
My mum feeds me well and looks after me too,
I've got my own towel for when I get wet.

I'm a black and white cat with a pretty pink nose,
I've got big green eyes and lovely white toes.
I'm quite independent and really quite proud
And when my mum is singing I join in quite loud.

I'm the boss and it shows, scared of nothing you see,
Well actually I'm scared of the Hoover,
I'm afraid that it might chase me.

I am not the only pet in the house,
There are two other pets with me,
A cute little dog and another small cat,
We get on quite well you see.

Gerald the cat likes to chase me,
I wish he would leave me alone.
I just want to get out of the house for a while,
I just want to be on my own.

Spike is a cute little mongrel,
He keeps himself out of the way,
I sometimes get jealous of Gerald and him
As on Mum's bed together they lay.

We once had a poodle called Toby,
He did love to play with me,
But as big as he was I beat him up,
I'm sure he was scared of me.

My mum sometimes gets quite unhappy
And I know it's a cuddle she needs,
So I snuggle myself right up to her,
Then she feels so much better indeed.

We all get plenty of cuddles
And plenty of kisses too,
So if you would like a good home
I'm sure she can find one for you.

Yvonne Buckle

Ode To Our felix

We lost our Felix yesterday,
The mice outside shout, 'Hip-hooray!'
The blackbird, robin and wren agree,
'The old lad's gone,' they cry with glee.

For many a year he'd ruled the street,
All other toms he'd roundly beat.
He'd seen them off into the night
And the she cats queued 'til the early light.

Jellicle cats did soon abound,
To prove our Felix had stud his ground.
Our own 'Mr Mistoffelees' without a doubt,
He'd lay by the hearth then he'd be out.

He'd tear around the house at incredible speed,
The dogs we'd hear whimper - he was into their feed.
Playing 'kitten' games for most of his life,
Never growing old - he tormented the wife.

Through his own little door he'd fly out of the house,
To return in the morn with a dead little mouse.
It was Felix's way of sweetening his 'mum',
For through nicking food he'd got one heck of a tum.

We've lost him now, he's dead and gone,
At thirteen years, he was ninety-one.
He'd lived his life and enjoyed it all,
Until he got that final call.

I bet he's battered down St Peter's gate,
To find the Jellicle cats to mate.
Not caring to rest or even to pause,
He'll see off their toms with his wicked claws.
And tho' St Peter's voice could well be vexed
Our lad's reply will just be - *'Next!'*

Gordon & Pauline Shaw

A Cat from My Next Door

You are not my pet
But you live in my house more
Than the one that feeds you so big.
I don't know what you like to eat
You never fancy my food.
You just like popping in my kitchen
Sniffing around my leftovers
Lying about on my dining table
And staring at me.

You are not my mate
But if there is somebody calling me on
You are the one.
Banging my door when the sun is out, the sky is blue
Scratching my window where you can see and reach me.
You simply like to come around
I simply like to let you in
Then we start to chat around
Miaowing away.

You are not the one I love
But you like to warm through my bed of double
Purring away and falling into sleep there.
You like me touching your soft, gentle body
You like me stroking your smooth, silky hairs
You like me holding your face and looking into
Your eyes so big and round.
And whenever I do I feel like
It seems it is only two of us
So close in this world.
You seem to be the one
To make a dark day of mine here
Seem bright.

Actually, in heart we are the same
We want to love and be loved
In this lonely planet.
When your master is not at home, out for work
I am the only one
Looking after you
Keeping you company, and
Putting you up.
But when you scratch and bite me
Bleed my hand,
I chuck you out.

Thiamkok Lau

My Best friend Twix

I have a cute pup,
she's a wonderful pet,
she's a golden Labrador,
not fully grown yet.

Her name is Twix,
she's whitish in colour,
without my good doggy
my life would be duller.

She has floppy ears,
she's 10 months old,
she's quite well trained,
so she does what she's told.

In the morning time,
Twix is up first
running to welcome you -
like she's going to burst.

She has a swishy tail
and big brown eyes,
she's a beautiful girl,
quite chunky - in size.

She's friendly and lively
and boisterous too,
if you met her,
you'd love her - just like I do.

I take her for walks,
before and after school,
my friends all love her
and think she's totally *cool*.

I give her healthy treats
when she has been good,
she'd eat all the time,
she really loves her food.

My angel Twix
is really quite funny,
she's my darling, my sweetheart
my little honey.

Jozie-Anne Smart (11)

Enchanting Faces

There are so many things, that make me smile,
Feeling happy and content, for the longest while.
Whether they are my own, or out on the street,
Those enchanting faces, you just can't beat.

There's Mary, who's eight, an Umbrella Cockatoo,
She's white, with yellow and her eyes rimmed with blue.
'You Can Get it if You Really Want', is Mary's favourite tune,
Her screaming and her laughing, you could hear it on the moon.
She sits on my shoulders and plays with my hair,
Swearing and chasing everyone, she doesn't seem to care.
A little bit naughty, and swearing most of the time,
Her voice very loud, sometimes, I wish she could mime.

My best friend, is a mix or cross, and she's nearly two,
Beside me all the time, you'll find my Lalley Leu.
She loves de-stuffing cuddly toys, won't stop until it's done,
Falling asleep, in her mouth, she holds her special one.
She sleeps beside me every night,
Under, or on top of the quilt, 'til the morning light.
She really is so silly, talking for some tea,
Going round everyone and asking, 'Is that for me?'

Bud, the Tokay Gecko, rescued was he,
Now so tame, he won't bite or flee.
In on his own, I think is best for him,
He's now quite fat, and not so slim.
Two baby Leopard Geckos, named Jade and Horatio,
Got as babies, to watch them bloom and grow.
Now left in her tank, still grieving is Jade,
Her lost Horatio, refused all help and first aid.

Fudge, my little kitty, in her boudoir is she,
No crazy plays or antics, but she's perfect to me.
She really is so lazy, sleeping all the while,
Her round and speckled face, always does it smile.
She doesn't miaow and rarely makes a noise,
Sitting and proudly showing, her most elegant poise.
A ninth birthday in June, has the tortoiseshell one,
Her orange tints, how they glow, like a burning sun.

No other joy in the world, has more power than this,
To not see, those enchanting faces, now that I would miss.
The love in my heart, that I show and possess,
Will always be more, and will never be less.

Heather Talbot

Sianny

Some years ago
I knew a tiny kitten,
Rubbing her tiny head
Close to mine
She showed the kind of love
The whole world needs,
Unconditional closeness
With harmonious seeds
Our mutual feelings
Fulfilled bereft of greed,
Until some stranger
Of well-intentioned deeds
Decided to feed her meat
Failing to remove
Its film wrapping,
Of course I paid
For surgery
A bid to no avail,
Her telescoped bowel
Repaired OK
But the anaesthetic
Was awfully strong
And her soul so frail.

I was out walking
In the country
The moment she died,
While above
A brace of seagulls
Cried out loud,
A special cry
Separate from the
Usual crowd,
Somehow I knew
She was above
Majestic on high
Up where they fly.

Now as this world
Unfolds evil
View by view,
I so much pray
For a landing,
Her resurrected love
To save the many
Not the few.

Chris Barnes

Kitty

(In memory of Kitty 13.09.04)

The cat sat on the deep blue cushion
His eyes tightly shut, no longer in action
He'd just come in with muddy paws
Glanced arrogantly at Mum; now snores

He will sleep until dawn
Arouse himself in the morn
We remember the day he was born
His sister drowned in the well, so soon

He is much older now, he fits in with us
Wanders in, wanders out, all around, visits
Spits at strangers, purrs at family
Growls at birds, roams round freely

He kills big birds no longer now
But the other day caught a mouse
One that had previously lived in the hedgerow
He ate it *all* just beside the house

In latter days he'd have loved to kill a pheasant!
Bring it home to us to eat, as a present
Never quite managed it, caught a blue tit
Chewed a whole snake, chased a rabbit

Once he chased a kitten right into our pond
Never seen *him* since, little minx
He goes over the fields and beyond
Hopefully he'll never bring home a lynx

No, he's older now, he lazily watches cows
Sleep, at night the owls, by day sparrows
One day his eyes will shut and never open
We want that day to be further away, not happen

Oh! Now he miaows, has to go out
Not again! I sometimes shout
Soon he will come in, stay in
Sleep here all night, be quiet
He keeps the day bright - our cat's alright.

Sheila Cheesman

Ollie, One In A Million

We chose him because of his massive feet
To train to 'go potty' took only one week
To teach to use dog flap took only one day
Mischievous and funny in his own way
Memories over the years such fun we've had
With our Doberman, such a 'big brave lad'

Walkies became a circus when
Ollie turned circles, barking and then
Out of the dog flap went bras and knickers -
A set of false teeth caused some sniggers -
One day a sleeping bag - oh yes -
How he got that out is anyone's guess

Along the seafront, twigs (no tree trunks) he carried
With Skye Rom and Sweep often he tarried
Ollie's best pal lived next door
A Jack Russell called Pip, one to adore
They protected each other, enjoyed playing games
'Little and Large' became their names

Ollie loved a scratch behind his ear
A stroke of his head gave him cheer
Bedtime was best when he got his cuddle
Being 'tucked in' and given a snuggle
Made him purr like a Cheshire cat
Wonderful memories are made up like that

Some people are frightened of big dogs but Ollie
Soon made friends by being so jolly
Seems such a short time since he was a pup
A heart full of love we didn't want to give up
Now in doggy heaven he really is at peace
We are thankful he had such a quick release

Janice Gibbons

My Lucy

My Lucy, the Yorkshire terrier is full of fun
She likes a fuss and is very friendly with everyone
She likes a game and to muck about
When she's had enough she lays flat out
Sometimes on her back with her legs in the air
Sometimes in a ball under a chair.

I want her to live forever
To lose her would break my heart
But I know deep down inside me
One day we will have to part.

We will enjoy our days together now
And not look at the grey times ahead
She looks so peaceful at the moment
On her back with her legs in the air in her little bed.

Linda Hunt

Little Megzy

At times domestic animals can teach,
If you want to know come see my bitch.
She teaches my baby how to watch,
Through the door they look out eating a fish.
If the door's ajar Megzy will wrench,
And utter with barks to visitors, a wish.
She's friendly, lovely and likes to punish
Any woman who's as scary as a witch.
Megzy is not just a dog, I believe:
If she's down with sleep, she'll still perceive
The fragrance of snacks that I receive.
Whenever I want to deceive,
Megzy won't allow me to relieve.
Even if I'm ready to conceive.

Bolaji St Ramos

farewell Straw

You had great green eyes,
Four white paws,
Always black and sooty,
From rolling about in the coal.

Purring content, you cherished me,
As I cherished you,
My constant companion.
With me all day through.

No more will you sit on the window sill,
Basking in the sun,
Never again will you hop and leap,
In the snow you thought was fun.

I'll miss your cheeky ways,
Tears sting as I place your toys away,
You've left a void in my heart,
And Gizmo your brother is distraught.

No more will I pity the fox,
That stole your life in vain,
Then left you battered and bloody,
Lying dead upon my lane.

Farewell my little friend,
Tears flow as I write these words,
I pray you have a peaceful rest,
Until such a time when we'll meet again.

Jane Margaret Isaac

The Kaffoon That Kaddanced In The Dark

With his baldy belly and his feet so smelly,
The Kaffoon is the daftiest dog there ever did was.
Oh the Kaffoon - the Kaffoon that kaddances in the dark.

He sleeps all day and he sleeps all night,
Just getting him out of bed takes all our might.
That's the Kaffoon - the Kaffoon that kaddances in the dark.

With his big wet nose and long pointy toes,
In-between sleeps he likes nothing better than to doze.
Wake up Kaffoon - the Kaffoon that snoozes in the dark.

His idea of exercise is a five minute stroll in the park,
When he kaddashes around in circles, chasing his tail for a lark.
That's you lazy boy - the Kaffoon that kaddances in the dark.

When his tea's on the table, he stretches and yawns,
In case he just might be able, to work up an appetite.
Get up now fatty - the Kaffoon that kaddances in the dark.

Kaffoon, Kaffool, Kaffooey or Kaffoodle,
We don't know your breed but you sure ain't no poodle.
You're our Kaffoon - the Kaffoon that kaddances in the dark.

Charles Christian

My Purrfect Little Friend

I love my little cat, she's my friend as well as my pet,
She always needs my loving and doesn't let me forget.

She greets me every morning with her head against my leg
She purrs as I serve her breakfast, she never has to beg

She sits upon my lap and we cuddle up together
I always like her to stay at home in cold and stormy weather

She looks at me and miaows, her eyes just seem to shine
I love to stroke her gleaming coat, I feel so proud she's mine

She's always very loyal, faithful and aware
Sitting there so patiently right beside my chair

She brings me so much pleasure, more than you could know
That's why she means the world to me and why I love her so

She's not a bit of trouble and is always there for me
I'll never ever part with her, she's my *purrfect friend* you see

Pauline Mayoh-Wild

432

friendly florence

Friendly Florence is mostly white.
She has a full set of smiley teeth
in her piggy head and
she supports hunting with hounds.

Friendly Florence has a bad memory
but she remembers the corgis -
those Welsh dwarfs with their fox-like
heads and short legs.

She remembers the one she clamped
in her full set of smiley teeth. It was
Grandma's favourite. Blood flowed
redder than a guardsman's tunic.

Tears flowed and upper lips quivered
in the garden when Grandma's
favourite was buried to the strains of
the Last Post and a one gun salute.

Next news: *Mordacious swine
Mistakes woman for corgi.*

But this time Florence has a watertight alibi.
So who? Was it Clarence? Or was it a pig?
'I really don't know,' said Alice, 'but
Florence is not to be invited for Christmas.'

Gwil Williams

A Wonderful Companion

I have a beautiful cat,
he's special in every way.
I adore him very much,
and love him more each day.

He brings me so much joy
and is such an affectionate boy.

His coat is so fluffy,
just like cotton wool.
My life without him
would be extremely dull.

He has lovely green eyes
and a cute pink nose,
gorgeous whiskers and tiny toes.

He is my soulmate, an amazing kind.
He really is a wonderful find.

Debbie Wynne

My Miracle

My miracle came to me, at a time I most needed, without me realising,
But as time went on my needs became greater.
I was desperate for an answer out of the rut I was falling in.
I couldn't see.
Then one day my comforter came to me,
He was there when I cried.
I sobbed, I wanted someone there but was too blind to see ...
Until one day, I had a great loss in my life.
I felt no one around me,
No one close by,
But there he was as loyal and faithful as always,
My one and only friend and support.
To you, Tyke,
My faithful and loyal companion,
Not just a dog ...
I thank you again.

Karen-Marie Falzon

Boddington's Job

I spend my time gazing, all the while lazing,
Watching the birds in and out of their box,
Wondering which way I can outrun, outfox,
Constantly flitting from tree to tree.
I wouldn't hurt birdies,
Oh no, not me.

When in the humans' house I'm quiet as a mouse,
Spending my days filling cat litter trays,
Scratching carpets and settee,
Oh no, that wasn't me.
Hiding under the beds, pulling out threads,
What a caper ripping wallpaper.
He's about to go mad is my human dad.
Oh, that wasn't me, I'm off for a pee.

The bird box beckons, I must go to it,
There may be a blackbird, a thrush or a tit.
I watch and I wait all the time lazing,
Upon potential prey quietly gazing.
I'll wander to another tree,
Oh, I won't hurt the birds, no not me.

Ellen Spiring

The Last Kindness

(Dedicated to Honey - 9th May 1993-18th October 2002)

Warm, soft head, cradled in crook of left arm,
lop-ears framing face, mouth twitching, tasting dandelions
but kind eyes closed in rapid movement
following dreams to fields of clover,
hind legs strong again to jump, twist,
flick joy into air brimming with sun.
Thin curve of body breathes heavy -
spending this last hour holding onto love,
in room he gnawed a hole in the dining table,
chasing round sofa, playing 'catch me'
when night-time and hutch beckoned.
'It's his time,' as the first injection, crystal clear,
brings immunity from pain to deepest sleep.
'It's the last kindness I can give him, isn't it?'
Tears punctuate words falling on cream, brown-tipped fur
resting on familiar blanket on knees.
Second injection brings total peace.
I place him gently as a baby down to cushion in basket
where lifeless body appears to rise and fall,
but wanting makes it so.
Payment made through blur, vet leaves
and waiting begins for Ian's return,
to dig deep, dark square by pink apple blossom rose
at garden corner, where he scampered to peer indoors.
Curled in death, missing him already,
racks its tortuous tempo on the heart
and tears will never be enough.

Vivien Steels

Titan

I fell in love with him from the start
That Irish wolfhound puppy that stole my heart
I always smile when I think of my boy
That gentle giant who brings so much joy
When he's lying stretched out in the hall
My house suddenly seems so very small
He pretends to be asleep but there's nothing he doesn't see
When I look down at him his beautiful big brown eyes are watching me
He tries to give me a kiss after a drink
Or when he's had tripe, what a stink
When we go for a walk people stop and stare
If he wags his tail items fly everywhere
He loves all animals big and small
But always manages to lick them even though he's so tall
He likes to smell the flowers when he walks by
Or sits watching the stars in the sky,
But he's the best friend that could ever be
That gentle giant who loves me

Melanie Merry

My Best Friend Ben

Fifteen years you've been my friend,
Since the start of your life, right up to the end.
When I felt sad, you'd make me smile,
You wagged your tail all the while.
Big brown eyes and long brown hair,
You'd always let me know you were there.
If you were good we'd give you a treat,
You puffed and panted in the summer's heat.
When you left we said goodbye,
You've gone to a better place in the sky.
There's an empty space where you lay,
In my heart you'll always stay.

Lindsay Clarke

Jeff

My name is Jeff
I am a ginger cat.
I like to sit in front
Of the fire on the mat.
I like to go out,
Depending on the weather.
Sitting out in the sun,
I am very fond,
Taking a sneaky look
At the fish in the pond,
Been known to catch
A few in my time,
Fell in the water,
That paid for my crime.
I like to sit
On anybody's knee,
Will stay for ages
if they will have me,
I'll curl up in your place
As soon as you go,
It is already warm for me
This I know.
The neighbour's cat
Has met his match,
I do not like him
Over on my patch,
I had an accident
A few months ago,
To the vets we had to go
To and fro,
A fractured skull
And stitches they did sew
But I still have eight
More lives to go.
I'm back to normal now
And still get my kicks
By getting up
To all my old tricks.

E Whawell

Jessie

How can I not but melt,
When you look at me that way?
And how can I not but put behind
All the bad things of the day
When you meet me madly at the door,
So happy that I am there?
And shower me with sloppy kisses,
That tell me how much you care.

And how can I not but close my eyes
At my once green perfect lawn,
Now a balding, muddy dog fouled mire,
And my flower beds all gone.
For you touch my heart, with that special look,
That says, 'It wasn't meant,
For after all I am, just a dog,
And you know that I am heaven-sent.'

Yes Jessie, you may be just a dog,
But you are my special friend.
For though you are often naughty
Your love can all wrong amend,
And it shows when you get close to pacify,
Aware of my illness, or fears,
When you nudge me on, with your cold, wet nose,
And kiss away all my tears.

My friend, so lovely and faithful!
You I can forgive, and ignore the mud
In my hallway, and tons of your fur
All over the living room floor.
For you will always win my heart
When you sneak your head on my knee.
And as I caress your velvet ears,
I know, my friend you will always be.

Beryl Joy

Young Tibbs

When I moved to Worthing two years ago
I had to let my young Tibbs go.

My dear faithful Tibbs, I loved you so well
And when you left, my pain was hell!

We really had fun when you lived with me
But now you're gone, my dear young Tibby.

I shall never see you ever again,
When I look at your photos it gives me great pain.

I shall always remember you with affection and love,
So farewell young Tibbs and goodbye with my love.

John Collard

The Fox Cat

The alert feline proudly exhibits her fine features,
Ready and eager for affection, interaction and fun.
Intelligence and curiosity are Somali characteristics;
Was an errant gene responsible for this elegant breed?
Standing on tippy-toes, the cat begs for a game,
Lovingly and skilfully she grooms her owner's hair,
The cat having a particular flair for this activity!
An exotic tail or 'brush' is displayed to great effect,
Earning the Somali cat the warm-hearted epithet:
Fox Cat.

Rose-Mary Gower

Martini The Devious Guinea Pig

She'll act all cute, and squeak quite sweetly ...
she'll pile her droppings up quite neatly ...
but gaze into those vacant eyes
and you will see through her disguise.

Behind the dainty leathery feet
there lives a pig who loves to eat.
Like some sort of rodent gangster,
she'll nick the veg and blame the hamster.

You can cuddle Martini but, undeterred,
she'll demand her water is shaken not stirred.
This pig is smooth, her posture's good;
she keeps me around to serve the food.

You never know what she is thinking,
those devious eyes are sparkling, winking.
I only hope it's nothing more savage
than a plot to get more cabbage.

Heather Child

My Kitten

I have a little kitten,
He is rather fat,
He eats all of his tea
And he'll soon be a cat!

I love my little kitten,
Very, very much,
I also have another cat
And his name is Butch.

My lovely little kitten,
Is very, very cute,
If he climbs the apple tree
He can eat some fruit.

Arron Hunt (9)

A Tribute To My Cat

For 12 long years I had a pet,
She was my friend as well.
She was so loving and so true
And so this verse I'll tell.
She had a lovely coat of black
With big green eyes so bright,
She was a star with eyes
That shone a long and lasting light.
My cat was very clever too,
She opened all the doors,
Then loved to jump from things on high
And landed on all fours.
My cat was always there for me,
No matter what the time,
She made me feel so happy then,
I'm glad that she was mine.
She left a broken heart behind
That was so hard to mend,
She gave me love that lasted
Until the very end.
And now I know she's up above
Where all the pussies go,
Where angels there will give her love
Because I loved her so.
To all the animals on this Earth,
However big or small,
Be kind to all and give your love,
Their blessings you'll recall.

Josephine Blackford

Oscar

I remember the day we chose you
Our samoyed cross collie, a soft ball of fur
Feet were your target
You grabbed and tugged at our bootlaces
With your small, delicate jaw.

We brought you home in a box
A cuddly new friend
You slept a lot to start with
But that was to be expected
As you were only a pup

The children used to chase you
But you, Oscar, would cling to their shoes
A bite, a chew, a shake would do
Kitchen cupboards were also a favourite
Gnawing contentedly, you'd chomp your way through.

Time has passed dear Oscar
A gentle giant you are
Nearly nine years old and built like a bear
You still bounce around like you're just three
A playful old boy

Still chasing birds when they invade your territory
Bumblebees annoy you
You pounce, you bite, you claw them
Those puppy eyes still warm our hearts
Sometimes look so sad
But we know our faithful friend is happy
When he nudges our hands with love.

T D Radley

Choose Me

I might not be
Pretty or handsome
As the case may be

I may be quite plain
Or even ugly
For your eyes to see

But look into my soul
And deep inside
I have a spirit
Waiting to be free

With your love and devotion
And time spent with me
With walks and some grooming
I'll outshine all the rest

You will be happy you chose me
Because I'll be one of the best.

Patricia Plumpton-Edwards

Our House

Our house, it feels so empty,
We sit, we wonder why,
It's because our little girl Cindy
Has gone up to the sky.
We love, we miss her dearly,
No one will ever know,
When the final day came along,
We had to let her go.

Lynne Merrill Jackson

Tarka

My little blue boy feels as soft as a toy
Scooped up for a cuddle the time flashes by
I squidge him and stroke him to show him I care
And bury my fingers deep in his fur.

His lovely big eyes are the colour of sand
I cradle his head in the palm of my hand
When I'm reading a book he miaows, 'Mum let me see,
Let me lay down on that, then you'll see only me.'

One time he was missing, I'd a feeling of dread
But he was just sleeping in his mummy's big bed.
He plays in his garden then sleeps warm and curled
He's the best little boy in the whole wide world.

Liz Brooke

Pearly's Antics

At night I lay my day clothes down,
Tidy, not in a heap,
So I can dress easily
When I return from sleep.

But Pearly, our cat, has other ideas
Which suit her plans instead,
She knocks them down and screws them up,
And with them makes her bed.

Then, when daylight comes, she wakes
And with a loud, 'Miaow,'
She springs upon the bed
And says, 'I want my breakfast, *now!*'

F Housam

Ginge

Lying softly curled on my duvet
Sunshine slants across her gilded fur.
A twitching tail the only sign
This feline lives - this cat of mine.
A wide yawn, a pink-tipped tongue,
another lick, her work is done.
I watch my cat sleep through the days,
In feline foetal position, my cat lays.
A wary heavy-lidded eye
Ensures the world passes safely by.
What catty dreams pass through her head
While curled upon my cosy bed?
The chances are that Ginger knows
Far more than even I suppose!

Jane Manning

A furry friend

This is next door's cat
Being as silly as can be.
The wind is blowing hard
And he is leaping through my tree.

He sees all sorts of things
That no one else can see.
The wind has driven him wild
And he stares from up the tree.

He twists and turns and leaps
His life is completely free.
The wind has driven him wild,
But he will soon come down for tea.

Rachel E Joyce

fish On A Dish

I don't have dogs, cats or bats
for I love fish, all orange and flat
you can have fish on a dish
but never can you wish
for my orange delights

crystal colours, shiny stone
that's their skin and I provide their home
they're no trouble to keep clean
for all their mess
filters through a little stream

I am not edible
and neither are my fish
so please don't ask
for any fish on a dish.

Kazina Pang

Missing You

It was cold, windy and wet
on the first day we met.
Your hair was a mess,
you looked in slight distress.
But from that day on
I couldn't disguise falling in love
with your appealing dark eyes.

We'd go for long walks,
you'd kiss, I'd cuddle.
We'd frolic and tease,
sometimes skip through a puddle.
My moods would differ from day to day,
yet yours didn't waver,
still greeting me
in your happy, exciting way.

I marvel at life's speed of time.
You've young ones of your own,
and you're in your prime.
I watch you sleep.
Sometimes I stroke your head,
admire your love for the young ones
who now share your bed.

You're growing old.
You sometimes look weak.
You're eyes still show me love, it doesn't
matter you can't speak.

Your life has ended.
I've had to give you up
but oh! how I wish I'd just met
my beautiful, dark-eyed, dishevelled pup.

Michael Spencer

The Cat I Love

There once was a cat
Who was as lazy as can be
And she sits next to me.
She sleeps all day,
Mostly in May.

She is white as snow,
But not so slow.
Only three, and she can climb a tree.
She is not so old,
And her collar is gold.

She sits on our beds,
And her hair sheds.
Her tail is like a panda,
And she likes my grandad.

The cat I am talking about
Is the cat that I love,
Because she is mine.

Heather Shea (12)

Thomasina

It has been two years since you went
to cat heaven, I think
your grave in the backyard serves
as memorial of your one-eyed wink

Cats have come and cats will go
but there will be only one of you
who was so abused and loved so much
but would never sit in a church pew

You were my best friend for a decade
and yes, I remember it still
that when I came in the door
you ran to meet me even if you were ill

Anita Marie Shirk

In Memory Of Tibbs

Tibbs, you were so special to me
You brought me comfort
And companionship.

You always knew when
I was in need of that extra
Loving touch.
You came to me like a dog
Sitting near me.

You visited me while
I was busy working in the shed.
If the weather was warm
You laid outside waiting for me.

While I was painting you would
Sometimes visit me
Lying on the landing.
In your well days
You were mostly nearby.

You had to go then
You were not well.
It was not right to hang on to you
I had to let you go.

We both knew inside
That day was to be the last.
Thank you for licking me
As you were dying
It meant so much to me.

Goodbye now Tibbs.

Julie Smith

Chula

(The tale of a Siamese cat)

I remember
Chula,
Our Siamese.
Warm fur
On bedclothes
Purring
Every morning,
Always answering
With a squeak to my,
'Good morning cat!'
Attacking rather
But all in fun!
Deadly claws
Bringing back
Starlings, mice
And other trophies
Of hunting.
Then tears
And weeping
From the busy road,
Blue eyes,
Snarling mouth,
In death's
Suspended animation.
Grandad muttering,
'Poor old puss!'
'Poor old Blacktail.'
Grave dug
In garden soil,
Wooden box coffin
And pebble marker.

Paul Wilkins

Rocky

Our stately tomcat, a regular tabby
or 'moggy' as registered by the vet
with stripy fur so silky and soft
his markings change as his mood
he is a fussy feline, forever grooming
vital whiskers twitching, golden-green eyes
and spiky ears on constant alert
his greeting sheer joy
as the tinkle of his name disc
especially when eating, tapping his plate
from where he came is a 'tale'
travelling alongside us
there and home again
Rocky's our pal and companion
a confidant and treasure
this precious sweetheart
we'll love forever

Shirley Pinnington

Spy Cat

I got burgled once.
The cat sat on the sofa
the whole time and watched.
He'd sat in the same position
from the time I'd left.

When I came home to
my ransacked house,
he sat calmly, licked his
paw and washed his head;

'Bald, quite tall, a funny scar
on his left cheek, probably from
a fight. He had a tattoo on the top
of his left arm of a skull.'

He jumped off the sofa, where
all night he'd
pretended to sleep;

'Give me some food and
I'll tell you
what he
nicked. But
you'll have
to stroke
me
for the
next hour.'

Jessica Hathway

Poor Pebbles

I was told by someone to keep you indoors.
It's a hard world out there for a kitten.
Cars, dogs and cruel people.
As safe as houses.
Then someone else said, 'How can you be so cruel?
A cat should be outside.'
She made me out to be a fool.
So I gave her to a dearest friend.
'I know a lot on cat care,' she told me.
But then she knocked on my door one day and said,
'I tried but I couldn't save her from the world outside.
Pebbles got run over and she's dead.'

Rachel Van Den Bergen

Hot Dog

Hot dog in summer is my canine lot,
To wear a fur coat in the tropics, cool it is not.

Hot flesh in summer is not much fun,
Wrapped in putrid fur, not the putrid bun.

My friend the Persian cat is clipped down to the skin,
She comments that zip-off furs are really in.

My owner and hers talk together a lot,
The result is a detachable fur with my tail in a slot.

But now the anti-canine, anti-feline comments are scathing,
'Hot dog and cool cat, arrested for naked bathing.'

Alan Bruce Thompson

Shedlen

You, the most brave and loveliest of pets
Deserving the highest esteem in the human breast,

A God-sent friend from above
To paint me the picture of love,

You who is not only a friend,
But a lover, a guardian there to defend,

You who knows how to obey, trust and rely,
And never seeking earthly glory,

You who will not take a sop, nor give
Door to robbers, thieves, or burglars to plunder me,

You who knows no slumber,
No pretence, no deception, no betrayer,

You who is lovely and queenly beautiful,
And has always remained so faithful,

I have but this poem to engraph thee,
As a monument more lasting than stone and marble,
Not just to any person, but more importantly to me.

Jakpa D Emmanuel

Teddy

(Dedicated to my Teddy)

My friend said, 'Get a dog for company,
then no more lonely will you be.'
To the animal shelter we did go
to see what they had to show.
Noisy barking running up and down
some wagged tails, others seemed to wear a frown.
Then from a kennel he came so slow,
rushed to the wire his eyes aglow,
we looked at each other in that way,
his eyes looked into mine as if to say,
please, please take me from this jail.
With head pressed to wire he looked up and wagged his tail.
We fell in love, that dog and I.
Take him? 'Of course,' I said with a sigh.
He seemed to know just what was said,
his look said, *thank you, thank you*, as home we sped.
We had some lovely days, Teddy and me,
the love and affection he gave was good to see.
There were times when I did not it return
and my sorrow for that pain in my heart does burn.
Now Ted has gone, my life is one that is so sad
but I know he is with another he loved, my dad,
his memory and love will never perish you see,
the time will come when again together we will be.
My love to you Ted will again be ever true
and long walks we will take, just me and you.

John Clarke

My Best Mate

We've been together for over five years
Through good times and bad, laughter and tears
Comforted each other, come what may
And lived to face another day

He's lazy and fat and doesn't do a thing
Just sits there staring 'til his food I bring
He licks his lips, I always give him the best
He turns his nose up at all the rest

He always sleeps in his favourite chair
No one else sits in it, they just wouldn't dare
His snoring is loud, a dreadful noise he makes
But if anyone disturbs him, he instantly awakes

He's loving, he's gentle, he's my best mate
When I come home from work, he waits by the gate
We sit and we cuddle whilst I drink my tea
He's wanting more - so he pats my knee

They say he changes when the sun goes down
A nasty creature, whilst out on the town
He stalks his prey, it's quite unreal
Not caring for his victims, whatever they feel

He's cruel and vicious and he's out to kill
Teasing and tormenting gives him a thrill
The creature lays dying, awaiting his fate
But whatever he's done, he's still my best mate

Proudly his victim is laid at my door
I get quite upset, but I know the score
It's animals' nature and I can't change that
But I still love him - my beautiful cat

Barbara M Beatson

Rodney's Cat

You sprawl, ears like the Sydney Opera House,
a Playboy centrefold, above the thwack and crawl
after catching mice, the sun.

A book in the gutter,
its dirty snow coloured pages flutter,
flutter. After a close look
I realise it isn't a book at all.

You curl, shift, stand and prowl,
bunched boxing glove hands punching,
punching. Furry moonface hunching
over haunches, looking for all the world ...

like a branch clasping owl.

Jonathan Chant

Jacob

Nervous at thresholds, suspicious of novelty,
he never tried his luck or staked a claim,
he didn't whine, no hunger made him bold,
theft was anathema to him. His mind tuned to omens,
he had an inborn sense of the forbidden
and we forbade him nothing. Spooked by the dark
he'd tiptoe into the garden as if entering a nightmare,
quivering and hissing at foes no one could spot.
And yet us, he trusted, as if our arms a home
to linger in, eyes closed, feet in the air like a dead bird -
he could take on bliss as a spell cast, as his sole motto.
A letting go we'd never seen in cats.
Then tiredness caught him, loosened his ginger coat,
made him giddy, distant, step out.

Judith Wilkinson

My Cat's In Love

'Awwww' you may say
But she is driving me mad
With the loves of her life
The night-time serenades
And days of disappearance

I worry you see
About her welfare
Tossing and turning at night
Calling her until the wee hours
Shaking bags of biscuits with a fury
But to no avail

Days later a miaow
And a rubbing against my legs
As if to say, 'Why were you worried?
Here I am. Now feed me!
And I love you still.'

Then 10 weeks pass
And little balls of fluff fill up her basket
And she looks at me in surprise
For romance should be all
Not motherhood as well
And as all good-time girls find out
A man will catch you out eventually

Ann-Marie Spittle

Treacle Treat

Treacle, Treacle
You are so sweet
Treacle, Treacle
You are a treat
Treacle, Treacle
I love your tortoise coloured fur
Treacle, Treacle
You're always there
Treacle, Treacle
I love the colour of your eyes
Treacle, Treacle
I hear your little sighs
Treacle, Treacle
I know you care
Treacle, Treacle
I know you miss me when I'm not there
Treacle, Treacle
You're always glad to see me
Treacle, Treacle
When I come back to thee
Treacle, Treacle
I love the way you growl when you hear
Treacle, Treacle
When anyone comes near
Treacle, Treacle
You're nearly 2 years old
Treacle, Treacle
I wish you were good as gold
Treacle, Treacle
Treacle-Treat, happy Hallowe'en
See the photo, see what I mean?

Michelle Knight

for My friend's friend

Maybe Muffin saw the bad years,
Maybe Muffin saw the pain,
And like some pretend St Bernard,
Through the blizzards of disdain
From the others who rebuffed you,
She would carry round her neck
An imaginary barrel,
With the writing: *What the heck!*

And the succour was her patience,
And adoring, knowing eyes
Which saw your push through illness,
Piercing straight through all the lies,
Yet, how strange it is, that fifteen
Years that held you firm, through strife,
Were to end, spirits transposing;
When she died, leaving you life.

Serena Waite-Shores

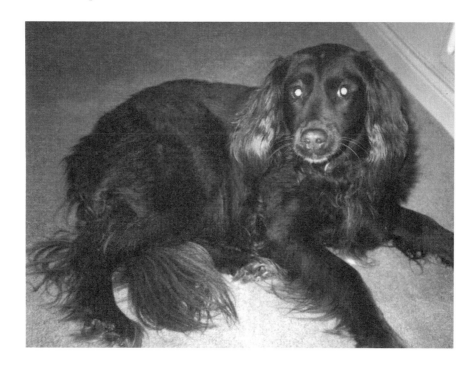

Untitled

Sparkle is a special dog,
We all love him to bits,
His waggly tail, his loving eyes,
He is so cute when he sits.
He was a rescue dog,
Looked so very scared,
We took him home,
From that day he shared -
Each and every day of our lives.
He's given so much joy,
His funny little habits,
He's a lovely boy.
We all love him,
From young and old,
We walk him, oh so proud,
He is the best dog in the world,
I want to shout out *loud*.

E M Gough

felix

I am a black and white cat,
Felix is my name,
Cats Protection Week
Promotion is my game,
I've subsidised the food
And goody bags are free,
All you need to do
Is adopt a cat like me.

Cat and kitten welfare,
That's what it's all about,
Be a volunteer,
Leaflets to hand out,
Rescue and rehoming
60,000 cats a year,
Helping us to live a life
Without neglect or fear.

5 million cats eat Felix
And I do the best I can
With donations and promotions,
'Happy cats' the master plan.

Beverly Maiden

Henry

H is for helpful, to which he is the complete opposite.
　　　Sometimes I think it is his sole purpose to make my life difficult.
E is for energetic. He is constantly mad.
　　　Bounding, springing, jumping - he never rests!
N is for naughty. He is the cheekiest, most disobedient
　　　And most stubborn animal I've ever met.
R is for really really stupid. He can't drop sticks, won't fetch things,
　　　Destroys toilet rolls and eats everybody's food but his own.
Y - Why if he is so unhelpful, naughty, stupid and stubborn
　　　Do I still think he's perfect?

One simple four letter answer ...
　　　　　　　Love

Harry Phillips

Love - A Little Doggerel

(For Issy)

Shakespeare said, ''tis not hereafter,
Much he made of mirth and laughter',
Shakespeare never lived to see
Loving like you show to me;
Two black ears and four white feet,
One pink tongue, expression sweet,
Amber eyes that softly shine,
Telling me your heart is mine.
Even the Bard had striven in vain
All your qualities to name:
Beauty, truth, and gentle nature,
Queenly grace and classic stature;
Zorro-mask, and tawny thigh-boots,
(Dare I add you're such a sly-boots?).
Silken ruff and dusky tresses,
Fairer far than gorgeous dresses;
Not Juliet, nor yet Cordelia,
Imogen, nor fair Ophelia,
Could by spell, or trick, or charming,
Steal my heart from you, my darling.
Not the greatest muse that erst
Guided pen or channelled verse,
Could in song or sonnet measure
All the joy or half the pleasure
That you bring me, day and daily,
Lovely Meg, my border collie.

Aideen M D'Arcy

Isadora's Tale

I travelled to Africa on a jolly elephant
Yes, he was very pleasant
And gave many friendly cheers
To roving zebras and similar-minded deers
As to the rest
Our meeting a lion was the best.

Susanne Södergren

Gretal And Heidi

I wake up in the morning,
My two goats Gretal and Heidi calling.
I come to groom them
And they chew my curly, ginger hair.
They want their breakfast
And then I put them out to grass
And they watch the birds and skip.
Evening comes and I put them away
And we say goodnight.

Margaret Palmer (9)

Faithful And Grateful Dogs

When you face hardships, to find loyal people around you,
To stand by you in your thick and thin alike,
You can count on dogs as your great allies,
In all your rises and falls, prosperities and poverties!

In the event of your becoming a pauper topper,
When all your relatives and friends desert you,
They would step into their shoes happily and spontaneously,
To guard you just like guards guard billionaires!

Even if you don't have any food to offer to them,
They would never make any barks of sparks against you,
But would kiss your wounds and lick your hands,
To exhibit their unabated affections to you!

When your riches take wings to fly to the height of skies,
Reputations dive to the abyss of deep seas,
They would steadfastly and ecstatically adore you,
Just like moon worships sun in its flights to Heaven!

When your luxurious six-door car of fortune drives away from you,
Making you crestfallen highly and heavily,
They won't ask for any higher privilege than to accompany you,
To strive hard for you to restore your glory back to you!

When you enact your heroic part in the last scene of the drama of your life,
When the Goddess of Death snatches your life in her dastardly wizard embrace,
And when your body is laid in the coldest ground in the coldest winter,
They would lie down near it with their heads in-between their paws!

They would never leave you even after you breathe your last,
However they would sit by your coffin to protect even your dead body,
As faithfully and gratefully as your active live body.
Crying endlessly and broken-heartedly to express their anguishes in your departure!

Davis Akkara

Animal Kingdom

The greatest of all is about to happen
The cock crows and the dog barks
What is going on in the animal kingdom?
They all gathered to celebrate a feast
The animals remember their early years
And they tagged the feast the young shall grow
And the poem goes like this ...
What was once a kitten is now a cat
What was once a puppy is now a dog
What was once a calf is now a cow
What was once a chick is now a cock
What was once a lamb is now a ram
What was once a piglet is now a hog
What was once a cub is now a lion
Every great individual starts from small
So also the pets in the animal kingdom
For the young shall grow if time permits
But not all of them can be a pet
Some of them are chosen to be a pet
Sharing an apartment with an individual
That cares and loves a pet
But what is a pet to me
Might not be a pet to you
Which means some animals
Have to have special attention
From the person that cares
And you keep on wondering
What they are doing with such a pet?
Well, that is what life is all about, surprises!
But no place can ever be like their place;
The animal kingdom.

Adejoke Austin Adedamola

Cat Hunting

When I'm twitchy,
I go cat hunting,
Which is silly
Cos when I'm twitchy,
The cat
Is very,
Very,
Cautious.
And waits ...
And waits ...
Until I calm down.

Then the cat is calm.
I'm calm.
We're both calm.

That's when I write.

And the c ...

... ow!

Rover!

Alex de Suys

for Paddy With Love

(In memory - to all people who have ever loved and lost their cats)

The people at the cattery
Are rather sad.

They lost the best cat
They ever had.

Paddy was his name
Their life will never
Be the same.

And now and again
They are heard to say ...
Do you remember when
Paddy did this, or that?

He really was our top cat!

Moira Jean Clelland

My Shadow Is A ...

P ersonal
R estful
E xciting
C hallenging
I ntriguing
O bservant
U ppermost
S ensitive

C aptivating
A dorable
T iddles.

Chris Batley

Mr Bigglesworth Biggles

(Aka Dog Eater)

Oh Mr Bigglesworth Biggs, in the house he sits,
And he's now coming out today.
He's a mean fuzzyfurker,
Leave the stroking to the mother,
He paws at the doors, in the house with the mouse,
He sleeps all day, and roams all night,
And he has nothing he wants to say to the likes of you, dog.
Bigglesworth's got you, oh the Bigg B's stopped you,
He'll take your hide out to town,
Fo shizzel, Biggs.

Alex Tabrizi

Muffin

Nobody owned our precious wee cat
she was everyone's friend
a cat like that
she followed the sun
and also her heart
gave us affection
which did impart the vital spark
that made us love her
everyone's cat

Margery Kayson

Mizey Cat

Yes, that's his name;
We love him a lot
Since to us he came

The next-door neighbour moved away,
She was worried he might decide to stray.
My son said ask her if he can live with us,
She said yes and we were chuffed.

He never went home much,
He was always with us,
Give him a home, I thought,
We really must.

His mother Molly met her fate
One evening when it was very late,
He's got a sister called Melody,
Her owner worked at the shop near me.

And there's a brother
By the name of Fizz,
What lovely names they have, gee whizz!

Our tabby is as good as gold,
He's coming on fine for three years old.
I love him and kiss his head
When I call him in and it's time for bed.

Rachel Mary Mills

from Sam

I am a little scaredy-cat but I have a special friend
He's strong and handsome, blond and kind
And to my faults he's completely blind when I bring him mice to tend

Our garden's rather like a forest, with trees and shrubs and things
There're lots of little animals and great big birds with enormous wings
Sometimes they swoop and frighten me
But I come in quick and have my tea

My biggest enemy out there is a very large fox with bristly hair
He has big teeth, he is fast and ghastly
My hair fluffs up and my heart beats fast,
I know he really doesn't like me

But my big friend comes running out
And chases the fox with the nasty snout
Then he puts his big paws around me tight
And gently lays his head so light
To protect me from harm both day and night
My very special friend.

Barbara Harrison

feathers

Feathers flying all around
As back from the shops we both were bound.
Opening up the door to see
On the carpet, there it be.

A grey-ringed dove was all forlorn
The carpet like a snowy storm.
Feathers all across the hall
A present from our Sam did fall.

My eyes did fill with tears to see
What our cat Sam had brought for me.
For although he knew no shame
To him it was his little game.

In my heart I cannot feel
That what he'd done was for real.
With large soft eyes and gentle purr
Did our Sam this dove procure.

But to this day I cannot say
How our Sam did bring his prey
Through his cat flap, large and fat
To then disperse dove on the mat!

Beryl Smyter

Rover

For twelve years you were loved by an unknown source
Your world shattered by illness,
Your burning fire at risk of going out
In a walk of shame you were led away
Your only belonging, an orange bone
Clasped tightly in your mouth

Surrounded by strangers
An unusual smell and place
Watching and hoping for your family to return
As soon as we saw you
We knew you were what was missing
Those beautiful eyes reflecting your forgiving soul
Trust would be difficult at an old age
To take you home would correct the injustice of humanity

You have become part of the family
Filling our home with love
An angelic presence breaking the silence
A formidable best friend to our intrigued cat
An undisputed forager
Sniffing out danger from the air

Your habits are endearing
A vision of vitality running down the beach
An innocent untarnished soul
Your vitality for life is unmistakable
This poem is for you Rover
To thank you for entering our lives

Tamara Burnett

Jasper

They could not afford to feed him
The vast quantities he ate.
On foot they walked the seven miles
And left him at the gate.

The rescue shelter where I'd hoped
To find another pet,
Was filled with sad and lonely dogs
And a worried looking vet.

'We have a mongrel here,' he said
'He really is quite good,
But needs a lot of exercise -
And love and hugs and food!'

The starving creature called to me
And looked me in the eye.
I knew I'd found my friend for life!
I knew I'd found my guy!

That ugly duckling mongrel pup
Became a shining swan!
He changed into a bearded collie
And made them all quite wrong!

His name is Jasper, my angel dog,
Protector, clown and friend.
He's filled with love and full of fun
Beside me till the end!

Ruby Rollins

Lizzie

She's prowling the garden looking for prey,
She takes no notice whatever you say
Lost in her kingdom of birds and mice,
She'll bring you one home, if you ask her nice.

She moves like a snake, close to the ground,
Eyes ever watching but never a sound
A rustle of bushes, she's waiting and glued
She will do as she pleases, she has an attitude.

Then there's the dog, who she just loves to tease,
Nipping his nose and making him sneeze
Invading his bed, his own private space
She'll settle beside him, and just smirk in his face.

She goes missing for hours, losing all track of time,
Asleep in the long grass, all thoughts left behind
If you rattle her plate or open a tin
You can bet on your life, she will stroll right on in.

Lizzie dear Lizzie, what a true pleasure you are,
A sweet little thing, a bright shining star
A poor lonely soul who started life all alone
But now you're a queen, and this is your home.

Sharon Cawthorne

Morning Song

My cockatiel sings incessantly
He speaks English too
Hi Taco, pretty bird
Gimmie a kiss, and I love you

He awakes every morning
With a brand new song
Kinda like me
How could we go wrong

We both like early mornings
The start of a brand new day
We keep each other company
And we both have much to say

This morning's a little different, however
Something's heavily on his mind
He's squawking up a migraine
And my sanity is on the line

I've tried to calm him down
I've given him some seed
Come on Taco, pretty bird
I've got revisions to read

My head is stuck in echo sphere
My nerves are wound up tight
If you don't bring it down a notch or two
You'll be demonstrating the freedom of flight

How can I be mad at him
He's only a bird
With his cute little rosy cheeks
And passion for the spoken word

Yes, mostly he's a charmer
A real feathered treat
It's a good thing I've got headphones
And a comfy computer seat

Holly DeLaughter

My Special Pet - Sally

Sally - a loving, helpful, playful, restful, friendly cat.

Sally is my loving cat
    she gives me lots of kisses,
    she lies down for tummy rubs,
    she gives me lots of cuddles,
    she purrs when she is happy.

Sally is my helpful cat
    she helps me in the garden,
    she helps me do artwork,
    she helps me do the dishes,
    she helps me on the computer,
    she helps me read my books,
    she helps me unpack the shopping.

Sally is my playful cat
    she chases birds, mice, moths and insects,
    she plays football with her red ball,
    she loves playing with feathers,
    she adores her catnip toys.

Sally is my restful cat
    she sleeps on my bed,
    she hides behind the sofa,
    she curls up in boxes,
    she rests under the trees and bushes,
    she dozes among the flowers.

Sally is my friendly cat
    she makes friends with old people,
    she likes children,
    she has a boyfriend called Tommy,
    she plays being a mother to Molly the neighbour's kitten.

Sally is my loving cat,
Sally is my helpful cat,
Sally is my playful cat,
Sally is my restful cat,
Sally is my friendly cat,
Sally is a special cat.

I love you Sally -
and God loves you too.

Melissa Harper (8)

If It Should Be ...

If I grow frail and weak,
And pain should keep me from sleep,
Then you must do what must be done,
For this, my last battle, cannot be won.
You will be sad - I understand,
But then don't let grief stay your hand,
For this day more than all the rest,
Your love and friendship must stand the test.
We've had so many happy years,
What is to come holds no fears.
Please take me where my needs they'll tend,
But stay with me until the end,
Hold me close and speak to me,
Until my eyes no longer see.
I know in time you too will see,
It is a kindness that you did for me,
Although my tail its last has waved,
From pain and suffering I've been saved.
Don't grieve in thought that it must be you,
Who has decided the right thing to do,
We've been so close for so many years,
Please don't let your heart hold any tears.

I loved you so with all my heart
And though we now at last must part,
Be strong, remember too ...
Look after yourself for me ...
For you!

Jill Nagra

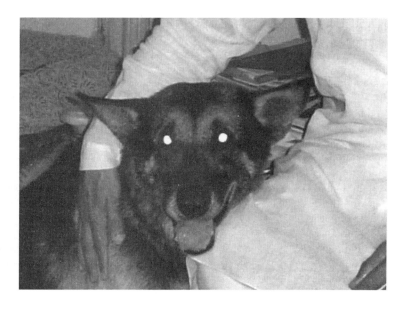

Sybil's Complaint

I have a few complaints to make
To you, my owners dear:

When you stagger downstairs at 7am
Crinkle-faced with lingering sleep
Don't head straight for that noisy room
To fill your drinking water deep.

So deep you can sit and splash in it
Now that's just being greedy
What about your poor old cat
Left thirsty, cold and needy?

Oh, you may say to me, 'Hi, gorgeous,'
Do that thing you call embrace
Meanwhile my tummy's rumbling
So shall we just cut to the chase?

Now you're walking out your door!
(Incidentally, it's bigger than mine)
Now I've eaten what will I do?
I'll have to sleep to pass the time.

You return, disturb my blissful snooze
But now that you are back
Make yourself useful, will you, and
Give me a good ol' scratch?

Take heed of this warning, Owners
My revenge will be so sweet
I'll sneak into your sleeping room
And pounce upon your feet.

But I don't want to sound ungrateful
So if you want to make amends
Stroke me for an hour or two
Then maybe we'll be friends.

Deborah Headspeath

Anchor Books Information

We hope you have enjoyed reading this book - and that
you will continue to enjoy it in the coming years.
If you like reading and creative writing drop us a line, or
give us a call, and we'll send you a free information pack.
Alternatively, if you would like to order further copies of
this book or any of our other titles, then please give us a
call or log onto our website at www.forwardpress.co.uk
Anchor Books, Remus House, Coltsfoot Drive,
Peterborough PE2 9JX
Tel (01733) 898102